Praise for
THE COLOR OF
GRACE

"Bethany is a force of nature and loves everyone in her blast radius with the kind of focused attention and compassion that Jesus gave to the people around him. Bethany doesn't just pass along some theories she's read about in this book. She shares the pain, the hope, and the wonder that have become her life. Buckle up. You're going to love the journey you're about to go on with someone who knows and lives what she's talking about."

—Bob Goff, author of *Love Does*

"I meet Jesus anew in Bethany's stories of these children. It is my prayer that you will, too. It is my prayer that all of us will know and believe that Jesus can turn our greatest pain into our greatest joy, if only we will invite Him."

—Katie Davis, *New York Times* bestselling author of *Kisses from Katie* and one of *Glamour*'s 2012 Women of the Year

"*The Color of Grace* by Bethany Haley Williams is an honest portrayal of her struggles and how she was able to overcome them and make a difference in young people's lives. Bethany has found her own way to connect with young people, and in that process of gaining knowledge and wisdom, the young people are able to heal and find purpose in their lives. With Exile International's trauma care program, Bethany uses art therapy to help youth who have been affected by war. Bethany is a true peace soldier and an inspiration to many."

—Emmanuel Jal, former child soldier, peace activist, musician, actor, humanitarian, and author of *War Child: A Child Soldier's Story*

"*The Color of Grace* poignantly addresses a lesson I learned long ago: when people are sick, homeless, or hungry, words are not enough. They need help for when they hurt. Drawing from her professional training and her personal experiences with trauma, Bethany provides that help for children who are wounded both physically and emotionally. This book will inspire you, inform you, and enable you to see God's grace in the midst of pain."

—Josh D. McDowell, author and speaker

"I couldn't put the book down. Bethany's words are raw and vulnerable. Each chapter made me want to read more and go deeper into the story of redemption. This book illustrates more than ever the beauty and healing that can spring forth from the most painful things in our lives."

—Esther Havens, international humanitarian photographer

"I recently traveled to Uganda with Bethany and the Exile team and was blown away by the impact art therapy can have on these young children. The pains of their past are unspeakable. But through Bethany and Exile International, I got to see the dreams of their future take shape right in front of my eyes. The powerful stories that we got to hear are now in this book, and they will surely have a profound impact on the lives of the readers, just as they did mine."

—Jeremy Cowart, photographer and founder of
Help-Portrait and See University

"How bad can life get? And how can people pull through when life gets beyond bad? This is the story of how Bethany Haley Williams found hope and healing from PTSD, and then brought that same healing to former child soldiers in Africa. This is a story of responding to God's grace and power. When I first heard Bethany's dream in 2008, I thought it would never happen. But that shows how little I knew about Bethany. A compelling read. Heartbreaking and inspiring. Overwhelming and uplifting."

—Dr. Harriet Hill, program director for the
Trauma Healing Institute at the American Bible Society

THE COLOR OF
GRACE

*How One Woman's Brokenness Brought Healing
and Hope to Child Survivors of War*

BETHANY HALEY WILLIAMS, PHD

FOREWORD BY *Katie Davis*

HOWARD BOOKS
An Imprint of Simon & Schuster, Inc.
New York   Nashville   London   Toronto   Sydney   New Delhi

Howard Books
An Imprint of Simon & Schuster, Inc.
1230 Avenue of the Americas
New York, NY 10020

Copyright © 2015 by Bethany Haley
Afterword copyright © 2016 Bethany Haley

Unless otherwise noted, Scripture quotations in this book are from The Holy Bible, New International Version. © 1973, 1978, 1984, International Bible Society. Used by permission of Zondervan Bible Publishers. All rights reserved.

Scripture quotations marked NKJV are taken from the New King James Version. © 1982 by Thomas Nelson, Inc. Used by permission. All rights reserved.

Scripture quotations marked NLT are taken from the Holy Bible, New Living Translation, copyright © 1996, 2004. Used by permission of Tyndale House Publishers, Inc., Wheaton, IL 60189. All rights reserved.

Scripture quotation marked NJB is from The New Jerusalem Bible, copyright © 1985 by Darton, Longman & Todd, Ltd. and Doubleday, a division of Random House, Inc. Reprinted by Permission.

First Howard Books trade paperback edition January 2016

HOWARD and colophon are trademarks of Simon & Schuster, Inc.

For information about special discounts for bulk purchases, please contact Simon & Schuster Special Sales at 1-866-506-1949 or business@simonandschuster.com.

The Simon & Schuster Speakers Bureau can bring authors to your live event. For more information or to book an event, contact the Simon & Schuster Speakers Bureau at 1-866-248-3049 or visit our website at www.simonspeakers.com.

Interior design by Davina Mock-Maniscalco

Manufactured in the United States of America

10   9   8   7   6   5   4   3   2   1

Library of Congress Control Number: 2014015337

ISBN 978-1-4767-6625-6
ISBN 978-1-4767-7383-4 (pbk)
ISBN 978-1-4767-6626-3 (ebook)

To the brave child survivors of war throughout the world: Those who are in the midst of battle as I write this. Those whose lives have been taken too soon. Those who are learning to live again. You are my heartbeat. May the world learn forgiveness, strength, and deep gratitude through your stories of redemption.

To my momma, the toughest and most beautiful cancer fighter I know. You and Dad are a part of me always. Keep fighting. All for the glory of God. Also, go Cats!

To Matthew, my love and my partner. You are a remarkable human for whom I have deep respect. You have taught me to love more like Jesus, and your surrendered life for these children humbles me. May we adventure through life together for eternity, dancing in the footprints of our Savior and kneeling at the feet of those we serve.

Out of suffering have emerged the strongest souls;
the most massive characters are seared with scars.

—KHALIL GIBRAN

Contents

Acknowledgments

My deepest gratitude . . .

To my wonderful family: Mom and Dad, your fingerprints are on my spirit. Fingerprints of faith, groundedness, goofiness, love, dedication, and honor to God and His word. If we ever lacked in material things, it was not noticed because we were abundantly rich in joy—making squash boats that would float through the trenches we made in grandmother's yard, singing as a family in the car on the way back from gospel meetings, and building forts in the woods. Thank you for reading every word and cheering me on to the finish line!

To my nieces and nephew: You light up my life. Although you never knew, I found much needed hope by simply being around you during my saddest times. Puppet shows, baking cookies, dancing to Mary Poppins, and reading books together in British accents might have just saved my life. You could live a thousand lifetimes and never fully understand how your laughter, play, and prayers kept me going. Never forget that all things are possible with God. He is your best friend. Always live in your imagination and walk in whimsy. You have been chosen to bring light to the world. Shine bright, young world changers. Your Aunt b loves you.

To my dearest Matthew: You were the most unanticipated surprise in both teaching me how to love again while also taming my stubborn spirit. Thank you for never seeing me for my past, but (as you always say) "only seeing Christ's righteousness in me." During this writing process: thank you for making sure I ate, for cheering me on through many sleepless nights, for the *countless hours* you spent reading and editing chapters, for giving wise feedback, for your silly accents that made me belly laugh when I wanted to cry, for bringing me ice to soothe my bulging disks, and for believing that I (we) could do it. Most of all, thank you for being my partner in justice, my best friend, and now my husband and the love of my life. I have overflowing respect for the man you are. It has not been easy, but—wow—has it been worth it.

To the Exile team, past and present: Jessie, never forget God brought you to us at the perfect time. You helped Exile International develop a solid foundation that will be built upon for decades. To those, being too many to name, who make Exile's work possible (our financial supporters, child sponsors, Restore Partners, church partners, prayer warriors), thank you for believing in these kids and this mission.

To our beautiful African teammates, the staff at the Peace Lives Center and Children of Peace Uganda: I could write volumes on what you have taught me. You give of your lives daily so these kids can find restoration. You have given up homes, security, and comfort to follow Christ's mission. I pray to be more like you. May God grant you an eternity of *posho* and cassava in heaven.

To the dear children and youth in DRC and Uganda with Exile International's programs: My heart overflows because of you. Thank you for teaching me how to be brave and for inspiring me to live. You have already overcome the world. I am excited to see what great things the Lord has in store for you. He beams with a Father's joy and pride for each one of you.

To the amazing editing team who walked through this labor of love with me: I wish each of your names could be on the cover. Philis, you are an amazing woman and deserve some sort of an award in heaven for your patience with me through this process. If there are gray hairs on your head, it's all because of me. Your wisdom, guidance, and chief editorial skills gave this project wings. Ciona, I'm deeply grateful for your creativity and friendship. You saved the day with your creative energy when my tank was dry. Cadence, your words speak life, and I'm so thankful they are found on these pages. Beth, thank you for your patience and for helping this newbie through the first stages of writing. Jonathan, thank you for believing in me and persistently pursuing me to write this book. It would not have happened without your tenacity.

Last, and greatest of all, to my Redeemer and my Lord: I have lived several lives throughout this one you have granted me. You have patiently taught me through all of them. Tears fall where words should be as I search for how to thank you. For you and because of you, I live, breathe, and have my being. To you I dedicate my life. I am dripping with Your grace and will only enter Your Kingdom because of Your kindness. I am Yours.

Foreword

by Katie Davis

No one laughs as loudly as my friend Beth. And when I am telling a story, no one is as quick to grab my hand tightly and say, "It's okay, you can cry." Beth knows real joy, the kind that comes only from Jesus. And Beth knows something that I am still just learning: the very deepest joy often comes out of our very deepest pain.

We see this to be true in the greatest miracle of all time, the story on which our entire faith is founded—the resurrection of Christ. Out of the ugliness of my sin, after the brutal beating and scourging and mocking, the Savior whispers, "Father, forgive them." And out of the black of the tomb, new Life emerges and new Light shines forth. Our very greatest joy—salvation—is born out of the very deepest pain and even death of our Savior.

This world would teach us otherwise: that pain is what ruins us. The world would teach us that once we are broken we cannot be used, that we should run from pain just as fast as we can. But in fleeing the pain and brokenness of this world, we might miss the joy of the Father's redemption. Beth knows that the Father's heart is learned on our knees, face-to-face with the reality of sin in a fallen world and thus face-to-face with the restoration found in Jesus.

We sit on the beach and I let my tears flow, raw and vulnerable, while children run and shriek happily around us. We sit in the hospital waiting room while my daughter undergoes life-altering surgery, and the joy of the Lord is so evident that we throw our heads back and laugh so hard that we have to excuse ourselves to the elevator. Beth listens long and speaks grace. I see Jesus behind her sparkling blue eyes as I lament my failures and tentatively share my hopes and dreams.

It comes as no surprise to me that children living in the heart of darkness also find safety to share both their pasts and their hopes for the future in her warm embrace. I know that here they are listened to and they are pointed to the grace and healing found in Jesus. They believe that they are cherished, not just by the life-breathing woman in front of them but also by their Maker. We are really all just longing to be known, for a safe place to tell our story, for a place to belong. Beth calls forth the life and strength of the one who lives inside of them, in each of us. Jesus enables their dreams.

She cries as she tells me their stories. She doesn't try to hide her tears as she shares with me the things these children have taught her.

And what strikes me most is that she doesn't just cry for them; no, she cries *with* them.

It's messier doing it that way. It's harder to cry with a real person, a real heart, than it is to cry about a hypothetical situation a world away. It is messy, this business of knowing those we serve, of learning from those we once hoped to teach. It is the harder choice, investing in lives and not just stomachs or bandages, knowing people and not just stories, letting these stories become not just our projects but also our lives. But people like Beth know that it's worth it. Not just worth it when we see the redemption in the hearts and lives of those we love, but also worth it right here, right now. Seeing Jesus transform the worlds and hearts of others is worth spending our very lives for. I am honored to be able to witness Beth spending her life on behalf of these children, these people, who have captivated her soul.

In these pages, Beth listens to her heart and learns that hope is greater than fear and that joy is bigger than pain. She teaches us to find strength in our weakness and joy in our suffering. She knows that we are not here to save the people we serve, but rather that they will point us closer to the Savior. Beth tells the stories of her friends. Friends whose hands she has held, whose tears she has wiped away. She believes that their pain will make them stronger. She believes that their stories will make us stronger. We learn from these stories that there is hope. There is hope for each of us that in Jesus there will be redemption for our brokenness and purpose in our wounds. Jesus weeps with these children, as do we. But He also promises to bring beauty from ashes, to restore hope, and with them, we believe His promises.

I meet Jesus anew in Beth's stories, in the stories of these children. It is my prayer that you will, too. It is my prayer that all of us will know and believe that Jesus can turn our greatest pain into our greatest joy, if we only invite Him to.

Opening Thoughts

Stories Are Lived to Be Told

There are some things in life that you are not supposed to survive, but you do. Some stories are so horrific that they beg not to be told, but they must be. Other stories are so beautiful that they transcend human understanding and embody a redemption rarely seen this side of heaven. These stories, too, must be shared. These stories—these realities—are lived out loud, by children who have survived war and slavery and by courageous men and women who have names—names that have been changed in this book to protect their identities.

Through this journey of stories, the Lord has revealed to me the deep places of the soul and helped me find answers to my greatest questions. I have found His glory in the reflection of my own tears, as I washed the feet of a recently rescued boy soldier, as I held the hands of young girls who had been raped as a weapon of war, and as I feared the death of children I love as my own who were hiding from bombs on the other side of the world. In these pages you will find wonderment, evil, survival, dancing, torture, redemption, adventure, and grace. In these pages you will find miracles.

By telling our stories and what we have learned, we step into the stories of others and give them hope for what the other side of pain can look like. In addition to the stories of these loved ones across the sea, I also tell a portion of my own story. Though it was difficult to reveal my own ugly past, if even one person's life may be altered as a result, it will be worth it. I believe that when we are courageous enough to be vulnerable, we encourage others to find the intimacy and freedom that come only through being known and loved.

> *By telling our stories, we step into the stories of others and give them hope for what the other side of pain can look like.*

In an effort to be candid, I have been careful not to reveal specifics of my story that may cause hurt to others. Because the details of my own trauma involve a long-dissolved marriage (to a person I no longer know but wish well), along with other events that are deeply personal, I have been intentionally vague about some details that led to my own counseling and admittance into a day-treatment program for post-traumatic stress disorder. But, more important, in God's beautiful plan, it was *that* journey of healing that remarkably intersected my path with the lives of former child soldiers, child survivors of war, and young sex slaves. More important than the details of a painful journey is what awaits us on the other side of brokenness. As you walk to the other side of the stories in this book, you will witness God's story of redemption—not in details of broken pasts, but in the radiance of survival and dancing in the shadows of suffering.

But this is not a story about me. I am not special or wonderful. I do not and have not done anything my dear friends and our teammates in Africa don't do *every* day of their normal lives. If there is anything good in me, it's because I have tasted the mercy of a patient and forgiving Savior. This is a story of the gospel and the redeeming power of Jesus, and it's a story of second chances that turn into third chances and . . . even fourth. I am not my own. I am a broken woman who is still in the process of being mended by the Creator of grace. Still falling. Still getting up. Still trying to learn how to live and love better, still often getting it wrong.

This is a story about grace—in all its many colors and wonder. One night when I was putting my niece to bed, she looked up at me and randomly asked, "Aunt B, if kindness were a color, what would it be?" She has an artist's heart and probably knew the word *magenta* before she knew *red*. "I don't know . . . maybe blue?" I said. She looked up at me and smiled. "Then if you were a color, you would be blue."

Her innocent question led to pondering, *What about grace?* What if grace were a color? What about redemption or love? I finally concluded that these words, these soulful gifts that only exist because of God, would be an array of colors too beautiful for simple words, and they can only truly be seen by living them.

And so I invite you into this story *with one request*: that you keep reading. Sometimes you may fully identify with what you read and it will speak hope to your heart. Sometimes you will smile and sometimes you will cry—especially as you read the painful details of a child who survived war. When those difficult stories come, you may want to stop, but I strongly ask that you do not. *Keep reading.* Keep reading until the end. By doing so, my prayer is that you will find treasures that will change you, and, by doing so, you will certainly give honor to these children's lives. I often tell myself that if these children can survive such atrocities, I can be strong enough to listen to their stories.

When I was asked to write this book, I accepted with a pounding heart and fear in my veins. But there was no doubt as to whether I would say yes—not because I necessarily wanted to, but because it was an act of obedience to the One who gave me a second chance at life and a responsibility that comes from being honored to sit with the world's most broken and learning from them.

Through living this adventure, I tasted blood in the marrow of life. This life-giving blood is not found in the shadows of comfort or in climbing career ladders. I found joy in the regions of poverty and forgiveness in the land of betrayal. I discovered life in those who have known death, and light in the heart of darkness. I saw hope reflected in the tears of an orphaned child and felt purity in the violated. I witnessed power in those whose innocence was stolen. I sensed peace in the middle of war and saw magic in the eyes of the dying. I found spiritual wealth and a richness of life in places most of the world pities. And I have come to realize that many of us in the West live in great physical wealth, drowning in the things that surround us, but suffer deep spiritual poverty and loneliness as we strive for more.

If we would learn forgiveness, resilience, gratefulness, and joy from these children, we would be radically changed. And these young survivors would be our greatest teachers.

Oh, and also . . . *keep reading*.

His, Bethany

SECTION ONE

Broken to Be Poured Out

Our souls will never rise to the heights of the spiritual mountains unless they have first descended into the valley of humiliation.

—Father Andrew, S.D.C.

CHAPTER ONE

As Sick as Our Secrets

Every saint has a past. Every sinner has a future.

—OSCAR WILDE

"Paper or plastic?" the grocery store clerk routinely asked. I didn't answer; I was focused on the lady in front of me. I watched as her manicured fingers slid her debit card into the neat slot of her wallet; the card sat perfectly in line with the others. She tucked her wallet into a perfectly matching purse, which coordinated perfectly with her suit, which already looked perfect with her peep-toe wedges. The shoes, of course, revealed that her pedicured toes matched her fingernails. Perfectly.

"Paper or plastic?" the clerk inquired again. I looked down at my hand to see the smudged remains of a hastily written reminder: "Wire food money to Congo for kids." The baseball cap on my head covered my hair, which was three days unwashed. The holes in my hat matched the holes in my shoes, but any other potential for perfect matching ended there.

My interest in the perfectly matching lady had nothing to do with envy, nor did I judge her. She was simply familiar to me. She reminded me of a woman I once knew.

I finished my purchase, finally choosing paper, and went straight to wire money so our team could purchase food for the former child soldiers and orphaned children in our care at the Peace Lives Center in the Democratic Republic of the Congo (DRC). After completing the transfer, I walked to my car, praying with each step. I had spent the morning with our Exile International team discussing the need to evacuate the children at the center, knowing the rebels were moving closer to them each day. After three days of deep prayer, sleepless nights, and helpless tears, I was exhausted. I paused when I got into my car and looked at my cracked fingernails as my hands rested on the steering wheel.

That perfect lady—I used to be her.

While my wallet never remotely matched my purse—and definitely not my shoes—I had been perfect at seeming so in control, so accomplished, so spiritually on point. But my "perfection" was in truth a daily mask that I had put on like makeup to cover the scars of shameful decisions. My mask had hid a life shriveling from the cancer of comparison, a life sick from so many secrets.

How was I ever that lady?

That lady—whose life had been sick with secrets—had found the courage to walk into the truth when she met children who had lived through horrors that begged to hide in the darkness. But these children found the courage to tell the truth, and their truth opened doors of hope and healing, not only for themselves but for you and me as well. Children like Devine and Nelson.

When Devine was three years old, her mother found her bleeding in the forests of Congo after being raped by rebel soldiers. Devine's mother scooped up her child and carried her two miles out of the forest. Unable to provide what her wounded daughter needed, she placed her in the arms of a man who took her to a care center for survivors of gender-based violence. Now a teenager, Devine is radiant. She is a leader among her peers. Her smile and song tell a story of survival. After all Devine has experienced, why is she so strong today?

> *When Devine was three years old, her mother found her bleeding in the forests of Congo.*

Because someone believed in her. Because someone believed she was larger than her past and stronger than her greatest pain.

Nelson is a timid yet strong young man who lives in Uganda. When he was ten years old, the Lord's Resistance Army (LRA) brazenly stormed his village in the middle of the night. Nelson woke to the sound of gunfire and the piercing screams of the mutilated. Smashing into his family's straw hut, soldiers jerked Nelson up from his mat on the dirt floor and screamed commands he could not comprehend. He finally understood the horrific orders as the soldiers repeatedly pointed to his parents and forced a machete into his hands. Nelson was spattered with the blood of his parents, and their screams battered his ears. His hands were tied above his head and his feet were bound with chains. For two days and nights, he was prodded by the butts of rifles and led deep into the forest.

Today I sat at his feet as he bravely shared the story of his art-therapy drawing in front of several other children who had experienced similar pain. We walked back to our huts, holding hands. During our final day together, he allowed me to wash his feet as a sign of renewal and redemption. We wept together.

Now a teenager, he dreams of caring for other orphaned children when he completes his schooling. Why is Nelson able to dream today?

Because someone believed in him. Because someone believed he was larger than his past and stronger than his greatest pain.

There is a little girl in the United States. She lives inside the body of a grown woman. A woman who, because of her past and her pain, had given up on herself and on life. But this little girl . . . this woman . . . found purpose in the story of a girl in Congo named Devine and a boy in Uganda named Nelson. Because of these children and many more, her greatest heartache turned into her greatest ministry, and grace came full circle.

Because God never stopped believing in her. Because purpose can come from pain.

I am that little girl. I am that woman.

My story led me to Devine and to Nelson, and so—as painful as my story is to tell—I begin here. For my story helped me understand theirs. And I hope it will help you understand yours. My story showed me the way to a healing that transcends culture and time. My story begins with dreams.

As a young girl, I loved life. Bubbly, imaginative, and stubborn since the day I was born, I wasn't the easiest child to reason with; but my parents were supportive, loving, and always pointed me toward God. Overall, my childhood was full of wonderment, joy, and laughter. I played in the woods, made mud pies, hoed rows of tobacco, went hunting, and ate juicy, red watermelons from Granddaddy's garden with my brother, sister, and cousins. As a kid, I liked my feet to be dirty and bare—I still do.

My grandparents lived next door, which in the country really means a cornfield or two away, and my cousins lived down the street. I grew up in Farmington, Kentucky, with my older sister and younger brother, who shared my same outgoing personality. We were loud and lively. My dad was kindhearted, wise, and goofy (I inherited the goofy part). He served as a minister at small Kentucky churches throughout my childhood. My mom had a nurturing, thoughtful spirit and served others by writing notes of encouragement to the hurting, making casseroles for the grieving, and hosting showers or get-togethers at church and home. We were all raised to be leaders in our communities, to honor the Bible, and to stand for what was right above all. Life was sweet and simple. My childhood was certainly not perfect, but it was wonderful.

Even as a small child, I had a unique love relationship with the Lord, and the desire of my heart was to serve Him and help others come to know Him. When missionaries came to speak at church, I sat bright-eyed in the front row, ready to hear every detail. I dreamed of serving overseas, especially in Africa. I remember asking Santa Claus for a monkey one year for Christmas—fully believing he would come through for me. To my dismay, the only animal under the tree that year was a stuffed chimp, holding a banana that fit in the pre-made hole in his mouth.

As a naive and giddy eighteen-year-old, I went off to a small Christian college ready to take on the world. Actively involved in campus life, I couldn't wait to get to know everyone I could—the outgoing kids, the kids eating by themselves, and those who didn't seem to fit in. My heart has always been pulled toward the lonely. Being an overachiever, popular, and a perfectionist, I constantly found myself striving to do and be more. I always seemed to be in charge of something, speaking at devotionals, or serving as an officer in a club.

I traveled on my first short-term mission trip to Zimbabwe, Africa, during my freshman year. It was a dream come true! I fell in love with the culture and the people I met in Africa. Every sight, smell, and story brought me life. Feeling at home there, I knew international work would somehow be part of my life. Even then, I began planning when I could return.

I hadn't dated much in high school; I was too busy soaking up life, leading pep rallies, and spending time with friends. To say I was a social butterfly would be an understatement. During college, I met a young man who was intelligent, very involved on campus, and admired by many. Unlike me, he was pretty reserved, but became one of my closest friends, as we shared much in common spiritually and in leadership. We began dating, and he soon became the first boy-friend I'd had for more than three months (which was a big deal).

We grew closer and closer—partially from the natural rhythm of sharing life together but mostly from an unhealthy dependency that came with repeated cycles of arguing, breaking up, and then getting back together. Believing to a fault that everything would work out, I was convinced we would be fine. We were both Christians and believed divorce was not an option in marriage—somehow we thought that made up for the emotional sickness that defined much of our relationship. Neither of us knew what healthy dating looked like, so we were blind to the signs of our dysfunction. Or maybe we just covered our eyes for fear that breaking up might mean having to start over with someone else.

So despite two tumultuous years of dating, we married in 1994, when I was twenty-one. We loved God and loved each other, but we did not know how to love each other *well*. Sometimes two very good people can have the best intentions, but without guidance on how to walk well together and love in a healthy intentional way, they fall.

From the beginning, the marriage was difficult. Arguing was our first language, and trying to be "good enough" became my calling. Sure, we had good times. We shared laughter,

> *Arguing was our first language, and trying to be "good enough" became my calling.*

good memories, and vacations. But the good times were overshadowed by a growing wall of power struggles, secrets, rageful nights, and an inability to cope with our own internal battles. One night in particular stands out in my mind—though it was not much different from many other nights. We'd both spent our days pretending to have it together, and that night a casual conversation about finances erupted into a vicious power struggle and a clash of strong wills. When we had exhausted ourselves, I stormed out of the room to sleep on the couch, slamming the door behind me.

In the midst of our pain, we both honed the skill of keeping the truth of our home life a secret. We were both climbing ladders in our professions—I was building a counseling practice and he was getting promotions in his field of education—and both of us were pursuing advanced degrees. We wanted things to be better, but we didn't know how to find the answers. We were much better at helping others than ourselves.

We were respected, admired, and sought out in both our church and community. We led a Sunday school class together and occasionally spoke at church and community events. Women struggling in their marriages looked to me for counsel; men admired my husband for being a leader in the community and in our church. As much as it pains me to admit it, I liked the view from atop the pedestal. It was comfortable. I liked the attention and the sense of accomplishment that came from being esteemed. Though we tore each other apart when we were alone, in public we bolstered each other's facades. If one of us fell, we would fall together, so we nodded in sympathy, dished out encouragement, smiled, and hugged. When people asked how we were, we would say, "Fine," and go about our business. We were masters of pretending.

Slowly, but in very real ways, I began losing myself. Feeling as if I were somehow the cause of all the emotional withdrawal, unhappiness, and anger, my confidence declined. My once-passionate fire for Jesus slowly started to fade.

Yes, we went to counselors, but we weren't completely transparent. I was fearful of openly sharing details about my husband's battles; he was a leader, after all, and I didn't want to shame him. These sessions gave us a sense of improvement, but the results were temporary. Previous patterns of explosiveness and withdrawal always returned.

I was on my knees regularly. I begged God to show me the answer. I placed sticky notes on my dashboard as reminders of what I needed to do to "be enough." I deeply desired to make my husband happy but felt totally unable to do so. But somehow my hopeful heart still believed we would be okay.

"Our marriage is like a lock," I would say to myself. "We just have to find the right combination to make it better; and when we do, we will help so many others who are struggling. God will use this for good."

As our fighting escalated and our secrecy simmered, we became the worst versions of ourselves.

But as our fighting escalated and our secrecy simmered, we slowly became the worst versions of ourselves. We both made choices from our most broken places, and the result left gaping wounds in our hearts and in what was left of our marriage. I will not venture into great detail here. My father once told me to be wise with my words because of the power they hold to give life or death. He also told me to always tell the truth. By withholding the salacious details that contributed to the outcome, I'm attempting to be both wise and truthful.

After around seven years of marriage, we started living two separate lives. Eventually, he started living upstairs and I lived downstairs; but no one knew. I mastered the craft of making excuses for why I went to activities alone, why my eyes were swollen from crying, why there was a hole in the wall, or why we weren't having children. I think bringing a child into that relationship was the thing I feared most; it would only amplify our issues.

Then one day I met a new friend who slowly became a confidant and support. He valued me—something I had not felt in many years. He ignited feelings within me that simultaneously excited me and terrified me. For several months I would successfully refrain from seeing him, but then I'd cave in and we'd spend time together again. In my heart I knew I should cut off all communication with him and fight off my attraction to him.

I tried, but I failed. And though I hadn't planned it and despite my desperately trying to end it, our relationship developed into an affair. What started out as friendship led to an addictive relationship and unfaithfulness to my marriage vows. The very things I had judged others for and the very things I had brazenly claimed I would never do, I did. Repeatedly.

I had my secrets and my husband had his, and our marriage spiraled into darkness. Sin has a way of shaming us. And shame and sin both love to feast on secrets, so we were a smorgasbord—we were as sick as our secrets. I hated myself and the entanglement in which I was living.

As if it were possible, our marriage became more volatile and unstable. I ended the affair, but the shame haunted me. We couldn't hold up the walls of our crumbling home any longer, and I confessed the truth to my husband.

It was the worst of times. Soon our secrets came spilling out to my family and our friends. Knowing that rumors were spreading in our close community, one Sunday morning, we went before our church, and I admitted my affair. I was unmasked, humiliated, and filled with shame.

Heartbroken over my actions and the hurt I had caused others, I immersed myself in guilt. There was no punishment I wouldn't take: I endured interrogations, being followed, and being verbally and emotionally torn down. The punishments deepened my shame and the break in my spirit.

The faces of those who once respected us and came to us for guidance were now filled with pity, confusion, and disgust. It was a scandal of the worst kind. In shame and regret, I left the church we had been part of for many years. My once-perfect dream lay crumpled on the ground, and I lay beside it, lost in grief. More than anything, I grieved for the plans God had for my life that I felt I had destroyed.

I moved out of the house to find solace from the war inside. After being forced to file for legal protection, I felt safer—but still racked with guilt. Then one rainy day in Nashville, at thirty-one years of age, I sat alone in a courtroom on a wooden chair, signed the papers that finalized my divorce, and ended my ten-year marriage. I walked back to the car in the rain, feeling as if my life was over. I had never imagined that divorce would enter my life; I was everything I hated.

Dangerous things happen to our psyches and souls when we give up on ourselves and allow our spirits to be beaten down. After the divorce I became trapped in a downward spiral. I was desperate for God's love and guidance, yet because I saw myself as damaged goods, I made even more impulsive decisions—decisions that would bring deeper trauma and regret.

A divorce is a lot like a basketball game. People think they have to choose sides and talk bad about the other team. When that happens, relationships are damaged, and you sometimes lose friends. I lost friends not only because some distanced themselves from me, but also because I isolated myself out of shame.

During those moments, I could not see that God's mercy is great and His love is steadfast, and I certainly didn't want to hear it from anyone who had not walked my pathway. I could only see what was right in front of me—a broken woman and a broken life.

The pages of my journal, which once held detailed dreams, were now stained with tears and ink blotches, as I cried out to a Savior whom I could not find. Depression enveloped me like a heavy cloud. I saw no way out of its shadow.

At the time, I had no idea that God was going to use the remnants of my wrecked life to point others to the redemptive hope found only through Him—and I certainly didn't know He would turn my silent, isolated mourning into dancing in a displacement camp with children who had survived war.

But He did.

And in the process, He saved my life, and walked me into miracles and wonderment beyond my wildest dreams.

Reflections from My Journal...

He Said No

"If I find in myself a desire which no experience
in this world can satisfy, the most probable
explanation is that I was made for another world."
                                                    —C. S. Lewis[1]

I remember being in gym class when I was about
eleven years old. I said something or did something.
I don't really remember what. But I do remember
what she said. I remember a girl looking at me and
saying, "You're weird."

And at that moment I thought, She's right. I am.
I'm not normal. But it's like I didn't care—or I didn't
know I was supposed to care. I mean, I wasn't a
social outcast. In fact, I was well-liked, receiving
high school superlatives and homecoming queen crowns,
but I seemed to be cut from a different cloth.

Not much has changed. And now it seems that
the more I pray for spiritual eyes, the more God
changes my lens and the more uncomfortable normal
becomes. It is a peaceful wrestling. But in my
wrestling, I sometimes feel a deep disconnection.

Like now.

I am lying on a beach chair, on my stomach, by
myself, in the middle of downtown Nashville—reading
a book and writing in my journal. I am surrounded by
chatter about the latest parties, celebrity gossip,

and fashion—people talking about how to make more money and climb more ladders. I have a cute hat on my head and black sunglasses covering my eyes. And I am crying. Crying after reading these words from Shane Claiborne upon his return from Iraq:

> I grew especially close to one of the "shoeshine boys"—a homeless boy around ten-years-old named Mussel [in Baghdad].... Day after day... we grew on each other. We went on walks, turned somersaults and yelled at airplanes "Salaam" [Peace!].... Mussel began internalizing what was happening. Nothing I could do made him smile... he mimicked with his hands the falling of bombs and made the sound of explosions, as tears welled up in his eyes. Suddenly he turned and latched onto my neck. He began to weep and his body shook as he grasped for each breath of air. I begin to cry... we wept as friends, as brothers, not as a peacemaker and a victim."[2]

And I wept with them. Lying in my chair a world away. Longing to be in the dirt with Mussel. Craving to be in the street with him. Dirty. There in Iraq. Who is with him now? He is not a name in a book. He is somewhere. He is somebody.

Some words should not go together: Children. Bombs. Guns. War. Slave. Just to name a few.

I close my eyes. By choice, I have become transparent. I've spent too many years wearing masks and hiding behind locked doors. Life is meant to be lived together and out loud. Not in the shadows with hidden tears. These days, I talk often about my fall from the pedestal. I talk openly about past struggles and am candid about poor choices that God has patiently used to teach me. He has taught me much, and there is no place I would rather be than at the foot of the Rabbi. Living. Learning. Loving. Even when it hurts. No, life has not been easy, and I am weary of many things. I am weary of coming home to an empty bed and an uncertain future. But I am not weary of Love. I am not weary of the heartache that comes from loving God's children. The deeper I go into His heart, the more I find the broken and the beautiful. In every letter from a child across the ocean, in every story I hear from the sofa in my counseling office, in every insight of wisdom I hear from the suffering.

I once believed a reflection of Jesus had to be pretty—even perfect. I believed that if I could not be pretty and perfect, then I could not reflect Him. Even worse, I could not be close to Him, and He definitely would not wish to be close to me. But I have come to know that God loves scars. And Jesus, while walking with the righteous, also surrounded Himself with people who could win awards for immorality. In His human form, Jesus Himself

loved perfectly and lived perfectly—but He bore
the scars of suffering, scars He did not hide from
others.

Imagining I am walking through the heart of
the Savior, I do not see only the pretty. I do not
merely see neat. I do not see married, 2.5 kids,
and a picket fence. I do not see pretty faces
and plastic smiles. I see the lonely. I see the
deserted. I see the depressed. I feel the pain of
those who are dying alone. I hear the heartbeat of
the homeless child who is shaken at night by bombs.
I feel the soft hand of the mother who longs to hold
the baby she has aborted. I taste the salt in the
tears of the father who was forced to say good-bye
to his son too soon. No, I do not see the pretty, the
perfect, the nice, or the neat.

Not in the broken heart of Jesus.

I see the woman at the well. Many men had known
her body, but only One knew her soul. I see Paul,
who persecuted Christians. I see the woman caught
in adultery. Condemned to be stoned, she stood
accused.

And He said, "No."

"No. I do not see you as they do. I do not see you
as you do. Not in my heart.

"You are not who you were or what was done to
you; you are not what you have seen or what you have
done. That is not what I see when I look at you.

"I see Me. In you. I am there. In the street.

In the shadows. In the nights of silent tears. In the mirror and the feelings of inadequacy. In the bombs. In the thinking you can't go on. In the hoping you won't. In the fear. In the silence. In the dirt. In the loneliness. In the hiding. I am there. And I see you. And I love you. Scars and all."

CHAPTER TWO

I Choose to Live

Nothing can hurt you if you can understand that whatever you are going through is your invitation to participate in the redemption of the world.
—FATHER THOMAS KEATING

Nothing in my life is as I had imagined, I thought. I was thirty-one, divorced, with no children and a scarlet past.

When the divorce was finalized in the spring of 2004, I retreated to the mountains of Colorado. I had visited Colorado only twice in my life, but I had fallen in love with the serenity of the mountains. The fact that I knew only one person in Boulder did not hinder or intimidate me. In fact, I knew I needed a fresh, safe place to mend—away from the fear of being followed and the whispers of gossip. I needed to be alone with my Lord to discover my worth again. There in the sheltering majesty of those towering peaks, I isolated myself in an attempt at self-preservation. I sought therapy in long drives up and down winding roads, pondering my future and grieving for my past.

Praying was difficult. For many years I had begged God to mend my marriage, but it was not mended. It was irreparably broken. Surrendering all self-created expectations, my primary prayer for many months became only these words: *Mend my past. Magnify my present. Mold my future into what you would have it to be.*

Beyond that prayer, I begged God for forgiveness. Over and over I pleaded. The shame over my affair had its grip on me and would not let go. Carl Jung says that shame is "the swampland of the soul."[1] This swampland had overtaken and wrapped itself around my spirit. I wept for my past decisions. I lamented disappointing my Lord. I flogged my spirit to punish myself for things I could not undo. Chest-deep in the swampland, I saw no way out. I absolutely and utterly gave up on myself, but somehow I did not give up on God. Even though I didn't always feel close to Him, I knew He was my only constant. Kneeling became sacred. But even in that position of petition, I often had no words. Sometimes I would sit in His presence, saying nothing. I longed to imagine Him holding me, but I felt He was too disappointed in me to be that tender toward me. I now realize that my compass for coping with my divorce, unfaithfulness, and shattered expectations was as broken as my life.

Going to church in Colorado was as difficult as praying. I felt dirty as soon as I walked through the doors even though no one there knew my story. But these kind people greeted me with love and acceptance. They knew only my present, didn't really care about my past, and wanted to walk beside me into my future. I slowly let them in. My new community of friends talked about their struggles openly and prayed for one another without judgment. This concept of authentic living was new to me. The church I began attending was known in town as the "me too" church. If you had struggled with something, chances were that someone at that church had as well. I often heard, "We are all sinners. We are all struggling or have struggled with something. You have struggled with lust? Me too. You are tempted by pornography? Overspending? Depression? Not feeling close to God or feeling inadequate? Me too." I was blown away and refreshed by their transparency.

In my previous life, I had not walked in true community. Surrounded by people who looked up to me for guidance and answers, I had hidden my secret struggles and distracted myself from reality. I'd found false value through volunteer work and other responsibilities. The authenticity of my new Colorado friends was scary. I wasn't accustomed to people who were so transparent, but these new friends wrapped their open, loving arms around me, taught me to walk in community, and helped me embrace the grace I had been pushing away. So I stepped out in weak faith and took my first, fumbling baby steps of healing in this safe and loving community.

That year of solitude in Colorado created room in my spirit for much-needed solace, and slowly—very slowly—I began to find grace.

I found a wonderful counselor who could see that I was struggling to forgive myself. One day he asked if he could share a scripture verse with me. He read it aloud slowly so each word would soak in: "For God has imprisoned everyone in disobedience so he could have mercy on everyone" (Romans 11:32, NLT).

"Do you see?" he said. "It's more about His mercy than your disobedience. He desires to have mercy on you. He orchestrated it that way. Let Him love you. Allow Him to be merciful and compassionate. That's what He does best."

Let Him love me? I thought.

Driving away from the appointment, I started to see that, from the beginning, God knew we would be disobedient. He is not shocked when we sin. Where sin rears its ugly head, His mercy rises up all the more powerfully. By allowing ourselves to accept the gift of His grace, we commune with the cross. I began to understand that the cross is not a reward for good behavior; rather, it is a bridge connecting a broken, shattered world to our loving

> *If sin is the conflict between humanity and God, then resolution is found by repenting and allowing ourselves to be embraced by our Savior.*

Creator. The goal of conflict is not distance; it's resolution. So if sin is the conflict between humanity and God, then resolution is found by repenting and allowing ourselves to be embraced by our Savior. And it's hard to be held when hiding.

Along with teaching me to receive His grace, God began calling me to give grace to others. I carried the burden of not forgiving my former husband—a weight I had carried even from the beginning of our marriage; I carried anger and unforgiveness toward those who rejected me after the divorce. I tried to forgive, but I couldn't find release. I knew God had called me to forgive as I had been forgiven (Matthew 6:15, NIV), but the pain was so thick I couldn't fathom cutting through it to real forgiveness.

For me, forgiveness began with a seed of humility, and that humility took root when I acknowledged my own need for mercy. Granting myself permission to walk this path slowly, I wrote in my journal: "Maybe extending mercy is an intentional choice that leads us into the process of forgiveness. When I look a brother in the eye and see his need for forgiveness, I realize I am looking into my own reflection. Mercy is a choice. Forgiveness is a process. Grace is a gift."

When I think of the hard work of forgiveness, I remember so many wounded people who somehow display heroic acts of reconciliation. I recall a moving conversation about forgiveness that I had with a friend I met in Rwanda. Aimee is a survivor of the 1994 genocide, which left hundreds of thousands of Rwandans brutally murdered because of severe tribal conflict and historical tensions. Family members turned against one another. Even church members killed one another. Some people say the devil took over the country during those one hundred days. Visiting one of the country's genocide memorials, I wept, surrounded by hundreds of skulls (children and adults) that had been kept as a reminder to never again allow such a tragedy to occur.

"I don't understand this forgiveness I hear about in Rwanda," I said. "How is it possible to forgive after such deep pain?"

Looking at me with gentle eyes and a peaceful smile, she replied, "We realized it was the evil within the man that did the killing and not the man himself."

What a sacred, beautiful way to view a human being! It takes a beautiful soul and a humble attitude to separate the heart of a person from his or her painful actions. During my time in Colorado, I worked to follow this example and train my heart and eyes toward forgiveness, but it was no small feat. After Nelson Mandela spent twenty-seven years in prison, he said, "As I walked out the door toward the gate that would lead to my freedom, I knew if I didn't leave my bitterness and hatred behind, I'd still be in prison." I was just beginning to learn how to walk in the freedom that forgiveness provides.

I loved Colorado and my life there, but after being there more than a year, I missed my family and nieces in Nashville. I was ready to be near them again. It was time to go back and establish a new, single life back home. And I was terrified. The timid part of me wanted to tuck my tail between my legs and take the easy route—live with my parents, give up my counseling practice, and find a job that required little interaction with others. But I had fight in me that didn't want the enemy to win, and my pride was still alive. As I prepared to return home, I wrote and carried these words on a piece of paper to remind me of my freedom . . . to remind me to fight: *Don't walk like a wounded warrior. Dance like a slave who has been set free.*

I longed to dance, but I was terrified to take a step. I wanted to live in grace and celebrate freedom from shame, but upon returning home, I was surprised by how ill-prepared I was for the intense fears that overwhelmed me.

In Colorado I could ignore these fears. I was safe and accepted. But when I returned home at the end of 2005, I was greeted by nightmares and flashbacks of my last year of marriage. I feared facing people from my previous life and not knowing what they would say. I was unprepared for this downward emotional spiral, and I am forever thankful to my family, who walked me through it.

I plummeted into a depression of emotional suffocation. My spirit gasped for air, battled for survival. I sometimes sat, literally shaking my head back and forth, trying to physically break free from the mind cloud. Simple tasks were mountains. I climbed, wrestled, and pushed past the pain to accomplish the daily activities that those around me breezed through.

On top of it all, I became increasingly disconnected. At times I felt as if I were living in a dream. Sometimes I lay in bed for hours, refusing to take on a new day. Most of the time, however, I tapped into depleted reserves and somehow pushed through.

Damning thoughts struck like a battle axe at my mind. *What if I am rejected by everyone forever? I have ruined my life. All the plans God had to use my life to bring others to Him are ruined. I am tainted. Who could want me?*

Blocking out as many of the blows as possible and attempting to dodge the others, I turned to writing. I wrote truths and Bible verses on note cards to carry around with me—truths such as: "God has not given us a spirit of fear or timidity, but of power and love and a sound mind" (2 Tim 1:7).

I wrote my thoughts in my journal—words dripping with laments and the scriptures I held on to for dear life. I wrote poems and creative writing that helped me process my thoughts, but mainly I wrote to God.

> Father, I am trapped. Trapped in this body and this life that I wish to shed. Trapped in the guilt and shame that is drowning me. To ask You to lift my guilt is to ask an undeserved blessing, and even approaching Your throne feels uncivil of me. I have failed You, Lord. If this is my punishment, my king, then I beg Your mercy.

Thoughts of suicide tempted me regularly. I couldn't believe I was thinking those thoughts, but the emotional pain was so dense, I felt I couldn't go on living. I knew I needed to reach out for help, but I had never done that before, and I didn't know how. I knew how to be a helper and a fixer, but receiving the help I desperately needed was uncharted territory.

One day, lying on my sister's bed, I asked myself, *Do you want to live or do you want to die? Are you going to fight or give up?* I laid there for some time—wrestling with these questions, emotionally fighting the darkness. Taking a deep breath, I sat up and looked this question boldly in the eyes, as if it were an animal threatening to pounce on me, and I knew the answer: *I choose to live. I choose to fight.*

When our level of desperation becomes greater than our pride, true healing can begin.

Getting up from the bed, I started looking for a treatment program. Having worked in a psychiatric facility for years as a clinician, being on the other end felt more than humbling. It was humiliating, especially because I knew so many psychiatrists and counselors in the field.

Stripped of any remnants of pride, I finally began a journey toward honest healing. Perhaps that was the key: when our level of desperation becomes greater than our pride, true healing can begin.

On that day, I realized that if I were going to live and live abundantly, I would have to fight. What I didn't realize was that fighting the darkness would take much more than a one-time decision. I would have to choose to fight again and again. Abundant life would not come easily or without a price. Wonderful things rarely do.

Reflections from My Journal...

Chasing the Tail of a Rainbow

I am lost. These mountains that surround me are my shield, and as I know only one real person in this town, the Flatirons of Boulder seem to be my only friends. Coming from ministry and teaching classes and being in the center of everything around me, I find this solitude a drastic change—a change I welcome. I know isolation feeds depression, and I am in the pit of it, but it feels comfortable. Too comfortable.

Saturday afternoon it rained. I hadn't eaten all day and needed to get out, so I went out to get food, or so I thought. Leaving the apartment, I noticed the clouds had cleared. The rainbows were on double duty. Looking up at the sky, I saw not one but two of the most beautiful rainbows I had ever seen! Brilliant. Bold. Magical.

So I set out to follow them—to find their end, actually.

I was on a mission and a chase, facing the clock before the rainbows disappeared.

What does the end of a rainbow really look like? I wondered.

I was determined to find out once and for all. I turned left and right, looking up in the sky and plotting my course according to where I thought the end would be. And then the end would move. And I would chase it again.

Chasing the tail of a rainbow is no easy task.

I did it for what seemed to be an hour. I couldn't believe the rainbows were still in the sky! It was like God was waiting on me to find them— giggling at me the entire time. He had me on a wild rainbow chase, and chase I did. I drove and turned and drove some more. I followed the back roads, wondering if I would ever find my way out again. I was getting closer and closer. Soon one rainbow disappeared, so now I chased the tail of rainbow number two, driving as fast as I could on a mountain road. And then I found it!

Driving around the corner, I came closer and closer to the end of the rainbow. It was right there. It just has to be right there, I thought. Just around here. Just around this corner. It looks like it goes into that field. Just... right... there.

And it did.

For a split second, I saw it. I parked on the side of the road, jumped out of my car, and bolted to the middle of an abandoned field. I ran to where the rainbow ended, and just as I got there, it faded into the field.

And then it was gone.

Was there a pot? No. Was there gold? Not a piece. There was only a slow, faint, colorful fade into an abandoned field. And then that was it. It was over.

The moment felt like the day after Christmas but held no disappointment. I was actually filled to overflowing. It was quite different from the emotional place I was in a few hours earlier. I was exonerated. Enraptured. Full. But that wasn't even the good part. Not even close.

It took me twice as long to get home as it took me to find the end of the rainbow. I was as lost as a southern girl could be in new western territory with absolutely no sense of direction. But it didn't matter. It just gave me more time to sing praise songs and thank God for this incredible joyride.

Which wasn't over.

I finally got home and opened the cabinet to get a glass for a drink. And there I found something pretty incredible.

Mom, the Chief Encourager, had left cards hidden around my apartment when she and Dad visited last week. Opening the cabinet, I found one of them.

I opened the card and read these words: "God puts rainbows in the clouds so that each of us—in the dreariest and most dreaded moments—can see a possibility of hope" (Maya Angelou).

Lesson learned: We strive and we plot and we plan for the end—the goal, the top of the ladder, or the "when I get there" moment. But that moment isn't actually where the gold is waiting.

There is no pot; there is no gold. When we get to that "I will be happy when" or "We will be okay after" place, guess what happens?

The place moves. Then we are left trying to find another rainbow to chase. Or... we can look back on our journey, kneel down in the middle of an abandoned field, and cry out to a God bigger than life, asking Him to teach us and change us to reflect more of His Spirit.

Maybe it's in allowing Him to change us in the middle of our disappointments that we find treasures. Maybe the beauty is found more in the becoming than in the striving.

CHAPTER THREE

With Truth Comes Redemption

Damaged people are dangerous. They know they can survive.
—JOSEPHINE HART

When drowning, your only concern is your next breath. You don't think about who is watching you or what they are thinking. You don't think, *Did they see me fall through the ice?* or *Are they judging me for being careless?* All that matters is finding that one breath . . . that one breath that will lead you to another.

I was holding on for one more breath.

Not only was I desperate for breath, I was also desperate for Jesus. Desperate for His hand, craving to be reminded that He still had a plan for my life. Every night before bed, I got down on my knees on the cold floor and prayed. Prayed for the fog to lift. Begged to feel alive again. Pleaded to be lifted from the pit and placed on top of the dry ground. God didn't magically bring me out of that pit, but He did something better: He taught me how to climb, and He showed me where my next step would be.

After extensive research, I found a highly recommended day program in Dallas for my much-needed treatment. I arranged it so that nobody in the program and none of my counselors would know about my profession; I wanted to be treated like any other person there. Gone were the days of my well-played role as the spiritual leader and the one in control. Gone was the cushion of educational degrees and the cheery personality that masked my pain. The wounds I had been trying to mend on my own would finally receive the care they needed.

I was diagnosed with post-traumatic stress disorder and clinical depression. Professionally knowing these clinical terms well, I could hardly believe this was my reality. Because these terms are typically associated with experiences of war, I had a hard time grasping that this was my diagnosis. But as my counselor illuminated several episodes of complex trauma in my life, I began to see the truth of my situation and how life can bring us wars of many faces. Without going into details that are not mine to tell, I can say that much of my trauma resulted from events in my marriage and the year following our divorce. I now know that experiencing this trauma alone and without support was almost as harmful as the events themselves. I wasn't alone for lack of people to reach out to; I was alone because I was too prideful and "strong" to be honest with those around me. I mistakenly called this bravery. But it's not brave to walk through life's most painful moments alone. It takes a lot of guts to ask someone to go through hell with us. When we're vulnerable and honest and invite a trusted person or people to walk with us, our burden is eased. Not because our situation has changed but because we are no longer alone.

"You are certainly as tough as nails," the counselor said, "but that isn't always a good thing. Sometimes you have to determine when it's better to bend than to break."

With the help of my counselor, I did find that next desperately needed breath. I discovered tools to fight my codependent nature and how to own my pathway to healing. I learned that blaming others, striving for approval, and letting others' opinions determine my happiness were sure-fire pathways to bondage.

During those six weeks in the day-treatment program, the surfaces cracked, and I found a place to be real and raw about my past and every hidden secret. Surprisingly, this new place felt strangely secure. I was able to be totally truthful *and* to be accepted and loved.

I would love to say that when I left treatment in the spring of 2006, I left as an entirely "fixed person," but I didn't. My journey toward healing was much more a two-steps-forward-and-one-step-back process (I'm still learning, even now), but I appreciate each tiny move forward. There were rarely moments of *total* release or *absolute* new beginnings. Each day required a renewed choice to live in authenticity and truth, and to take full responsibility for my life. Similar to that day on my sister's bed when I made a choice to live, I must choose to fight for wholeness time and time again. Sometimes broken spirits heal much more slowly than broken bones.

> *Sometimes broken spirits heal much more slowly than broken bones.*

But something remarkable happened during my time in Dallas—a life-altering encounter that would lead me into my lifelong mission. Having sold my car to pay for the treatment center care, I was on foot. The weekend after I completed the day-treatment program, I walked to the nearest church to attend worship. When I walked in, the voice coming from the front reminded me of friends from my previous trips to Africa. My ears perked up.

The gentleman's name was Celestin Musekura, and he spoke about living through the Rwandan genocide. He shared his story of surviving near-death experiences and how forgiveness had brought healing and life. As a result of the pain he had experienced, God placed within him a passion to help his people. Out of that passion, he founded an organization called ALARM, Inc. (African Leadership and Reconciliation Ministries), which teaches leadership and reconciliation skills and provides trauma care in several African countries. My eyes lit up, and my heart started to race. I had been praying that God would weave together my counseling skills, my love for international missions, and the lessons I was learning in my own recovery from trauma. I dared to wonder if this might be part of God's answer to this prayer.

After church, I introduced myself and asked for an opportunity to meet with him the following day. He kindly agreed. I met Celestin and his wife, Bernadette, for coffee and loved hearing their hearts, their stories of hope, and the ground-breaking work ALARM was doing in Africa. They were as inspiring as they were endearing. Having a heart for children, I asked about the youth in these areas and if they also needed support. We began conversations about trauma care and children, and I quickly learned about the vast need of children in these countries for counseling. We discussed the possibility of my joining ALARM on a future trip to provide counseling to traumatized children. Knowing it would take time before I would be well enough to provide trauma care to others, I dreamed cautiously—but dream I did. For the first time in a very long time, I felt passion in my spirit again.

Returning to Nashville after the counseling program was like walking on new legs. Limping. Falling. Then trying to figure out why I fell and doing things differently the next time. Sometimes I ran. Sometimes I didn't. When I couldn't walk, I crawled.

Unlike the counseling center in Dallas, where I was part of an intimate community whose wars were similar to mine, back in Nashville I felt misunderstood, and the instinct to prove myself returned. I lost much of my community during the divorce, so I had few friends. On top of readjusting to "regular life," I had no car, no place to live, and I was deeply in debt. Some friends actually recommended that I file for bankruptcy, but I refused. I knew the path to financial stability would be long and hard, but I was determined to stay the course.

This time around, I forced myself to reach out for help in as many ways as I could. Asking for help was embarrassing and made me feel vulnerable, but it also felt hopeful. I was doing something I had never done before. I connected with various support groups, I continued counseling, and I became involved in women's Bible studies and active in church again. Although I continued to struggle with depression, I found healthier ways to live. My wonderful family stood by my side, welcoming me back home to live with them while I slowly got back on my feet.

I define "failure" quite differently now. I no longer believe it means not completing a task or not reaching a desired outcome. Failure happens when we fall but refuse to get back up. It means not learning from our struggles and our poor choices. If making mistakes leads to growth, strength, and intimacy with Jesus, is that not, somehow, wildly successful?

I read a story once about a little girl whose aunt took care of her one day. As the child got ready for school, she wrestled to put on her dress, getting her arms caught and unable to get her head through the top. Her aunt stepped in to put the dress on for her, but the girl resisted.

"It's okay," the little girl said. "I'll eventually get it. Mommy and Daddy let me struggle for a little while before I get it right."

I smiled the first time I read that story. With the best intentions, we want the quick fix that will make it all better. We may think ourselves incompetent when we "fail," when actually it is our struggle, our falling, that reminds us to alter our steps and our stance when we get up and try again. In a journal entry, I wrote:

> Some of the most beautiful cravings in my soul—
> the most painful—were when I was immersed in my
> own insignificance and feelings of worthlessness.
> Slowly the darkness began to fade, slowly my eyes
> adjusted, and slowly I felt found. Not because I was
> ever lost. Not really.

For can we really be lost when someone always knows where we are? He knows. The Lord always knows where we are. We try to hide behind the trees in the garden, ashamed of our choices and our secret lives, but He is there—loving us, believing in us, seeing us, asking us, "Where are you?" He is seeking to be with us... even in our shame.

I am at ease in Your arms, Lord. May I rest in You. Speak to my dry bones and bring them to life again. Make me Your instrument to be played humbly for Your glory. May my wounds serve as Your resting place and my scars speak of Your beauty. May my song be Your story and my death sing of Your life."

Back in Nashville, I began to find life-altering ways to practice authentic community. I chose to share life with people who had high standards of purity, and I came to understand the importance of honesty and accountability. I also learned that I stink at both! Being vulnerable and accountable are the most difficult lessons for me because they are the most unnatural. Naturally I am strong and independent. Naturally I go at it alone—just a girl and her God. But God showed me that the things I need most are the things that may not come naturally.

> *I came to understand the importance of honesty and accountability. I also learned that I stink at both!*

During that season, I let go of expectations I had been clinging to, starting with the tear-filled release of my expectations of marriage and children. I was not certain that I would never remarry, but I had to be open to that possibility. If marriage (and, even more, a fulfilling marriage) was a requirement for happiness, then it seemed a good part of the world was bound for unhappiness. There had to be more than sitting and wishing for what I didn't have and waiting to receive it to find joy. I knew I had a long road ahead of me before I would be emotionally ready for a relationship.

I came to see that striving for perfection (which is unattainable) only leads to more attempts to prove ourselves worthy and increases feelings of inadequacy. When we pursue perfection, we completely miss the point of the Gospel. But when we embrace our imperfections and inadequacies, we catch a glimpse of our dependency on Jesus to sanctify us. We are imperfect. I am inadequate. We need Christ. I need a Savior.

So at the age of thirty-four, physically healthy, youthful, and in my prime, I decided to take the entire year of 2007 off from dating so that the Lord could further heal my heart. That difficult decision provided freedom to discover my identity in the Lord without the false sense of self-esteem that often comes with attention from the opposite sex. I concluded that a wonderful marriage is a bonus, not a necessity for joy, and that only God could fulfill my need for a soul mate. I placed a ring on my left hand and committed to the Lord that I would be married to Him unless He made it evident that His will was for me to be married to someone else. Yes, some people thought that was a little radical, but people thought Jesus was radical, too, so

I just assumed I was in good company. More important than what others thought, I can say it was one of the most pivotal decisions in my healing.

As I write this, I am looking at a beautiful tree my sister painted on the wall beside my bed to remind me that God is trustworthy. It takes up the entire wall and shelters me each night as I sleep. The tree is a replica of a print I bought when I was in the treatment program in Dallas. The leaves of the tree are not leaves at all. They are painted doves, and they represent the peace that passes understanding. On the doves I wrote the words that have taught me most along this journey: *Authenticity. Rest. Beauty. Truth. Community. Forgiveness. Surrender. Courage. Faith. Forgiveness. Believe. Freedom. Prayer. Purpose. Redemption.*

When the painting was finished, I wrote these words on the trunk of the tree: "With Truth Comes Redemption. With Story Comes Song." I read those words each night before bed.

With fierce determination to never be so broken again, I picked up a pen and paper and started rewriting a creed for myself that I began during the divorce. This creed, a living dedication to an intentional life and an understanding that I will never be perfect, serves as a reflective guide to lead me back on point when I struggle. I fall short in meeting its declarations every day, and that's okay. The creed changes often and is a constant work in progress. As am I.

Reflections from My Journal...

Excerpts from My Creed (in part, and in lifelong transition)

I will find my self-worth only in the eyes of my Creator, remembering that my honor is not dictated by the approval, love, or actions of another human.

I will laugh—loudly, with passion, and unashamed.

I will learn to receive Jesus' undeserved grace as a treasure rather than refusing to accept His gifts. I will learn how to let Him love me—even in the center of shame and feelings of unworthiness.

I will embrace the art of just being with my Beloved as my painting of peace.

I will dance in the middle of the storm.

I will not allow the actions of another person to steal my joy or crush my God-breathed spirit.

I will remember that if others are to honor me, I must first honor myself.

I will find purpose in my pain, wisdom through my weaknesses, and growth in my mistakes.

I will create expectations for my life out of God's will rather than my own wishes.

I will climb trees rather than ladders.

I will choose daily to surrender myself at the feet of my Father, asking for His will to be done in all things—not my own.

I will choose to be a human being rather than a human-doer, remembering that it is in the silence of rest that the voice of God is loudest.

I will learn to rest as hard as I work—and play even harder, remembering that I cannot give away what I do not have.

I will not sacrifice the Creator's plan or will for any earthly relationships, selfish ambitions, or temporary gratifications.

I will see His new mercies in the spirit of every sunrise.

I will not overanalyze situations to the degree that I lose the experience of the moment.

I will not interpret the heart of Christ by the mistakes of His children, for our flaws are not a reflection of His.

I will seek to forgive, recognizing that there is always a story behind each imperfection and an intention behind each action.

I will choose to love without condition or agenda, realizing that I have been gifted the same love in return.

I will never wait for someone to believe in me before I believe in myself.

I will see the less fortunate as blessed in ways I am blinded to, praying daily for spiritual eyes and thankfulness of heart.

I will not allow disappointment to create persistent pain; I will instead choose to use my hurt, anger, and confusion—responding rather than reacting out of pure emotion.

I will harvest hopes rather than expectations, prayers in place of worries, and requests instead of demands.

I will embrace that being single does not mean being alone, and being alone does not mean being lonely, and that it is only in finding my wholeness in God that I may promote wholeness and health in any other relationships.

I will remember that many problems are solvable and most people are tolerable, and that I have a Father who simply wants me to ask.

I will show kindness to the coarse, give to the taker, forgive the unforgivable, and see brilliance in the broken—attempting in this to have the heart and mind of Christ.

I will see wealth as having little yet basking in contentment.

I will see honesty as the foundation for all relationships; without it the entire union is smoke and mirrors.

I will learn to speak softly and listen loudly.

I will attempt to be a woman of character, choosing to do what is right, not because it feels right but because it is right.

I will treasure the wisdom and truth of scripture.

I will refuse to walk like a wounded warrior. I will run as though I have been healed, stand as I continue to grow wiser, sing as though a symphony lives inside me.

I will seek maturity by developing the ability to delay gratification and practicing reservation of thoughts, behaviors, and impulses.

I will understand that making mistakes breeds opportunities for growth, but refusing to learn from them breeds destruction.

I will value the person God created me to be, and remember I was formed in detail by the fingers of the Almighty, praying that the hands of the Potter will continue to mold me and shape me into the woman He wants me to be.

And with God as my Soul Mate—my partner in intimacy—I will overcome.

SECTION TWO

I Will Not Look Away

Keep me away from the wisdom which does not cry,
the philosophy which does not laugh
and the greatness which does not bow before children.

—Khalil Gibran

CHAPTER FOUR

Looking Darkness in the Eye

Although the world is full of suffering, it is also full of overcoming it.
—HELEN KELLER

"How did his parents die?" I asked the tall, thin man who stood before me.

He pointed toward the forest with one hand over another and one finger pointing out, as though he were holding something.

"You know," he said. "You know . . ."

His English was better than my Swahili, but not good enough to find the right word. He held his hands up again and pointed. "You know."

Being a deer hunter and having shot a few, I knew. "Guns?" I asked, already knowing the answer.

He was laughing now. "Oh, yes, yes. The guns. It was the guns. It was the forest. It was the rebels and the war."

In the summer of 2008, two years after I'd completed the thera-peutic day program in Dallas and had that first contact with ALARM, I found myself in Congo—a place often referred to as the very heart of darkness. I welcomed the opportunity to travel on a short-term mission trip with ALARM to help lead a trauma care conference for recently displaced war survivors. God was answering my prayers to use my counseling skills, my personal journey through trauma, and my love for missions in one place. I had been to differ-ent African countries on short-term mission trips, and I had seen poverty and despair, but I was in no way prepared for what I was about to encounter.

Our team was made up of ten ladies from the United States. We were there to love, listen, and provide care to women and children emotionally wounded by the ravages of war. We were also there to learn. I met the little boy whose parents died in the forest at an or-phanage. When he was eight years old, he found himself orphaned and navigating the streets of the city of Goma for three years all alone. No parents. No family. No shelter. Just a year before I met him, he learned about the orphanage and walked five miles to get there.

I looked down at the smiling, hopeful face of this young boy, who couldn't have looked any more different from my eight-year-old niece back home; in him I saw her face—her gentle, carefree smile as she played and dreamed the innocent things children should play and dream. I tried to imagine her here in front of me, living this boy's life. I blinked away tears.

This boy's parents were brutally killed in the bush by rebels, and yet the orphanage administrator spoke casually of it. He laughed as if it were a familiar mistake, like tripping and falling over a tree stump in the woods. As if murder were as simple as a familiar mishap.

But murder in the forest of Congo was common for him and his community. This was their normal.

"It's not normal!" I cried in the privacy of my heart. I could have used all kinds of adjectives to describe his story. *Normal* was not one of them.

The day after we met the children in the orphanage, we visited five different displacement camps. I quickly learned the difference between an internally displaced person (IDP) and a refugee. Refugees have been forced to flee their country in search of safety. IDPs have fled their villages to seek safety within their own country. Both are forced to run due to armed conflict, violence, or human rights violations. The displacement camps consist of miles of squalor, overflowing with thousands upon thousands of tiny shelters constructed with sticks and mud and covered with a United Nations–issued tarp. Many of these straw shelters house one or two adults and four to six children—often two or three of those children have been orphaned and taken in by families. These tents and shacks are poor substitutes for "home" for the thousands whose houses and land have been stolen or destroyed in the war.

> *I could have used all kinds of adjectives to describe his story.* **Normal** *was not one of them.*

Since the war began in 1996, 1.5 million Congolese have been displaced, and 2.5 million have been made homeless. Another 1 million were forced to flee to neighboring countries as refugees. An estimated 5 million people have died from the violence, hunger, and disease resulting from the war,[1] and some reports indicate that almost half of these are children. Approximately 400,000 women and girls are raped each year.[2]

I began the day overwhelmed with the basic physical needs of those around me—these strong, mighty, tenacious people. My heart was completely dazed by the thousands of malnourished children, the rampant sickness and looming death, and the lack of basics that sustain life, including water and food.

The first displacement camp we visited held eleven thousand people, all forced to flee because of rebel fighting—all visibly worn and wounded. We climbed out of white vans with full stomachs, wearing clean clothes and carrying three-hundred-dollar cameras. All eyes were on the white women from America who had come to witness their tragedy. These people had walked miles to get to this camp, carrying mattresses and possessions on their heads and babies on their backs. Their faces revealed raw grief from having lost loved ones just days or hours earlier to starvation. But in a displacement camp, where makeshift huts seem piled on top of one another, there is no space to grieve. There is only space to survive.

"The food supply has been cut in half because of the lack of funds," one of our Congolese team leaders explained. "At least one woman died yesterday of starvation. She had three children." I looked down to see a child nursing on the breast of his frail, thin mother. His eyes were fixed on her, looking to her for life. The noises of the thousands around me seemed to drift away as I realized how precious this one little life was.

Not long after we exited the van, a crowd of children rushed to say hello—maybe the only English word they knew. They were curious about us. They gathered as close as they could, kicking up black dust with their bare feet, stretching tiny hands toward me to touch my skin and pull at my clothes. I smiled at the sweet faces on emaciated, underfed bodies. Their ripped and soiled clothing was likely the only clothing they owned. My mind raced. *Children this young should not know war like this*, I thought as I pushed back tears. I saw the burns on the face of one little boy in front of me and wondered if he had been burned when the rebels burned his hut—a common tactic used to destroy villages. I wanted to know these children and their stories. But there were so many. Where would I begin? As far as we could see, stunning ebony faces stared at us, faces etched with the strength that suffering gives.

Slowly we came to life, recovering from the shock of what surrounded us. Over the next few minutes, along with the wonderful ladies in our group, I played with the children, sat with the kind women who welcomed us, and looked curiously into their eyes. Their eyes—what have they seen? Their hands—what stories could they tell? I knew I had no words to give them. Even if I did, I couldn't say them in a language they would understand, except for one Swahili phrase I memorized during a previous trip to Kenya:

"*Yesu yuko pamoja nawe.*"

"Jesus is with you."

Over and over and over I said it. Holding hands. Touching faces. Praying they felt the hand of Christ. "Jesus is with you." Feeling small and helpless in the middle of this war zone, I spoke those words to the little children and to the older ones, to young women carrying their babies, to old, weathered women, to the men of scars, to the young people whose true youth had been stolen. They needed to know Jesus was with them. If they knew nothing else, they needed to know that.

The smiles those words ignited were priceless. The laughter that erupted at my attempts to speak Swahili seemed to lighten the shadows of despair. The songs the children sang that day, despite their surroundings, were fresh and necessary, like rain during a cruel drought. As we drove away, a girl ran beside our van, waving goodbye, with a smile bright enough to end any war. She ran as far as she could, then stopped and continued waving until we were out of sight. Still smiling.

The second camp we visited held approximately eight thousand people, practically living on top of one another. Though that camp bore a great resemblance to the first in the way it looked, smelled, and operated, I quickly realized that I wasn't just walking into the same place. They were different. Each woman and each man in each camp had a unique story that deserved honor and dignity. Each child had a name and a heartache, a joy and a soul. Each one was just as important as our own children. In fact, had we been born in another country—they could be our own. This could be our life. And if they were our children, what would we do? No person was just like another. These mothers and fathers, sons and daughters had individually suffered brutality. They were not a mass;

> *If they were our children, what would we do?*

they were distinct humans, and each had felt real pain. They deserve better than a description that lumps them together. All survivors of war deserve better than that.

But my *experiences* there were similar to those at the first camp. Some of the children reached out to touch my skin to see if it felt the same as theirs, tracing the veins that showed through my thin white skin. The girls tousled and braided my blond hair, stifling giggles all along. Some of the babies cried in terror because we were the first *mzungus* (white people) they had ever seen. It's a strange feeling when an infant screams in terror at the sight of your face. "Do not worry. They only fear the skin," our guide said as he laughed.

By the fifth camp, I was dazed and nearly numb. Throughout the day, so many people had asked us for food. Some women even tried to give us their children. Others had asked us to help them "go home." Home—a place where I would be in a week, with all of the luxuries afforded to me in the United States. It struck me hard: I could leave this place. In fact, I definitely *would* leave. Even that night, I would return to a safe, comfortable bed. In only days, I would return home with absolutely no fear of bullets or rebel raids. I would walk in the door where I would flip on a switch to receive light and turn a faucet to receive water. Instantly. I would open my refrigerator and there would be ample food. And I would have to do basically nothing to have these luxuries. I could leave, but they could not. Stuck in that awareness for a moment, I stood motionless. In the stillness, a young boy who seemed about ten years old approached me. With a look of longing in his big brown eyes, he held out his hand. But to my surprise, he did not ask for money or food.

"Bible? Give me a Bible?" he asked in broken English.

His request actually startled me. *Considering all that he needed, he asked me for a Bible?*

I had started the day with a desperate desire to feed, clothe, and tend the wounds of children just like this boy—to give them bread. At the moment the little boy asked for a Bible, I began to see my surroundings differently. I realized that the clothing I would give him and his friends would soon tear. The food I would give them would be gone by tomorrow. The cup of water I would hand them would leave them thirsty again. But the Bread of Life on which we all sustain our lives is eternal. It is hope.

Of course, the children's physical needs must be met, too. But to cope with living in a war-torn world and to heal from their pain, they need more. They need to know a mighty God who loves them and gives them strength in the middle of the storm, who holds them as they wash away their grief with salty tears. They need to know Someone who believes in them when the rest of the world turns its face away.

I lay in bed that night thinking about my own life. My fellow Americans and I live in a country of "peace," but we struggle greatly with internal unrest. It's true. We live in one of the most emotionally depressed countries in the world.[3] We may live in a peaceful country, but are we a peaceful people? We cannot have peaceful nations if we are at war with ourselves.

Some of the people I had met that day didn't even have a word for *suicide* in their native tongues. The thought of taking your own life must seem strange if you are fighting merely to survive. I started to wonder if I was short-changing myself when it came to hope.

Perhaps it was time to redefine what hope and happiness truly meant to me.

I was born to be Pollyanna, sprinkled with Mary Poppins, topped with David the shepherd boy, all wrapped up in the heart of God. Not normal. Actually, it's a little weird. I'll admit, the toll of past hurts had jaded my Pollyanna just a bit, but it was still there. Coming face-to-face with the darkness, the death, and the desperation in this African nation challenged everything I had ever thought or known—specifically my definition of hope and happiness.

We Westerners define happiness as achieving or gaining what we want. In our definition, we're happy when life is smooth, when we are on top of our game, when our marriages are fulfilling, and when we are reaching our goals. But the more we have, the more we want, and we begin to ride the deadly wave of hyperconsumerism. We fill our insecurities from the outside in, rather than the inside out. Christians are not exempt. I have done the drive-by to the mall on the way home to get a new "something" to make me feel like "someone," forgetting that I was actually someone the whole time.

And what of hope? We hope for financial security, a happy family, a nice home, to be in love, to have well-rounded children, and not to die of cancer. But what if we get none of these things and our desires are unfulfilled? Are we then enslaved to hopelessness or to live a life of unhappiness?

On that first day in Congo, I saw *true* hope. I looked into deeply weary eyes and saw them smile.

Hope came from watching twenty children laugh and scream as they kicked a makeshift soccer ball of plastic bags tied together with string, in the middle of a displacement camp. Hope stirred in me as I heard the children sing in one of the world's most dangerous places to be a child. Hope is not about getting what we want or ask for. Hope is choosing to believe in something bigger than we are and beyond what we can see or touch: love, joy, play, gratefulness. It is knowing that light extinguishes the dark. It's holding the hand of pain and sitting at the feet of suffering, knowing that heartbreak can actually be one of our greatest teachers if we choose to learn from it. Though the cause of our despair was as different as the languages we spoke, I had come to know the same hope my new friends relied on. Hope speaks across the universe.

The next day was the beginning of the trauma-care conference. Forty women from each of the displacement camps we'd visited attended. We wanted to help these brave women deal with the emotional pain that they and their children suffered. The women came to the conference excited and wearing the very best clothes they owned. We, too, were overjoyed and honored to be in their presence, to dance with them in joy despite their surroundings, and to listen to them sing songs of praise in their native tongues. Strong women, though weary from being displaced the past six months, were oozing with gratitude and cheering as they received food and clothes. The Congolese are, indeed, a beautiful people.

When the time came for me to share my message, I stood in front of two hundred women who had fled from rebel militia, and I spoke in general terms about my "dark time." Knowing it was only a droplet of pain compared to their oceans of trauma, I was cautious not to compare the two. I shared about healing from the wounds trauma had inflicted and what God had taught me in my own journey. It was the first time I had spoken about my experiences publicly, but being in Africa and away from the realities of home made it easier. Strangely, I don't remember being afraid. I remember feeling peaceful—like I was doing exactly what I was called to do. I was embarrassed to call it a dark time, because I knew that my experiences paled in comparison to their suffering, but the women seemed to come to life when I spoke about my struggles. At that moment, we were connected. Our skin color, our homelands, and the semantics of our hardships did not matter. We shared the same Redeemer, and our stories joined hands.

I talked about how God showed me the freedom that comes with forgiveness. I told them I had given up on myself because of my past, but that He reminded me of my worth in Him. He used my own story to lead me to their country, to stand in front of them to speak words of hope, I said. I did not have to draw from textbooks and psychological research alone; I was able to share what God had taught me through my own trials.

We ended our time by inviting the women to lay down their burdens at the foot of the cross. We had instructed each woman to pick up a stone from outside the church, then we had explained that the stones represented their pain. I was taken aback by what happened when we invited them to come before the cross to surrender their stones and pray. All two hundred women came up at once. I remember seeing hand over hand laying down their stones and then hearing the sacrifice of prayers they offered to the Lord as they knelt almost in unison. And after the silent prayers came the cries to their Savior. Weeping, they lay in surrendered positions on the floor lamenting the pains life had bestowed upon them. I will never forget the image of the floor after the ladies slowly rose and walked away. Wet with their tears. Damp from their sorrow. They had given it all to Jesus.

After our time together, an older woman limped toward me, leaning on a long stick. She smiled, saying, "Today, you have given me medicine for my soul." I looked into eyes that had certainly seen more than my imagination could bear and simply pointed up. It wasn't me. "He is the medicine," I replied.

> *"Today, you have given me medicine for my soul."*

After I got to know my traveling companions during our week-long trip, I felt a unique bond with them. These nine genuine, compassionate new friends did not simply speak the Gospel but truly lived it. These ladies quickly became my kindred spirits. In their company I found acceptance and value. They were genuine and authentic, and I felt safe with them.

Around the dinner table on one of the last nights, one of my teammates, Ann, quietly said, "I have to ask. What is your story?"

I guess her question caught me off guard. Even though our bond on this journey was quick and unique and though they had heard me reference my "dark time," I had not shared my full story with them. As I quickly considered how I would respond, other questions flashed through my mind. *Will they still love me? Will they lose all respect for me?* Fear bounced around inside my head, but I remembered that God had taught me to be brave and to stand forgiven. The truth started spilling out of me.

The more I shared, the more questions they asked. They were not intrigued because they craved drama. They inquired because with every detail, they could see how God was redeeming my past. They could see how He used my pain for a purpose. I was taken aback by how loved I felt, even after baring all the ugly, messy details of my story. They witnessed my scars and saw beauty in them.

Instead of extending judgment, these ladies extended grace. It was the first time I had shared the secret details of my story outside a counseling environment. God had to take me all the way around the world, to the middle of a war zone, for me to tell the truth in a real-world setting. It was terrifying. It was freeing. He does crazy, beautiful things like that. Crazy, beautiful things like taking our deepest pain and giving it meaning in the craziest, most beautiful ways possible.

Reflections from My Journal...

The Strong Ones

As we first drove from the airport into Congo, I felt
as though we were entering another world. On the
way to our destination, the realities of this country
came into focus for me—as though I were looking into
a camera and adjusting the lens. The road was filled
with holes surrounded by chunks of volcanic rock. Half
of the road was there; half had disappeared over
time. Truckloads of soldiers with guns and handheld
missile launchers drove past us with angry faces.

People. People everywhere. So many people.
Women walking beside the road with babies tied to
their backs, wearing brightly colored head wraps
while balancing anything you can imagine on their
heads. Children running barefoot with torn clothing
half on, half off. Playing. Laughing. Unaware—for a
moment—of the war around them.

Looking around as we drove through the city of
Goma was overwhelming. On the way back to the
place where we were sleeping, we listened to a
Congolese pastor talk about the village where he
was raised.

"There was nothing left," he shared with us. "It
was destroyed, never to be lived in again. During
the attack on my village, the people fled. They could
not save anything. They ran with only their lives.

Now the village is no more. It is only a forest, so we fled to another country for safety. But when we were exiled, we realized that God ran ahead of us to wait for us there."

God ran ahead of us. Wow. What faith. What courage. What respect I have for them.

It reminded me of one of my favorite verses, Deuteronomy 31:6: "Be strong and courageous! Do not be afraid and do not panic before them. For the Lord your God will personally go ahead of you. He will neither fail you nor abandon you."[4]

Yesterday we met so many women and children in the IDP (Internally Displaced Persons) camps. We came to visit them, but we refused to be spectators. We would not be just one more group of mzungus who came and saw and shook their heads and left. No. We would sing with them. We would dance with them. We would love them. We would pray for them. Tomorrow at the trauma-care training, we will provide food and clothing. We will share with them about the hope and healing of the Lord. This is more important than anything else we give them.

This poverty is more than I've ever seen or known, and it reminds me how important the Bread of Life is. I realize I cannot give them enough food. I cannot make their government less corrupt. I cannot stop the raping. I cannot calm the fighting or make sure anyone gets back home. That's something they hope for every hour of every day. They are truly living in exile—literally and figuratively. But I can give them a hope of heaven and the beginning of healing. I can sit with them and listen to their stories and show them the honor they deserve.

One thing stood out to me yesterday—one strange thing that happened over and over. While we were praying in the middle of the displacement camp, in groups of hundreds, we often became teary. Voices cracked; sniffles were heard; tears were seen. And looks were given. These looks were the blank stares of confusion from those who lived in the IDP camps. At least on two occasions today I got "the look." The stare. Me—with tears coming down my cheeks, slowly and unashamedly, as I was praying. I glanced up at one point and saw a twelve-year-old girl staring at me as if to say, "What's wrong with you?"

At one point she tapped her friend and pointed to my face. If her look were words, I think they would be, "This is our world. Why are you crying? This is our reality, and we live in it every day."

What did I see today? Strength as I have never seen it.

What did I feel? Humble admiration.

And in witnessing their strength, I realized: In our American quest for comfort, our resilience muscle has been weakened. In our desire to have things "quick and easy," we have atrophied our ability to thrive and survive. So we now have quick, and we now have easy, but we have less strength to cope with life when it becomes difficult.

In our quest for comfort, we have weakened our ability to be uncomfortable. Funny how we think we are the strong ones.

I have found the strong ones. I am surrounded by them.

CHAPTER FIVE

They Belong to All of Us

Let us be the ones to say we are not satisfied that your place of birth determines your right to life. Let us be outraged, let us be loud, let us be bold.

—BRAD PITT

When I was a little girl, I wanted to be Little Orphan Annie. I went around my house dancing and spinning with my arms outstretched, singing about the sun coming out tomorrow and dreaming of a head full of tight, red curls. I must admit, I still kind of do that sometimes.

Then there was Anne of Green Gables. Again, red hair. She was spunky and bold, and she viewed life through the lens of a hopeless romantic mixed with an idealistic dreamer. She saw the good in everything and had a fight in her that weighed more than she did soaking wet. And she had been orphaned.

Ironically, I rarely heard about orphaned children when I was young, except when people at our small church in Kentucky spoke about the orphanage we supported a few hours away from our town. I honestly didn't even understand what an orphanage really meant back then.

My world was safe and warm. I climbed trees, caught lightning bugs, and all was right with the world. Almost all of my friends lived with both of their parents, and family roots ran deep. Sure, I read where Jesus spoke about orphaned children, but I had never met an orphaned child. Until I grew up.

I was thirty-three when I visited my first orphanage, in Haiti. I went with a local church group from my time in Colorado. We walked into a dull, lifeless building where the walls were gray and the children seemed distant. There was no joy in their eyes or toys lying on the floor. I felt loneliness in the pit of my stomach when I saw so many children lined up in one small room. One after another, with so few people to love them. Crib after crib. Baby after baby. The place was sterile like a hospital, but it was their home. Because there were not enough caregivers to watch the children, they could not go outside the building until they could walk. Because they were kept in the baby beds for so long, sometimes walking didn't happen until they were close to two years old.

This was not the glorified setting of a redhead betting her bottom dollar that tomorrow would bring sun.

I visited an orphanage again in 2008, during that first trip to Congo. We actually made it to two orphanages—a girls' orphanage and a boys'. Before the other ladies and I could even get out of the van at the girls' orphanage, about a hundred precious girls, ages three to eighteen, rushed toward us. They ran as though we were their long-lost mothers, as though they already knew us. They didn't know us at all, but they knew we would provide loving arms.

When that group of girls reached us, I felt pulled in four different directions. So many sweet little fingers were trying to hold on to my one hand. The ground on which we stood was a sea of broken lava rock from an eruption outside Goma in 2002. Yet many of the girls were barefoot, walking on the jagged ground as if it were sand. The leaders at the orphanage had taken the larger pieces of lava rock and made a wall around the center. To me, it symbolized God creating

> *They were as starved for touch as hungry people are starved for food.*

strength from life's eruptions. Some of the older girls were pushing the younger girls away so they could grasp our hands. They were as starved for touch as hungry people are starved for food. Looking down, one of the little girls caught my eye. She had something in her mouth.

"What's in your mouth, sweetie?" I said, pointing my finger to my open mouth so she would understand. She reached inside and pulled out a piece of glass she had been sucking on. These girls had been through hell, and their toughness proved it.

I later found out that more than half of these young girls had been sexually violated in unspeakable ways, and the scars on their bodies told the horrific story. A local pastor found many of them in the bush, terrified and traumatized, after they had been raped—some when they were as young as four years old.

It's not uncommon for young girls and women, wandering

through the woods looking for wood to build fires for cooking or fetching water near the lakes, to be raped by soldiers or rebels. In eastern Congo, 40 percent of the women have been sexually violated.[1] Rape in the Congo is particularly brutal and knows no limits. It is also not uncommon for women and young girls to be raped with guns, shards of glass, or other objects. Rape is used as a weapon of war, to create fear and gain power.

To double the trauma, when women or children have been raped, they are often ostracized by their husbands and families, losing both their innocence and their dignity. The women are often sent away from their homes to care for their children alone, with no support. "Never speak of it," the girls are advised for fear that they will never marry if anyone knows. They can tell *no one*. Ever. So that's what they do. They tell no one, and they bury their secrets— something I was familiar with.

But on this day, the girls were singing and laughing, welcoming all the love, grace, and kindness we could give them. For me, the highlight of the day was teaching some of the girls to blow bubbles. I gave the girls a couple of brightly colored plastic bottle of bubbles and showed them how to open them and dunk the wand into the liquid. They squealed with excitement as they watched the bubbles float in the air around them. Chasing them and popping them with our hands before they touched the ground, we laughed together as though we had known one another for years. Play and laughter are universal languages that bond spirits together—even without words. I longed to tell all these girls how beautiful they were and that God had a plan for each of them.

On that day, the team's schedule permitted us to stay with the girls for only a short period. I had taken paper and markers to leave with the caretakers at the orphanage. Having used art therapy in my counseling practice and seeing the fruits of art in my personal recovery, my hope was that these girls could take their first steps toward healing by expressing their feelings through art.

Wondering how I could explain the concept of art therapy in five minutes across a language barrier, I pulled the two primary caretakers aside.

"I am a counselor," I explained. "I counsel children who have gone through suffering and sad times. Sometimes it is difficult for children to talk about their feelings; it may be easier for them to draw how they feel, to draw their stories. If they can express their feelings through their drawings, it will help them. I brought some paper and markers for you to give the girls so you can invite them to use art to express their feelings."

The caretakers' eyes were bright and full of gratitude. Wishing I had days to spend with the girls rather than minutes, I joined the team as we all piled into the van for a visit to the boys' orphanage. Our experience there would be quite different from our time with the girls.

Approximately twenty-five boys greeted us with singing and dancing. We gathered on one side of the open-air pavilion, and the boys sat on benches across from us. Most of these boys had been found on the street, living alone. Some had been dropped off because no one wanted them; others had been orphaned. Some were former child soldiers who had nowhere to go after they escaped or were rescued from the rebel army. In awe of them, I felt the freshness of their heartache as if it were my own.

One of the younger boys used two small tree branches as drumsticks. Passionately beating them against the side of the bench, he was in perfect rhythm with the songs of survival flowing from their hearts. Joy and excitement filled the air as the boys shuffled their feet and clapped to the beat of their music and welcomed us to their home. They beamed with excitement as they shared their performance. When we applauded, they seemed to feel honored to simply be heard. In Africa, singing and dancing are almost as important as breathing. They are signs of life.

> *"We will pray that you become soldiers of peace rather than soldiers of war."*

In typical African etiquette, the caretakers asked one of us to "give a word of encouragement" on the spot. My team member Shari spoke up. I don't remember everything she said, but these words stood out: "We will pray that you become soldiers of peace rather than soldiers of war."

Wow. Yes. Something jumped inside me. *That is beautiful*, I thought. The boys' faces lit up. Those words gave them vision to see past their surroundings. Though I didn't know it at the time, those words were seeds planted in my heart. By God's hand, Shari's prayer would blossom into something remarkable.

All too quickly, it was time to leave, and our group started walking to the van. Suddenly two boys approached me. The older boy pointed to the younger and said, "He is a child soldier." Caught off guard, I looked at the younger boy. His eyes were determined.

"I am his brother," the older one said, pointing at his chest.

I looked back at the younger boy, and noticed he seemed afraid. Nervously, kicking the ground, he began to speak. His English was better than his brother's, but he still struggled to communicate. Out the corner of my eye I could see my friends getting into the van to leave. I could only stay with these boys another minute.

Stammering, the child soldier began to explain that he and his brother were orphaned. The older brother kept stopping him in mid-sentence, even pushing him at one point and scolding him. "No. You are doing it wrong," the older brother said.

Desperately trying to understand what they were trying to communicate while cutting my eyes toward the van where everyone was waiting for me, my soul felt torn. It was as though the boys had rehearsed what they were going to say. I looked at the van again and then back to the boys.

"We want you—" the young one began. "We want you—to be our—father. To be our father," the younger boy stammered.

Looking at them blankly, I thought, *What did he say? Did he just say—?*

"No, you are doing it wrong!" The older brother pushed the younger one again.

Frantic to make everything all right, if just for that one moment, I said, "No, it's okay. He's doing fine. It's okay."

By now the people on my team were calling me from the van to leave.

I finally understood. The younger brother was the spokesperson for the duo, and his job was to convince me to take them with me. It was as though they had practiced this stunning request for a long, long time and saved it for just the right moment. And the older one felt the younger one was messing it up.

As I heard the van's ignition, I looked at these courageous boys, brave enough to ask a total stranger to become their parent. The team yelled for me to come. I was caught between two worlds. I gathered the boys together, held their hands, and prayed for them, thinking, *Every child should belong to someone.* They should belong. We all should belong. Somewhere. To someone. And they do belong to God. I know this truth, but do they know it? I said good-bye and ran to the van, wishing I could have done more.

Thinking about my experience with the boys as we drove to the guesthouse, I asked myself, *What do you do with that? What do you do when two children who have been orphaned by war ask you to be their parent?* In what category do you put that in your head or in your heart? There is none. My heart was broken.

> *Could we ever put a name to the feeling of belonging to no one?*

The fact that more than forty times in the Bible God mentions taking care of orphaned children and widows is noteworthy. The world is full of so many who are wounded and in pain, so why does He specifically mention those who have been orphaned? Because they are the most alone. They are the most easily forgotten. They belong to no one. They have no one to protect them and no one to lean on.

What does it feel like to be orphaned? Could we ever put a name to the feeling of belonging to no one?

Eventually I realized that these children do belong to someone. They belong to God. And if they belong to God, then they belong to all of us.

Returning to my room that night, exhausted and with my heart stretched in ways it had never been stretched before, I wrote this in my prayer journal:

> This is their reality, Father. This is their life. They have wounds so deep their emotional blood supply has been cut off for mere survival. I don't know how or by what means their lives can get better, but I know You know, and You will use this for good—because You are bigger than this. And that is what I will trust.
>
> I think of the hundreds of thousands who have been orphaned in this country. Some on the street as I write this. Some lying in bed alone in the few orphanages that are here. Help them feel You, Father. Help them to know You are their forever Father who will never leave them or forsake them. I think about my own heart years ago and how I also felt spiritually orphaned—as if, somehow, I didn't belong to You anymore. But just like I can never stop being my own father's biological child, I can never stop being Your daughter. I know that now. Help them to sense that, Lord. That they are Yours. That they belong to You.
>
> I know something can be done to help, and I wish to be a small part of that answer. Laying my life at Your altar, I will wait. With an open heart, I will

wait. Waiting on You to renew my strength so I can mount up on wings as eagles. And I will run and not grow weary. And I will walk and not grow faint. For You are my God, and I am Your servant. Honored to be used by You, humbled to be Your daughter.

My first week in Congo had been a full one. As I prepared to leave, I remembered being in the middle of the last displacement camp, looking around and thinking, *How, Lord? How? How can you use me? How can I even begin to help?* I left Congo not knowing the answers, but having been forever changed, feeling that God was opening a set of curtains to reveal my new life.

On our last night, the Congolese minister who was leading our group looked at our team and said, "Please take with you our hearts, because we have given them to you. We ask you to leave yours here so that you will return one day."

Looking the darkness of their situation in the eyes, I not only saw deep pain, but I also saw resilient strength and a beautiful dependence on God—like nothing I had ever seen. And my journey was just beginning.

Reflections from My Journal...

Reflections from the Heart of Darkness

What do you do when you look darkness—the sheer despair of war, murder, rape—in the eye? What is a person's natural reaction? We look away. We look very far away. Why? Coming face-to-face with darkness makes us feel uncomfortable. It makes us feel uneasy, disturbed. I have only been back home from Congo a few days, and I can easily say that on many levels, I have looked darkness in the eye. From that deep gaze have come many thoughts and questions. The most important one is this: What am I to do with all of this? I think about my experiences—the stories shared, the sights seen, the tears cried. I ask Him, What would you have me to do with this, Lord?

I think about the mother I sat with—the mother whose baby the rebels literally snatched from her arms as she ran away from her village.

I think about the hollow eyes of the little six-year-old boy who witnessed something so tragic that he has disengaged from the reality around him.

I think about the women who tried to give us their children because they yearned to see them physically nourished and tended to.

I think about the IDPs and refugees in the

camps where the food supplies had been cut in half, leaving barely enough for survival.

Darkness. Heaviness. Twisted as it is, I realized every day that everything I saw in Congo was their normal. Though their trials overwhelm me, I am equally amazed at their strength, at their smiles, at their joyful worship.

Resilience. The widows who have several children of their own and care for two or three others who are orphaned. Many of these widows have started their own business of selling flour made from tree roots so all of them may eat each day.

Joy. I think about the laughter of the girls at the orphanage after I showed them how to blow bubbles and then chase them. I think about the smiles on the faces of the displaced women as they left the conference after learning for the first time how to begin healing from their heart wounds.

And then I think back to my first few days in that war-torn country. I remember feeling so small compared to the size of their pain and questioning whether I could make a difference at all. It was all so much bigger than me. I think about these things—seeing their faces, remembering their stories, and I ask: Lord, what do I do with it all?

This is my answer:

I will do something. Some thing. There is much I cannot do. I cannot stop the violence, violation, starvation, or government corruption. But I will not let that stop what I can do: something. I will see the fact that I am here in the United States and they are in Congo as a responsibility. Now that I know how they are living, I am even more responsible to act. I will resist the temptation to place my knowledge in a grocery bag and cram it under the bed, pretending these things don't go on, just because the thought of them makes me uncomfortable and even disturbed. Yes, I am tempted to file these things away like vacation photos—but not tempted enough to forget.

No, I will not feel small. I will feel. <u>I will feel.</u> I will be courageous enough to sit with all of this in prayer, asking how God can make baskets of bread out of the tiny loaves in my hands. My part may be as small as sponsoring an orphaned child so he or she has food, medical attention, and an education—being fed and clothed along the way Home. Or it may be as large as developing a trauma-counseling curriculum to be used with the children of war-torn Africa.

Regardless, I will do something.

CHAPTER SIX

"It Is Bigger Than We Are"

Suffering and death are not enemies, but doors
leading to new lives of knowledge and love.

FATHER THOMAS KEATING

On my way back to America, I felt trapped inside the plane, unable to get away from my thoughts. My mind was spinning as I reviewed everything I'd experienced during my first week in Congo.

I looked at my feet, still dirty from Congo's black volcanic dust. I had not showered in a few days. I smelled bad. But I didn't care.

Looking out the window at the clouds, I remembered one of the last times our team debriefed together. A specific theme kept coming up among us: "It is bigger than we are. How do we even begin to help? Can we make any difference at all?"

I felt a tap on my shoulder. The soft-spoken man sitting next to me asked politely, "Would you mind if my son sat in your seat for just a few minutes? He would like to see the sunset."

I had met them earlier. They were from Kenya. This sweet, kind boy with an autistic nature appeared to be about five years old. I was happy to be distracted from my thoughts. The boy and I switched seats, and I began to point out the shapes of clouds to him. Smiling, he delighted in seeing the sun from so high, and I delighted in his excitement. Somehow, for a moment, I felt closer to God.

As he looked into the heavens, the boy started repeating a phrase over and over again. Quiet at first, then a bit louder.

"It is bigger than we are," he said. "It is big. It is bigger than us."

I stopped and looked at him. He was echoing my exact thoughts. It was as though God were speaking to me through this little boy, confirming His voice in my spirit. Yes, it *is* so much bigger than we are. The despair. The brutality. But it is *not* bigger than all of us together. It is not bigger than God. They are His children, and He loves them more than I could begin to. My eyes filled with tears as I smiled at this young, wise new friend sitting beside me.

Adjusting to life back in the United States was difficult. For three days after I returned home, I barely left my bedroom. I did not want to see or talk to anyone. I had no words—only heartache for what I had seen and tears for those I had left behind. It was as if God had pulled back a curtain to reveal levels of hurt and pain that I hadn't known existed. I didn't know what to do with what He had allowed me to see. Finally, I went for a run to ease my racing mind. I felt as though I were running from something I could not get away from. Perhaps because I was not supposed to.

There is a beauty that comes from sitting with our pain—a

beauty we miss if we run from it. The pain was uncomfortable and uneasy. My instinct was to distract my mind from the reality I had seen. It hurt too much to remember.

But I finally came to the convic-
tion that God did not want me to run
from my experiences in Congo. He
wanted me to sit with their reality, to
look the darkness dead in the eye and

> *There is a beauty that comes from sitting with our pain—a beauty we miss if we run from it.*

wrestle with it. I could not go back to "normal" and block out what I had seen and learned. I *would* not go back to comfort. I knew too much now.

These children are worth more than my comfort. My own jour-ney through trauma bonded me to the Congolese people. I tasted just a tiny drop of what they were feeling, and I wanted to tell them to hold on. In one of my lowest periods of depression, I wrote a few words on a postcard and carried them with me for a year: *It will not be this bad forever. Hold on.*

I read those words at least twenty times a day, willing myself to believe they were true. Because if they were not true, I did not want to live any longer. I could not keep living. But those words were true. In time, things *did* get better. They always do—if we hold on long enough and reach out for help.

Though I was blinded to it at the time, I now know there's simply too much beauty in life to quit. Depression and trauma blind us from the beauty—but it is there. In truth, we are constantly surrounded by joy and wonder, but sometimes we cannot see it until the fog clears. In those times we must choose to believe the beauty is there, until we can see it with our eyes once again.

This is one of the many truths I learned from my own pain and a truth I wanted to share with the boys and girls, men and women of Congo and beyond.

Once I finally acclimated to being back in the United States and was ready to see people, I met my sister and nieces at an ice cream shop as one of my first social outings. Julia, my then-four-year-old niece, sat on my lap, and I held her more closely than usual. Both of my nieces, Julia and her older sister, Haley, radiated innocence on that day, but as I sat there with them, my mind traveled back to Congo.

Only a week earlier, I had been surrounded by about forty children orphaned by Congo's wars. Our team met with them at the ALARM office to give encouragement, pray with them, and give them gifts. They sat eagerly in plastic chairs, anticipating the gifts our team had brought them. Soon their laps were overflowing with toys and other goodies, and they had sacks full of rice and beans to take home to their host families (the families who cared for them). Most of the children were overjoyed, with smiles so large you could almost hear them bubbling over with excitement. But not all of them.

One boy, about Julia's age, stood out to me. Having worked with children who had been traumatized, I noticed that this young boy showed every sign and symptom of severe trauma—on a level I had not previously seen.

Surrounded by the laughter and giddiness of the other children, he stared at the wall blankly, as though no one were around him. But the room was full of people, hustle and bustle, and loud, joyous conversations. This child moved in slow motion and showed no emotion. It was as if his spirit were frozen.

I went to our translator and asked, "What has happened to that boy?"

"That one? During the war, he saw his father murdered in a brutal way. He has never been the same. His father was his best friend," she said quietly.

Haley's laugh jolted me back into the present moment. She had ice cream on her nose, and Julia was trying to wipe it off. We were far away from the vacant-eyed little boy whose father had been massacred before him.

For a few months, I wrestled with the two worlds: my heart was in Africa; my body was in America. I felt God calling me to do something, but I wasn't sure what.

A passion stirred inside me, and I knew it had to have a purpose. Crying out to God to show me what that was, I wrote in my prayer journal:

Lord, they are there and I am here. And I confess I feel I have abandoned them. I am here in my world of comfort. They are there in their world of pain. Rape, running, guns, erupting volcanoes, abuse, hunger. But there has to be more. Surely there are answers. Your light is bigger than any darkness. I choose to believe that. Show me the way, Jesus. May my hands be Your hands. May my heart be Your heart. May my will be Your will. I am Yours.

One night, as I grappled with my thoughts, I sat on the floor beside my bed and opened my Bible to Isaiah 43. As I started reading, I realized it was the exact chapter I read during my time of leading the trauma-care portion of the conference in Congo, where so many brave faces and broken hearts stared back at me.

> *Do not be afraid, for I have ransomed you*
> *I have called you by name; you are mine.*
> *When you go through deep waters, I will be with you.*
> *When you go through rivers of difficulty, you will not drown.*
> *When you walk through the fire of oppression, you will not be*
> *burned up;*
> *the flames will not consume you . . . you are precious to Me.*
> *You are honored, and I love you.*
> —Isaiah 43:1–2, 4, NLT

> *On their backs they had carried their sleeping mats, cooking utensils, and whatever else they could manage. But mainly, they carried their children.*

My eyes drifted to the annotations in my study Bible. I saw these words about Isaiah 43: "Written to the Jews in exile in Babylon."

In exile, I thought. *Yes. In a way, they are.*

I remembered the thousands of people who swarmed our team in the displacement camps, saying over and over that they just wanted to go home. Begging for our help. Some had walked for days with small, dying, or malnourished children to get there, forced to leave their homes as the gunfire from rebels was literally at their feet. On their backs they had carried their sleeping mats, cooking utensils, and whatever else they could manage. But mainly, they carried their children.

I thought of the stories I had heard firsthand. Knowing they were true haunted me. I thought of the boys who had been snatched from their families in the middle of the night and led deep into the forest to be trained as soldiers. Those too young to actually fight were placed on the front lines to act as human shields for the rest of the soldiers. Guns, machetes, and knives were thrust into their innocent hands. Any child who was too tired or fearful to perform his task or who fell under the heavy loads they were forced to carry was brutally punished. Some children were sadistically forced to cut off the ears, arms, or feet of villagers—nothing was off-limits. If a child tried to escape, the other children were told to kill the escapee in front of their peers after they were caught. And those who remained alive and were a bit older had to invade *other* villages in the middle of the night and abduct *other* children, who would then join their nightmare. If the children were fortunate enough to escape and return home, they often were *not* welcomed with open arms. Instead, they were rejected by their fellow villagers and seen as little rebels—outcast and worse than shunned. Sometimes after they escaped and returned home, they were killed.

The girls at the orphanage came to my mind. I closed my eyes and I could see them as if they were beside me, holding my hand. Some of them had been orphaned because their parents were killed in war, but most were young survivors of gender-based violence.

Used as sex slaves for the soldiers, they were brutally raped—even at the young age of four. I had trouble even understanding how this would be physically possible, but it was possible. I knew it now. It was not only possible, it was right in front of me. If these girls are ever able to return home, they, too, are shunned by remaining family members and often are doomed to live life alone, for few men will marry a violated girl.

I think of the women who were raped in their own villages and then exiled in shame by their husbands—forced to leave their homes and care for their children the best they can . . . alone. If they are open or seek help for the physical or emotional wounds from the brutality of rape, they risk losing support and love from their families. So they bury their pain inside the secrets of shame.

They all just wanted to return home or be with their families again. And they were all crying for peace.

Peace: It is the cry of the Congolese people. It is the cry of the exiled. And what is God's answer?

He says, "Do not be afraid, for I have ransomed you. I have called you by name; you are mine. When you go through deep waters, I will be *with* you. . . . You are precious to me. You are honored, and I love you" (Isaiah 42, NLT). Every day since my return from Congo, I had wrestled with one question: *Where was God in all this pain?*

At first I couldn't find Him. I searched His heart in confusion, wondering how He could allow this to go on. He—the Almighty One. But I finally understood where He *was* and where He was *not*. He was *not* the one inflicting torture on His children. He was *not* the one displacing the Congolese people. He was actually right beside the children when they were kidnapped and trained to be soldiers. He was with them as rebel forces raped them when they were eight years old. He walked with them when they were forced to carry pistols at age seven because they were too small to carry AK-47s. He was *with* them. And He intensely grieved at the evil inflicted on them by cruel men. He was with them, just as He was with me when I had given up; He held their hands just as He had held mine when I felt alone.

God does not promise there will not be pain. There will be. Deep pain. But He *does* promise He will never leave us or forsake us. Even when we cannot feel Him or see Him, He is there. As I began to resolve some of the initial struggles following my life-changing trip to Congo, I stopped wrestling with the question *Where is God in all this pain?* Slowly, the answer became clearer. Promising He will never leave us or forsake us, there is no doubt that His tears of sorrow over this brutality were greater than my own. I began to ask another question. A stronger question that I could find an answer to. The question was not *Where was God?* The question was *Where were we?*

> *The question was not* **Where was God?** *The question was* **Where were we?**

Reflections from My Journal...

Exile

Blanketed by moonlight and shadowed by stars, I read poetry aloud around a campfire a few nights ago. My body was there, but my mind drifted. I remembered Congo.

My drifting thoughts led to praying, and praying led to writing, and writing led to tears, tears for which I will no longer apologize. Are these people not worth my tears? Am I too prideful to shed them?

When I left Congo, I made a promise. I promised to "go and tell," to tell their stories, to bring their voices out of the darkness into light. I will go, and I will tell. Their stories are more than worth telling; their hearts are more than worth healing; and their lives are more than worth saving.

Yesterday I picked up my Bible and read one of my favorite verses, Jeremiah 29:11. "For I know the plans I have for you, says the Lord. They are plans for good and not for disaster, to give you a future and a hope." Next to the heading of Jeremiah 29 I read, "A Letter to the Exiles." Just like the passage in Isaiah 43. God has a way of speaking clearly to me through scripture.

Yes. Exile haunts me: the presence of exile, the feeling of exile, the existence of exile, the word exile.

But Jeremiah 29 proclaims hope—hope for the homeless, even the hope of forgiveness for the heartless. And are we so different? I think of some of my clients who are as lost emotionally as the children wandering in Africa's bush. I remember. I felt the same exile in my own heart after being distanced from my community—partially by my own choice, partially through the rejection of others.

Exile. It is a powerful word.

Looking through spiritual eyes, exile is the absence of intimacy—the absence of connection. It is isolation; it is being lost and away from home. Once we understand exile, the answer to exile becomes simple: the answer is in being found, walking with others, and discovering what it means to be loved and safe.

The answer to exile is intimacy. Simply said, intimacy means "into me see."

Without the ability to be real about our secrets and our pain with those who fully love us, we will never be free. If we cannot admit we are lost, can we ever truly be found? If we refuse to allow ourselves to be vulnerable, will we ever feel the familial bond that comes from togetherness?

I believe every heart has that yearning and every heart asks, "Do you see me?" "Am I brave enough to let you in?" "Can I trust you?" "And if I trust you with the real me, will you still love me?" The answers to those questions just may be the key to releasing us from our lostness and bringing us to the place of being found.

My favorite Swahili word is <u>pamoja</u>. It means "unity" or "together." The African people are teaching me about community and the power that comes from intimacy: Intimacy with others. Intimacy with ourselves. Intimacy with God.

This is a culture of circles—eating together, living together, laughing together. A wise, elderly African gentleman once said, "How can you walk by your loved one and not stop and greet them? To see if they are well? We are all brothers and sisters. We are all one."

God sees. He sees the African children in the bush. He sees them orphaned on the street. He sees us when we pull away from Him, either because we are upset with Him or because we believe He is upset with us. Yet He loves us still. Longing for us to accept His love, wishing we would love ourselves.

Though God is not pleased with every choice we make, there is nothing we could ever do that would cause Him to stop loving us. And as He loves us, He wishes for us to love others—as we walk in the shadow of the Rabbi and dance in the dust of His footprints. Breathing in His grace and using that breath to live one more day as we were created to be—together.

SECTION THREE

Stepping into Their Stories

*If we knew how deeply we were loved by God,
we would never feel lonely again.*

—Author unknown

CHAPTER SEVEN

A Little Pencil

*You can't stay in your corner of the Forest waiting for others
to come to you. You have to go to them sometimes.*
—WINNIE THE POOH

Soon *exile* became much more than a word to me. It encapsulated
the stories of hundreds of thousands of children—some who were
being held captive by cruel and demanding soldiers; others who were
running frantically in the bush, trying to escape their captors; and still
others who lived on desolate streets yearning for a home to which
they could return.

*The endings of their stories can look different from the begin-
nings,* I thought. I've heard it said that "where there is breath, there
is hope," and they were still breathing, so I knew hope was alive.

Doing nothing was no longer an option. Not because I was fearless, but because my hunger to do "something" had become stronger
than my fear.

My fear told me that the problems in Congo were too massive—that we couldn't make a difference in the midst of a violent oppression that had gone on for decades. But my heart told me the true story: The children who had survived war across the world were deeply treasured by God. They were precious and valuable, and it was our responsibility—my responsibility—to make a difference.

Praying for God's direction and reflecting on the lives I'd encountered, I felt a calling swell deep within my heart. I now know this calling was influenced by all God had walked me through: heartache and redemption, trauma and recovery, doubt and faith, naïveté and wisdom. I could no longer turn away or pretend I had not seen what I had seen.

Mother Teresa once said, "I am a little pencil in the hand of a writing God."[1] She was changed when she came face-to-face with the dying and the poor of Calcutta. I was changed when I looked into the eyes of children orphaned and hurt by war. I am *certainly* no Mother Teresa. I am simply someone who had an open heart and open hands.

Yes, God. I can be a tiny pencil. Your pencil, I thought.

I began researching and searching for answers to big questions such as:

"How many child soldiers are there in the world?"

"Who are the rebels fighting?"

"Why are the children kidnapped, and what is being done to help them?"

The more answers I found, the more madness I discovered. It was like watching a horror movie I could not turn away from. Somehow I had to help make it stop. Even as I write this sentence, old journals are strewn around me. Each is filled with ideas, thoughts, research, prayers—and stories, so many stories. . . . I read about the history of violence in Congo and the scars left behind after the genocidal exploitation by Leopold, king of the Belgians. I learned that the exploitation of conflict minerals such as gold, diamonds, and coltan partially fuel the continued warring. In researching the 1994 Rwandan genocide, I discovered how the tension of its aftermath remains alive in Congo even today.

Sitting with Congolese men and women now living in America, I listened closely to their experiences, which gave me further insights into decades of violence in the region. They helped me better understand how rape is used as a weapon of war to create fear and cripple communities (more about this in "A Brief History of the Wars" at the end of this book). I also learned that there were more than three hundred thousand child soldiers[2] in the world and more than one million who had been orphaned or separated from their parents because of war.[3]

After researching the few trauma-healing programs being used with war-affected children, I traveled to meet with leaders in international mental health care. I was thankful for the pioneering work of dedicated caregivers, but in the end, my findings were disturbing: I discovered that very little was being done to help children find emotional restoration, and even less was being done to teach them peace-building skills—something I strongly felt could foster a change in the course of war. If these traumatized children did not receive help, they would likely grow up to be traumatized

adults. I believed we needed to begin with the smallest children—
to bring healing to the hearts of the youngest lives and teach them
about peace and reconciliation. In building a new generation of
peace leaders, there was a chance that whole communities would
eventually be changed. The dream of witnessing a generation of
children healed and leading their
families, communities, and regions
was grand—but I felt it was worth
striving for. And, with God, I felt it
was completely possible.

> *I discovered that very
> little was being done
> to help children find
> emotional restoration,
> and even less was being
> done to teach them
> peace-building skills.*

As I shared my dreams and vision
with close friends, the possibilities of
forming a nonprofit to address the
void I had noticed grew and grew.
Not being skilled with details, I clearly needed assistance with the
paperwork, budgets, and the logistical portion of the process. I was
much better at leading groups of children in art therapy, offering
counseling to survivors of war, dancing in displacement camps, and
developing long-term programs. I was a psychologist with a private
practice in counseling who was jumping into a new adventure I
wasn't sure I was ready for. So I set up meetings with founders and
leaders of successful nonprofits, asking for advice and guidance and
seeking wisdom.

With their help and that of loyal friends, Exile International was
formally established in the summer of 2008. I gathered a small team,
including passionate and talented friends willing to donate their time
and skills to the details I wasn't gifted to handle. We formed a small

board of directors and began raising funds to purchase art therapy supplies and to create an art therapy/trauma care workshop to be led by counselors and local leaders on the ground.

The mission of Exile International was and is empowering war-affected children and former child soldiers to become leaders for peace through art therapy and rehabilitative care. My original plan was to travel with small teams to the most war-affected parts of Africa to provide art-therapy workshops to children who had experienced the trauma of war and to offer trauma-care trainings to local leaders. Had I known how much *more* God had planned for my small ideas and tiny footsteps, I probably would have covered my eyes and run the other way! Thankfully, sometimes, He only calls us to put one foot in front of the other. That much I could do.

I was passionately propelled in my work with Exile by one thing: the thought of hundreds of thousands of young boys and girls who were abused, scarred, and enslaved by brutal rebel soldiers. While I sat at a red light in Tennessee, little girls were being raped in the forests of Congo. While the media reported on the latest drama in Hollywood, boys and girls were being forced to kill their own parents. As I posted on social media, little boys were being coerced at gunpoint to cut off the ear or even eat the flesh of a "disobedient" fellow soldier. And the world was turning away. For me, this was no longer an acceptable option. I could no longer *not* do something. I had to do anything I could do to help.

I asked myself over and over, *What if these were my children? What would I do?* I knew I would go in and get them. To fight for them. To rescue them.

And as I made plans to help, God persistently whispered that these were His children first, not mine. I was not there to save; I was

> **God persistently whispered that these were His children first, not mine. I was not there to save; I was there to serve.**

there to serve. He was the leader of this new organization, and I would learn to surrender all decisions to Him. From the beginning, I did not look at Exile International as if it were "my" ministry or something "I" was starting. Exile was God's mission, and I, His servant. This was not my organization; it was His.

Early on, He impressed two scriptures upon my heart:

> *At that time I will deal with all who oppressed you.*
> *I will rescue the lame; I will gather the exiles.*
> *I will give them praise and honor in every land*
> *where they have suffered shame.*
> —Zephaniah 3:19, NIV

> *I myself will tend my sheep and have them lie down,*
> *declares the Sovereign Lord.*
> *I will search for the lost and bring back the strays.*
> *I will bind up the injured and strengthen the weak,*
> *but the sleek and the strong I will destroy.*
> *I will shepherd the flock with justice.*
> —Ezekiel 34:15–16, NIV

These scriptures brought me great hope and direction as my friends and I began this new journey.

And even beyond my vision for the children, I found myself simply praying that the warlords would come to know the Lord. I wondered what it was like to be inside the head of a rebel leader and how changed his heart would be if he served the Prince of Peace rather than a lord of war. I had heard stories of rebel leaders leading enslaved child soldiers in "prayer" before going into battle. I read other stories about leaders twisting scripture to manipulate the children into believing they were doing God's will. But I also heard, firsthand, stories of warlords surrendering their lives to Jesus and becoming Christians. It had happened to some, so I believed it could happen to others. Even hearts drenched in hate can learn to love. The issues were deep and wide, with many tangles, but I knew I didn't have to understand them all; I just needed to take the first steps in doing something more than was being done.

One of the first things I did as part of Exile International was to write a trauma-care workshop specifically for war-affected children. Sitting down with pen in hand and paper in front of me, I started praying: "Lord, what did you teach me? How did you help me through my own trauma?" And then I started writing. I wrote a counseling workshop designed to be shared over one to three days with twenty-five to fifty children at a time. The workshop invited the children to share their stories of pain through art therapy drawings of both the darkness and the light in their lives. Using storytelling and activities of expression, song, and dance, the children would be encouraged to voice their heartache while being reminded that God was with them in their brokenness. Not only would they be able to share the secrets and shame they had been hiding in their hearts, but they could also experience a safe environment in which to grieve and begin healing, alongside other children who also had experienced similar atrocities. As the children learned to share, breathe, and pray through their emotional pain, flashbacks, and trauma, I hoped they could—together—take steps of healing from their pasts while they envisioned a beautiful future as peace leaders in their countries.

Although I used my research and background as a psychologist—taking into account the current work in this narrow field, relying heavily on narrative therapy, and using art and expression techniques—this workshop was written as much from what God had taught me through my own journey toward trauma healing as from what I'd read in books.

The pivotal part of the workshop involved guiding children to draw their pain and their dreams on large, white handkerchiefs. Explaining that handkerchiefs are used to capture our tears—an expressive symbol of God keeping track of our sorrows and collecting our tears in His bottle (Psalm 56:8)—they would be given two handkerchiefs: one on which to draw a story of their sad tears (painful memories) and the other to draw their happy tears (joyful memories or their dreams for their lives). By drawing their heartaches and their dreams, they would have a tangible, color-filled storyboard to help them find the words that seem to leave us in times of deep trauma. I had used art therapy often in my past ten years of counseling children, and I found it to be a remarkable tool in helping children express their stories and emotions. Looking over the workshop, I realized I was missing one important piece. They needed to know they were not alone. They needed to know that Jesus was *with* them during their heartaches and their moments of joy or dreaming of their future. So the idea came of asking them to draw God in the middle of both of their handkerchief drawings as a reminder that they had not been abandoned. That realization had given me a welcomed peace in my own healing, and I prayed the children would experience a taste of that same tenderness from the Lord. And so the finished workshop began with hope, then moved through heartache to healing and back to hope again.

After the workshop was complete, I began actively praying for an opportunity to return to Africa and lead child survivors through this time of healing and to begin the work of Exile International. As a nonprofit, we were just getting on our feet, so I was thrilled when I was invited to join a short-term mission team from a local church in Nashville that would be traveling to a remote village in Sudan (now South Sudan). My role and privilege would be to provide emotional and spiritual care to children and villagers who had suffered trauma from tribal wars. As always, and just as important, my role would be to listen, learn, and be present as these strong souls taught me.

Sitting down with the church's team leader, Michelle, I realized God was answering that prayer. Not only was she thankful to have a psychologist come alongside the team to provide trauma care to this village, she also immediately took a special interest in Exile's vision. We quickly discovered that we shared the same love for missions, and her support was like water to my soul. She even offered to travel with me to northern Uganda the week following our time in Sudan to research child soldier rehabilitation. Gulu, Uganda, already had several projects specifically for child survivors of war, and there was much to learn. Little did I know that God was using this new friendship with Michelle to provide encouragement that would nourish me for years to come.

So in the fall of 2008, I joyfully joined this team of educators, Bible teachers, and artists traveling deep into a remote village of Sudan. Approximately twenty-four hours after flying out of Nashville, we landed in Africa. After spending one night in Kenya, our team (which I had already grown to love) crammed into a tiny seven-passenger plane. We traveled for seven additional hours before arriving in the remote village of Lietnohm. Our anticipation grew with each minute as we flew over pristine forestland that looked untouched by human hands. I had heard about the wars in Darfur and mourned the approximately four hundred thousand people who had lost their lives,[4] but I had never visited Sudan before, and I felt honored to have this opportunity.

The small plane circled once simply to scare the goats and chickens off the dirt "runway," then made a second circle to land. The runway in Lietnohm was a narrow dirt strip just a stone's throw from the villagers' huts. The whole village (and many nearby) came out to greet us, as though we were dignitaries.

Stepping off the plane, we were surrounded by hundreds of Sudanese villagers dancing and singing with joy. The scarred markings on their deep ebony faces represented the Dinka tribe's beauty and strength. Joyful villagers beat frenetic rhythms on wooden drums covered in animal hide. Tall, thin women clad in brilliant colors raised narrow wooden crosses above their heads as they sang praise songs to God. We received floods of hugs and handshakes from kind people we had never met. I had never felt more welcome in my life. We waved good-bye to our small plane and joined in the celebration of this new and primitive culture.

The children were the shyest at first, unsure of what to make of our foreign white skin. Some even cried and hid behind adults, thinking we were ghosts! But it did not take long for them to warm up to us, nor did it take long for their bright faces and welcoming spirits to melt my heart.

The Lietnohm people are kind and gentle. This village was, by far, the most primitive I had ever visited. Instead of money, goats or chickens were used for payment. Many villagers did not know their ages. Time was communicated with hand gestures representing the movement of the sun. To say "noon" would be to hold one's forearm directly up (the location of the sun at noon at that latitude).

After landing, we walked through the village and toward our housing accommodations, holding the tiny hands of our new little friends. I soaked in my surroundings—rounded mud huts; naked babies with emaciated faces and bulging, malnourished stomachs; and *huge* smiles.

Hearing children reciting phrases in unison, I looked to my left to catch a glimpse of about thirty eager faces staring back at me. The canopy of a tree was their classroom: broken plastic chairs were scattered about, an old, wobbly chalkboard was propped against the trunk, and goats intermingled with the students. Standing in the harsh sunlight, a dedicated teacher raised his voice above the bellows of the cows. Some of the children sat in the dirt while others sat two to one chair. A damaged school building stood nearby, but it was too small to house all the students, so the tree became their center of learning. I later learned that leaders in this village, as in many impoverished cultures, viewed education as a treasure and valued it almost as much as they valued food.

"How many orphaned children are here?" I asked one of the Sudanese leaders who hosted us.

"Oh, too many to count. Because of the fighting, so many of the parents have been killed," he said.

"Where do they go? Who cares for them?" I asked.

"They have nowhere to go. Some sleep in the school. They try to find food wherever they can. Some families take in the children as servants if they can feed them. These children are lost," he replied.

> *"These children are lost," he replied.*

I felt my heart break as the gravity of the problem overwhelmed me, but my mind began to stir. I wondered, *What if we provided funding for families to take in these children? What if we provided school fees to children who couldn't afford to pay? What if people were taught about God's plan to take care of children who had been orphaned as though they were their own children, rather than as slaves? What if they learned to serve and care for the orphaned children as though they were taking Jesus into their homes?*

Change is possible, I thought. There was much work to do.

The following day, I and two of our team members—David and Emily—gathered up the few materials I had brought with me for the workshop and joined the children under the tree. Also joining us were several chickens, goats, and a few cows.

When I work with children, I usually separate them into groups according to age so they can address issues most relevant to their age levels and so they can better connect and relate to one another. When I told the translators we needed to group the children by age, they looked at me with blank faces. All fifty children looked at us in confusion. No one understood what I wanted to do. I then remembered that many of the children don't know their ages because they don't know the day or even the year in which they were born. They rarely, if ever, celebrate birthdays. When you are fighting to survive, some things—such as birthdays—are often forgotten.

Finally, the translator smiled as he began to understand and took two children by the shoulder—one child who was tall and one who was shorter.

"You mean this size?" he said, pulling the shorter one by the shoulder and laughing.

"Or this size?" he said, placing his hand on the taller child.

Of course, I thought. *Sizes. Not ages, sizes!*

"Umm, maybe this size and taller in one group, and this size and shorter in another," I said, laughing with him.

After all the children were seated, I turned to the translator so he could introduce me to the children. Fifty pairs of dark brown eyes stared expectantly at my face. I couldn't help but smile, and when I did, smiles began beaming back at me from throughout the group—

from children who knew the secret of being joyful even in this war-torn place.

Our conversation then turned to more serious things. We discussed the difficult time they had experienced during the past few months of tribal fighting. Trying to validate their fears, even though I knew nothing of the pains of war, I knelt down so I could look into their eyes. I began, "I know many of you have experienced much pain and heartache in the past months. You have seen guns shoot and kill your loved ones. Many of you ran into the bush for safety when the clashes came, and some of you hid there for days with no food—all alone. You are so brave, and I am so sorry for what you have seen."

I looked into their tiny faces and at their small bodies, and a flood of grief came over me. These children should be running and climbing trees; they should be daydreaming about all things safe and wondrous. But they are here under this tree, and we are having hard conversations about bullets, homes being burned, and war.

After my time of sharing, David, Emily, and I handed out crayons and paper for them to draw their saddest memories—their greatest heartaches. Exile didn't yet have handkerchiefs for the children to draw on—but that didn't hamper the expression of their feelings. It was as if their memories had been trapped inside their heads, screaming to come out at the first opportunity. They may not have had the words to tell their stories, but they were able to use the crayons as their megaphones, and details came pouring out.

As they began to draw, silence descended over the group. It happens every time I offer children the opportunity to draw their pain—a peaceful, quiet hush falls upon the group. It comes without fail. My time with the children had begun with loud laughter and chatter and my best attempts to keep them quiet. But when they received pieces of paper and a few crayons, their minds went somewhere else, to another time, and perhaps another place.

I walked among them and peeked over their shoulders as they drew. Guns. Dead bodies. Blood. Soldiers. Burning huts. People running. They drew these horrific images in telling detail.

> *When the children received pieces of paper and a few crayons, their minds went somewhere else, to another time, and perhaps another place.*

As the children drew that day, they gave their stories color and life. Not only did their stories come to life, but as they processed their heartache, the children come to life as well. I never cease to be amazed at the power of art therapy—regardless of culture or location.

After the children finished drawing their pain, we handed out red, construction paper hearts. I asked the children to draw God on their hearts. Inviting them to hold that paper heart to their own hearts and close their eyes, I asked them to picture Jesus beside them in their memory, holding their hands or even hugging them tightly. When they closed their little eyes that had seen too much and held the red paper hearts close to their own, I could feel God's healing presence.

After we finished, it was time to release their heartache. We held hands and prayed a prayer for new beginnings. For peace. For forgiveness. And then, in closing, we danced! And then we sang and danced and sang some more, praising the God Who had saved them and given them life.

"The more you share your story of pain, the more God can heal your heart," I told them.

Struck by this new culture, far removed from the world around them, there was one word that stood out to me: *joy*. We awoke every morning to the sounds of someone in the village singing a praise song to the Lord and playing a drum. We went to bed with the same accompaniment. Surrounded by extreme poverty and preventable disease that took the lives of many of their loved ones, the villagers were somehow still living in a rare form of joy—and I was immensely thankful to be welcomed into their world.

Reflections from My Journal...

My Heart Beats with the
Rhythm of the Drum

Today I was able to lead about fifty children who had been affected by the recent violence in their village through the new trauma-care workshop. As we balanced ourselves on broken benches and old plastic chairs under a tree, I realized how far this world was from my office in Nashville, Tennessee; but I loved it even more! Goats gathered around me, scattered cows wandered aimlessly, and government soldiers peered from around the neighboring trees to see what was happening. And, somehow, I felt at home.

During the program I shared a verse that had gotten me through some very dark times. Second Timothy 1:7 says, "For God has not given [me] a spirit of fear, but of power and of love and of a sound mind" (NKJV).

These sweet children listened as I told them that a strength lives inside them that no one can take away. No one. Man can burn their homes, kill their families, or force them to do things they would never, ever normally do. But man <u>cannot</u> take away the strength that lives inside them. We only lose our strength if we give it away. I told the children that we believed in them and that God believes in them. And then came my favorite moment.

Those badly wounded children straightened their shoulders, lifted their heads, and stood together, grounded in an almost tangible strength. I asked them to hold each other's hands as brothers and sisters in the Lord, as a family, and to shout the Lord's promises in their native tongue: "God will never leave me! God will never forsake me! God loves me!"

If nothing else is true, this is. If our world crumbles and all that we believe is real fades away, if all those we think we can depend on leave or die, or if our homes burn and our dreams disappear, there is one thing that will never cease to exist or go away: God.

Watching the children draw their pictures of pain was difficult. Yet even among such obvious pain, their joy was evident. Their needs are great, but when I looked beneath the surface, I could see something greater: hope.

I walked away from that tree and those goats and those dusty benches knowing that these children, whom I had taught, were actually teaching me. The most valuable gift they gave me was seeing their joy in the midst of all their pain and growing in my belief that my own pain could be overpowered with joy.

Tonight, beneath this vibrant star-filled Sudanese sky, I lie under my mosquito net in bed and listen to the drums in the background. Villagers sing

praises in African harmony, and the smiling moon
serves as my only light. Children have come to sit
outside our window. Their voices join in the chorus
of this symphonic evening. Oh, and there is a family
of bats chirping above my bed; they do not wish to
be forgotten in the choir. The children sing louder
now as the drums beat stronger. My heart beats in
rhythm.

CHAPTER EIGHT

To Chase Away the Fear

If we are to teach real peace in this world, and if we are to carry on a real war against war, we shall have to begin with the children.

—GANDHI

After my time in Lietnohm, South Sudan, I stayed in Africa for an additional week to do research with Michelle in Gulu, Uganda. Just a few hours across the South Sudanese–Ugandan border, Gulu was only beginning to recover from more than two decades of war and violence that had displaced millions of its people. The key perpetrator was Joseph Kony's Lord's Resistance Army (LRA), a militant movement that began in northern Uganda and mercilessly spread into neighboring countries. Kony was forced out of Uganda in 2005. It is believed that the LRA is responsible for more than one hundred thousand deaths and approximately sixty-six thousand child abductions. As if the numbers are not horrible on their own, the LRA is also known for using witchcraft as well as cutting off the ears, noses, and limbs of their victims as a means of torture.[1]

Through my recent research and journey toward understanding how Exile could serve these war-affected children, I had heard about the work being done by organizations such as Invisible Children and World Vision. I also learned that Gulu was one of the best places to investigate the current rehabilitation practices for former child soldiers. So during our time there, we visited an organization dedicated to serving child survivors of the LRA, the appropriately named Village of Hope Uganda. When our plane landed in Uganda, several children from one of the camps met us at the airport, along with Village of Hope's founder, Cindy. Packed into the van with us, the children sang praise songs and laughed with us as we attempted to learn their Acholi language. They were full of life and beauty! They radiated survival.

When we arrived at our destination and the children were out of earshot, Rose, Village of Hope's Ugandan director, began telling us stories of their survival.

"Almost all of them have either seen their parents killed by Joseph Kony's army or have been forced to kill their parents. They have all been orphaned by the war," she told us.

Rose's voice was kind and soft, reminiscent of the flower after which she was named. She spoke candidly about the atrocities the children had experienced, but with a calm, casual demeanor, as if referencing clouds moving across the sky. The people of this ravaged area often speak of horrors as if they are talking of common things and with little emotion. In her gentleness, I could see Jesus.

The children in these displacement camps filled the air with life through their dramas, songs, and performances of their Acholi traditional dances. Dancing is my second language as well, and after just a few minutes I was joining right in! The dirt formed clouds around us, and the sunlight covered us with delight. The children beamed with so much life that it was difficult to imagine the bloodshed this land had experienced just three years earlier.

That night, I watched the children smile and laugh despite their losses. I sat in adoration as they covered their eyes with both hands as a sign of reverence to their Savior when they prayed before bed. They actually knew what it meant to be saved from slavery—physically saved from war and violent captors and spiritually set free as new creations in Christ. They showed great joy in being close to our team, and we treasured each moment with them.

Rose not only knew how to help children heal from their wounds of war but also had personally lived through them in her own life. She had even been at the meeting where Joseph Kony turned from a "God-fearing," trusted man of the community to a murderer of his people—all in just minutes. The accounts of that day from the local Ugandans I've spoken with are surreal.

"The local people didn't know who to trust or who to turn to, so when this man came, everyone trusted him and saw him as a great savior," one woman recalled. "We were suffering . . . had no homes, no food, no medicine, so when he came and disguised himself as a God-fearing man, performing what seemed to be miracles, it was very easy for him to win the hearts of the vulnerable people. He preached the gospel, and this helped everyone to trust him."

One leader in the community went on to explain that Kony had designated a certain area as a "holy ground" and told the people that no bullets or enemies could come beyond that point. This place was designated as "the yard," and people traveled long distances to come to see it.

"Until one day when he announced there would be a special, miraculous night and that people should come from all around for this special night of prayer."

Hundreds came from nearby villages, believing it was their day of miracles, but that day would be the end of many lives. One eyewitness, Ruth, recalled that many were worshipping and praising God. After a large explosion, Kony asked those who had gathered to close their eyes, and all of a sudden there was a huge fire in the front of the yard.

"We heard the people crying so loudly from the front. Several were being cut using machetes and others started running toward the back, where we were. People realized that several at the front were being killed, so they took off running for their dear lives. By the morning, many people, children included, were killed. That marked the beginning of his [Kony's] brutal operations of killing, abducting both old and young—cutting off people's ears, lips, and burning their homes."

As a former counselor at the World Vision Rehabilitation Center in Uganda, Rose had stayed with the children through many dark nights, sometimes even sleeping on the streets with groups of children when there was no safe shelter from Kony's rebels. Earlier in the war, thousands of children had become "night commuters," walking from their villages into towns at night to find safety from the LRA's nighttime abductions in their villages.[2]

"When they are able to dance, draw, and sing," Rose explained, "they can be children again. They can dance out their pain. They can sing out their pain. They can draw out their pain. But they must find a way to get it out of their hearts. There is a great difference in the hearts of the children who have received counseling and those who have not."

I was deeply moved to find out that Ugandan counselors were also using art and expressive therapy in their work with former child soldiers, and I loved seeing how intertwined dance and music were with their culture. As I watched the children in the displacement camps dance, I felt like I was watching a scene from the National Geographic Channel. Using calabashes (gourds) as instruments and bicycle spokes as drum sticks, they moved rhythmically and perfectly in their circular formations as the girls twirled in their colorful traditional skits. The culture of northern Uganda is rich. One time our team was asked by the children to perform one of *our* traditional dances from America. After much discussion, our team could only come up with the electric slide performed to the music of Alan Jackson. Though gracious, I do not think the children were impressed.

> *"They can dance out their pain. They can sing out their pain. They can draw out their pain. But they must find a way to get it out of their hearts."*

I had come to Gulu to discover more about what had been successful in the emotional healing of former child soldiers and child survivors of war in Uganda, and I was hungry to learn more of their work. I dreamed of bringing that healing to the tens of thousands of child survivors of war who still lived in a traumatic state because of horrific memories, who were still unable to sleep because of nightmares, and who were still rejected by their communities in this area of Uganda. At the time, Gulu and the Republic of Sierra Leone were two of the few places I knew of in Africa where former child soldiers were being successfully rehabilitated. My hope was to take what I would be learning from the current rehabilitation programs in Gulu and establish rehabilitation programs, groups, and workshops for children of war throughout Africa.

There is something divinely healing about using our hands to draw and our feet to dance and our mouths to sing. These expressions tap into a different part of the brain by bypassing language. Recent scientific research indicates that our bodies actually release a bonding neurotransmitter when we dance and sing together.[3] Dancing and singing are universal languages that connect us. I had seen this power in art and expressive therapy with my clients back in the States, as well as in Sudan the week before. Seeing the freedom it brought was refreshing.

Children do not have the same vocabulary as adults. They have images and memories and heartaches that they often do not have words to express. Artistic expression is a unifying language in Africa—whether it's dance, drama, drawing, singing, or storytelling. It is a language of beauty and a natural pathway to healing. Actually, the Bible itself is full of poetry, song, stories, and parables. Sacred acts of symbolic expression are found in communion, baptism, Jesus washing the feet of the apostles, and Elisha telling Naaman to wash in the Jordan River seven times to be clean. These actions are tangible expressions that tie the spiritual and emotional self to the physical self, and they also change the heart.

I sat with Rose and Cindy for hours. I wanted to soak in as much knowledge as I could—not from books, but from people who had actually lived through this madness. While still at the World Vision Rehabilitation Center, Rose had spent years providing art and expressive therapy and rehabilitation to LRA child survivors. At the time she worked with World Vision, the abducted children were still coming from the bush by the hundreds after escaping the LRA. She welcomed formerly abducted children after they had been rescued and prayed with them after they laid down their military gear. She taught them how to be children again. She, like several others along the way, became a mentor to me as I learned from her work and began making plans to provide similar care to more war-affected children in central and East Africa who had received no care at all. Some of Rose's stories were almost unbearable—I didn't want to hear the end. I didn't have a place to let them settle in my head, let alone my heart. *But,* I thought, *if these children can endure it, how can I not be strong enough to hear it?*

She told us horrific stories about children she had counseled who were forced to bite other children to death and eat human flesh as a means of torture.

"There are many children here who cannot eat meat because it is a reminder that they were forced to eat flesh while in captivity," Rose explained.

She told accounts of Kony's LRA forcing children to disfigure their own siblings, making them chop off and collect body parts of villagers. If they did not comply, they were tortured or killed. She shared details about the witchcraft and the oil the LRA witch doctors smeared on the children's heads as an occult ritual.

A small, horrified voice inside me said, *This cannot be true.* A part of me wanted to believe that the things Rose told me were legends of sorts, stories that had been passed down and manipulated. But they weren't manipulated. They were true. Each of these stories matched a child who had a name and a face and a spirit of strength: Grace, Dennis, Wisdom, Gloria.

"But I don't understand! *Why?*" I exclaimed.

I will never forget her response: "Man cannot think up the evil that has been done to these children. It is not within a man to think up such things."

> *"Man cannot think up the evil that has been done to these children. It is not within a man to think up such things."*

As I contemplated the horrors I heard about in Uganda, I wrote these words in my journal:

In Congo, yes, I saw darkness. But greater than darkness, I saw hope and resilience. A hope that will slowly and surely become stronger with time.

In Sudan, I found a joy and a spirit of gratitude that continues to humble me. They praise a God of faithfulness in the middle of a disaster for which many would blame Him. They fast from food they do not have in order to petition the grace of a great

Savior. They find strength in their weaknesses and joy amidst great suffering.

In Uganda, even in those who have endured horrible torture, I've found life. I have heard the sounds of a country rebuilding from war and children who were beginning to dance again. The guns have gone silent here, and it is time to live again. For all of this I am deeply grateful, Lord. So honored to be used by You. So humbled to simply be Yours.

I go to bed with the memory of being sweaty and dusty after dancing until sunset with the children in the displacement camp in Uganda. Resting on a tree root to catch my breath, I turned to a man sitting beside me and said, "I was told that many Africans continue to dance in time of war. Why is that?" He smirked and replied, "You know—it is to chase away the fear."

During my time in Uganda, I began to feel a discomforting connection to Joseph Kony. The more stories I heard about him, the more real he became and the more I knew I must play a part in stopping him. I learned that although the LRA had left Uganda in 2006, they had not stopped their rampage in other parts of Africa. Even as I write this book, they continue their attacks in the northeastern Democratic Republic of the Congo, South Sudan, and the Central African Republic. Fortunately, the children of northern Uganda are now safe from the LRA, but their heart wounds remain deep.

After a few days with Rose, I spent the rest of the week seeking out people who could help me learn more. Friends from agencies in

America had provided names of local organizations that were providing trauma care and counseling for former child soldiers, and I wasn't leaving until I had sought them out. So I spent my remaining days on the back of a *boda* (a small motorcycle) and knocking on doors of people I didn't know. That stubborn spirit that always kept my parents on their toes can come in handy sometimes.

I had one criterion: I wanted to meet only with Africans. I had not been raised in the war, nor did I bear the scars of a machete. I did not know what it was like to run from rebels or to live in fear of being captured. I felt the best way to find out how to help African children was to speak with Africans who had learned how to help their children. Uganda was the sixth country in sub-Saharan Africa that I had visited. Though I knew a significant amount about the overall culture of the region from my travels, African people were obviously the experts in their own culture, and I was humbly eager to learn more. I was there to listen, and I was honored that they would allow me to enter their stories of survival.

On one of the last days of the trip, I was on the back of a boda checking off my list of places to visit. In this region, bodas and boda drivers were everywhere. The process of getting a ride goes something like this: You go to a busy corner in a town, flag down a boda driver, negotiate the price from one location to another, jump on the back of the bike (skirt and all), and trust they'll get you where you need to go. Hopefully there won't be chickens tied to the back of the boda, but if there are, you just go with it and try not to disturb the chickens (they may be someone's dinner that night). No, most of the time you do not know the person driving, but yes, sometimes they speak English. On this particular day, the driver, Sam, was patient with me and went above and beyond to help me reach the remaining destinations on my list.

We were searching for places neither Sam nor I had ever been. At one point I realized that Sam and I had stopped five times to get directions in an attempt to find our way to a particular organization. I was hot, tired, and covered in dirt—and I loved it. We were on a mission and would not be deterred.

When we would finally arrive at one of our destinations, I would climb off the boda and rap my knuckles against the large, metal gate guarding the agency's entrance. Someone would come to the gate to greet me, and I would explain that I was a psychologist from America in town for just this week, trying to learn more about the counseling being done with former child soldiers so I could learn how to help.

In return, I would then usually receive a blank stare revealing little emotion. I assume they were thinking, *Why are you, a white American woman, here in our country to help our children?*

Often I sensed an air of distrust and encountered looks of confusion from the people with whom I spoke. But when they finally replied, they often said three words: "You wait here."

They typically disappeared for several minutes as Sam and I waited in the sun. When they returned, they gave me one of two answers: "There is no one here," or "You are welcome"—which, to my delight, meant "Come inside."

Everyone I sat with was distant at first, wondering why I wanted answers to the questions I asked. Some, in their wisdom, asked what I was going to do with the information they gave. Others asked if I was a Christian. Learning I was a sister in Christ helped bond us, despite our differences in skin color and accent. I found the people of northern Uganda to be warm, kind, and loving. Many of the Acholi people are soft-spoken and gentle. They have survived ugly brutality and torture, and yet they seem to live in joy with radiant smiles and laughter.

By the end of the day, Sam and I were tired, and my notebook was almost full—full of notes, ideas, and a deeper understanding of what was on the other side of this war and how children could find a new life after brutality. I soon came to understand that assistance of all kinds was needed in surrounding communities that were still recovering from centuries of war. War destroys the very fiber of nations: Education systems are wrecked as children miss years of school in instability. Poverty sets in as food and water become scarce. Families are separated, and the psyche is wounded as a result of the fear and memories that are etched in the minds of young and old. Some villages had yet to receive any support at all—especially in remote villages of northern Uganda.

Through the people I talked with, God taught me that lasting healing for children of war is found in *long-term* rehabilitation programs. Seeing the power and success of group counseling with children, I learned that the most effective programs provided safe places for former child soldiers to come week after week. These children needed places where they could learn how to be children again with other youth who have survived war.

Although the war had ended in northern Uganda, the LRA was still abducting children in surrounding countries. The madness I had heard about was still continuing, and there were countless children who needed help. A fire welled within me, and three words kept coming to mind: *this must end.*

I thought about the children in the Democratic Republic of the Congo, Central African Republic, and South Sudan—and about how they would love to meet their fellow war survivors in Uganda. *Maybe one day they can,* I thought. *Maybe one day they can pray with one another, dance together, and dream of changing their communities as peace leaders.*

> *A fire welled within me, and three words kept coming to mind: this must end.*

Little did I know that my dream of "one day" was close to reality.

Reflections from My Journal...

Gloria

She captured my heart on our very first day in Uganda. Her smile was not an average one. Her eyes were radiant—and there was something about her I couldn't quite put my finger on. One by one, each of the children from Village of Hope's safe house came up and gave me and Michelle a hug, as though each hug were custom-made and gift-wrapped especially for its recipient.

This little girl's embrace was as special as her smile. It was a shy, side hug, and she looked down as she gave it.

"What's your name?" I asked this girl who appeared to be about eleven years old.

"Gloria," she said timidly. "My name is Gloooria," she repeated, in her gentle Acholi accent.

Gloria. That she was. I had watched her on and off throughout the week and often found her standing next to me or seated right beside me in the van. She was subtle in seeking my attention, yet she sought it nonetheless, and I so desired to give it to her. I asked Rose about her story. All the children had a story.

"She and her parents were abducted by the rebels," Rose explained. "She watched her parents die, but was spared and then went to live with

her auntie, who died the next year from AIDS.
She then went to live with her grandmother, who
also died soon after. Gloria was found living in a hut
alone."

"Did she have any siblings?" I asked.

"No. None."

Alone is such a powerful word. Cutting. Deep.
Barren.

I watched her tonight as the children had their
nightly Bible study, said their memory verses aloud,
and placed their small hands over their eyes as
they prayed diligently. I was humbled by the honor
they showed their Savior. It seems this war's
heaviest violence has been unleashed on Uganda's
children, but still their young faith could move
mountains.

I watched Gloria gaze around the room with a
certain look in her eyes. She seemed buried in
her "lostness." She was searching, as though she
were out of place. I watched her as she prayed
and recited her memory verse. She watched me
back.

As my eyes followed her, I couldn't help but
remember a song that must be playing about now,
at Christmastime, back in the States. A song that
captured her—a song God must sing as He looks down
on her every day, remembering her story. Most, if
not all, of the other orphans were in sibling groups,
but Gloria was alone. Wearing her green tie-dyed

tank top and her red corduroy pants, her smile covered a world of pain. She seemed to be missing something, yet if it were not for Village of Hope, she would simply be missing. So I watched her, and I hugged her good-bye, and I hurt for her, singing that powerful Christmas song in my head over and over on the ride home.

"Glooooria in excelsis Deo."

And I thought about all of the orphaned children there. Why did I hurt for her? Why?

She was alone. She was in a room full of children orphaned just like her, yet she was alone. There is little worse in life. Isolation, left to fester, will kill—if not the body, then the spirit. When I got back to my room that night, I opened my Bible and looked down to see what I was to read for the night. Matthew 1. The first page of the book. I looked down and saw four words underlined. Four words:

"God is with us." The preceding sentence was this: "She will give birth to a son, and he will be called Immanuel." Yes, He never ceases to amaze me.

What is the answer to being alone? It is simply to be with. That's it. So simple. To simply be with. When asked what my favorite part of the first week in Sudan was, I said it was giving each of the children a red paper heart and telling them it represented God's presence. I had asked them to hold it close to their chests while they thought of their heartache and to then picture God being there—somewhere—with them.

You know, there are many names that God could have given Jesus. Many names with many different meanings. But out of all of those thousands upon thousands, He chose one. God is with you—and me—and Gloria. He so wanted us to know this that He came down to show us. Maybe we had to see it for ourselves. Maybe it wasn't enough for Him to just tell us.

There is a quotation of unknown origin that I have struggled to believe. In times of my own depression and loneliness, I read it often. "If we could truly grasp how deeply we are loved by God, we would never feel lonely again." Is it true? I have come to believe this: The question is not whether it is true. The question is how relentlessly do we seek to understand the depth of His love? How diligently do we pursue it? How welcoming are we to receive it? If we could pursue His love enough to grasp it—well, it would just be...

Glorious.

Note: At the time of this writing, Gloria is surrounded by more than two hundred brothers and sisters at Village of Hope Uganda. She has a "house mother" to care for her. She is a leader, she is doing well in school, and her smile becomes more beautiful with age.

ABOVE: Children in southern Sudan welcoming us to their village. (2008)

ABOVE: Homes in the Internally Displaced Persons (IDP) camps near Goma, DRC. (2008)

ABOVE: Taken on my first trip to Goma, DRC. (2008)

ABOVE: Art therapy in a Ugandan displacement camp with children orphaned by war. (2008)

RIGHT: Dancing with children in a displacement camp. (Uganda, 2008; photograph by Michelle York)

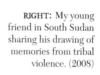

ABOVE: A young village girl holding her art therapy drawing while also holding her baby sister. (Lietnohm, South Sudan, 2008)

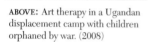

RIGHT: My young friend in South Sudan sharing his drawing of memories from tribal violence. (2008)

LEFT: Sudanese boy visualizing God beside him during his sad memories of war. (Exile International's Art/Expressive Workshop, 2008)

ABOVE: A lovely young lady who ran beside our van, waving good-bye. (DRC, 2008)

ABOVE: One of the boys dressing up like a rebel soldier during a reenactment of their abduction, using drama therapy. (DRC, 2010)

LEFT: Feet washing and big smiles in Haiti. (2010)

RIGHT: A time of art therapy with former child soldiers. They would later become the first members of the Peace Lives Center. (DRC, 2010)

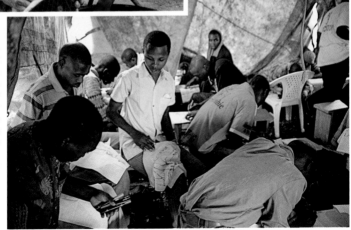

LEFT: Washing tiny feet at the girls' orphanage as an expression of our love for them. (DRC, 2010)

ABOVE: Exile's counselor Janelle providing care and encouragement to young girls in Congo, many of whom had been victims of sexual violence at young ages. (2010)

LEFT: In a Ugandan displacement camp, these children held hearts (representing God's love) to their own, remembering that God is with them, even during the most difficult times. (2010)

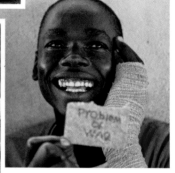

ABOVE: Young survivors of Joseph Kony's LRA rebel army dancing in spite of loss or heartache. (Photograph by Cindy Cunningham, Village of Hope, Gulu, Uganda, 2010)

ABOVE: During the workshop, children were asked to write something that caused pain in their hearts on "seed paper." This paper is then buried underground and watered. The wildflower seeds in the paper soon sprout, symbolic of God making beauty from our pain. (Uganda, 2010)

LEFT: Uplifted arms during a time of song and worship after group counseling. We could learn so much about dependence on God from these children. (Goma, DRC, 2010)

ABOVE: Rose praying with the children before they lay down their burdens at the foot of the cross during an art/expressive therapy workshop at Village of Hope. (Uganda, 2010)

LEFT: Traditional Acholi dancing by child survivors of war in Uganda. (Photograph by Cindy Cunningham, Village of Hope, Gulu, Uganda, 2010)

ABOVE: In Haiti, with children who had been orphaned by the recent earthquake, teaching them how to take deep breaths when experiencing flashbacks or when feeling emotionally overwhelmed. (2010)

ABOVE: Big smiles after the art therapy workshop. Releasing burdens brings freedom! (Goma, DRC, 2010)

LEFT: Jane and I at the International Criminal Court for the Thomas Lubunga trial. Lubunga was the first warlord tried and convicted at the ICC for the use of children in armed conflict. (International Criminal Court in The Hague, Netherlands, 2011)

RIGHT: After the Children in Armed Conflict symposium at The Hague, with Luis Moreno Ocampo (ICC former prosecutor), Jane Ekayu, and Jason Russell—in conjunction with the Thomas Lubunga trial. (2011)

LEFT: Honored to share time with these two world changers. Once child soldiers, now leaders for peace, Ishmael Beah and Emmanuel Jal. (The Hague, 2011)

ABOVE: Congolese counselors trained in Exile International's trauma-care program. Ready to bring emotional care to hundreds of survivors of war. (2011)

LEFT: Construction of the first dormitory at the Peace Lives Center, which provides housing for former child soldiers and children orphaned by war. (Goma, DRC, 2011)

ABOVE: Former child soldiers display the handkerchief–art therapy drawings of their emotional wounds that came from war, along with the dreams they have for their lives. All of these boys are now in Exile's sponsorship program, receiving education, food, housing, and trauma care. (DRC, 2011)

ABOVE: Reviewing the Young Peacemaker care plan with Exile's counseling and management team at the Peace Lives Center. (DRC, 2011)

ABOVE: Bahati was abducted twice by two different rebel forces. Thankfully, he escaped and found care at the Peace Lives Center. Here, he's praising Jesus for his life and for keeping him safe. (Goma, DRC, 2011)

LEFT: Dancing with our Congolese teammates with one of the Village Peace Clubs. In Congo, dancing is a requirement for a long life! (Kibumba, DRC, 2012)

ABOVE: New beds! Most had never slept in their own bed and many had slept in the bush for months or years. (DRC, 2012)

RIGHT: A sweet little one at the girls' orphanage drawing hopes and dreams for her life. (Goma, DRC, 2012)

ABOVE: Gabriel trying to teach me how to play guitar. "I gave up the gun for my guitar," he says. "Now I only want to sing songs about peace and praises to God." (Goma, DRC, 2012)

LEFT: Singing and dancing after a time of group counseling with boys who'd been recently rescued or had escaped from armed groups. (DRC, 2012)

ABOVE: Peace ceremony/celebration in Kibumba, DRC. Young Peacemakers washing the feet of recently rescued boys. (2012)

ABOVE: Birthday celebration with my nieces and nephew after returning from Uganda with malaria. (2012)

LEFT: Bahati (a Young Peacemaker Program participant) washing the feet of a recently rescued boy soldier and praying for him in a ceremony of peace. (DRC, 2012)

RIGHT: Janelle and Matthew giving Exile's BELIEVE T-shirts to the girls at the orphanage. These T-shirts are a tangible representation to the children that we believe in them and God believes in them. (Goma, DRC, 2012)

ABOVE: Newly rescued child soldiers receiving their first Bibles! (DRC, 2012)

LEFT: A Peace Club youth in Uganda preparing for a drama about his abduction and rescue. (Photograph by Jeremy Cowart, 2012)

ABOVE: Children served by one of our partners, Children of Peace Uganda, kneel before the cross to lay down their drawings of war and pain during Exile's art therapy workshop. (Photograph by Jeremy Cowart, 2012)

LEFT: Many Congolese are proud of their rich culture, and these young ones were proud to perform their traditional dances in their village. (Bishange, DRC, 2012)

RIGHT: Exile International's Congo team and boys of the Peace Lives Center. (2012)

ABOVE: Visiting my friend Katie and her thirteen beautiful girls in their home in Jinja, Uganda. (2013)

ABOVE: My family. (Photograph by Michelle Crouch, 2013)

ABOVE: My sister (Angela), my brother (Jason), and me at the "concrete skidittle," where we had picnics and played in the creek when we were kids. (2013)

ABOVE: Time with the Peace Clubs in Lira, Uganda. Presenting them with a quilt, each square an encouraging note from a church in the United States. (2013)

RIGHT: Leading a Peace Club in northern Uganda with our partners Children of Peace Uganda. (2013)

LEFT: Shalom packing his things into the car in preparation to return home after graduating Exile's Young Peacemakers Program at the Peace Lives Center in Congo. He is all smiles! (Goma, DRC, 2013)

RIGHT: Reuniting Shalom with his family after he graduated school and the Young Peacemakers Program. He grabbed me for a big bear hug after giving him his "full circle" bracelet. (DRC, 2013)

ABOVE: Team meeting in Congo—full of laughter, dreaming, planning, and fun! (Photograph by Matthew Williams, 2013)

ABOVE: Members of the Peace Clubs paint what they would tell the world about peace. (Children of Peace, Lira, Uganda, 2013)

RIGHT: Playing with the community children outside of Exile International's care center in Goma. I have never found a child who doesn't love to be swung into the air. (Photograph by Matthew Williams, DRC, 2013)

LEFT: Youths using dramas during a peace-building and conflict-resolution activity. (Peace Lives Center, DRC, 2013)

RIGHT: Clean water for the center! Before this system, children were fetching water at 4 a.m. each morning. Funds for this water catchment system came from Living Water. (DRC, 2013)

LEFT: Exile's first Help Portrait (brain child of Jeremy Cowart). Children received their first photo of themselves to remind them there was no one like them on earth! (DRC, 2013)

ABOVE: A common scene in Goma, DRC. Strong women carrying unbelievably heavy loads, often as they run from their homes because of rebel activity in their villages.

LEFT: Dancing and drumming with all their might at Exile's Peace Lives Rehabilitation Center. They are drumming on the "Peace Lives" drum, which is painted on the instrument. (Goma, DRC, 2013)

RIGHT: These wooden *chukudus* are seen all over Goma. They're used by boys (young and old) to transport heavy loads to and from town—sometimes for many miles.

ABOVE: Metal stamping project by the orphaned children and former child soldiers at the center in Congo. We love to sell these as necklaces and bracelets to raise funds for Exile's work in Africa.

RIGHT: Another common scene around Goma. This bicycle driver was carrying charcoal twenty-five kilometers to sell in town.

ABOVE: The eldest Young Peacemakers wash the feet of newcomers to the center—a sign of new life and an extension of love. (Goma, DRC, 2013)

LEFT: Mount Nyiragongo (volcano), near Goma, destroyed significant portions of the city in 2002, leaving the town covered in volcanic rock and ashes.

LEFT: Dennis's tears mingle with the colors of his drawing; his story inspired the Mercy Fast.

BELOW: The LRA would often tie the children to each other and force them to walk barefoot for days. The child also depicts the sad image of the LRA killing his mother (in the top right corner of the handkerchief).

ABOVE: Geoffrey depicts the common practice of the LRA cutting off limbs and decapitating victims. The green heart is his reminder that God was with him during this dark time.

LEFT: In Swahili, *Yesu* means Jesus and *watoto* means children. The character in the center is Jesus, a loving reminder of His presence.

LEFT: *Tumaini* means hope in Swahili.

RIGHT: *Amani* means peace in Swahili. The hope and joy that is evident in these children's lives is beautiful evidence of God's great work in their hearts.

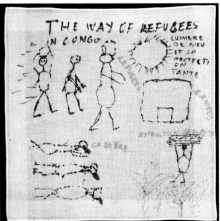

RIGHT: Judith, a former girl soldier, draws her hopes and dreams, which include becoming a psychiatric doctor to care for other traumatized children.

CHAPTER NINE

I Am Changed

Despair happens when we believe our pain has no purpose or no end.
—MAX LUCADO

I am amazed. I am bewildered. I am dizzy and I am drowning in something fathomless.

But I am not blind. I am not blind to this calling, and I will not look away.

These past few months have been an adventure, to say the least. I have traveled to three different countries that have been wounded by war: Congo. Uganda. Sudan.

The reasons for the wars differ. The rebel groups that kidnap these children have different names and reputations and vary in size. Each militia group tends to have its own agenda, fueled by power, money, revenge, and evil. But I have seen two consistencies in all three of these countries: children who have lost the innocence of their youth to the desecration of war and an incongruous spiritual richness in the hearts of the suffering and the impoverished.

My mind is a spinning top. But when it settles, I return to the same spot, to the same place in the dirt. I'm looking over the shoulder of the Savior as He drew in the sand, pondering before He spoke to the stone-holding crowd that surrounded Him (John 8:1-11). I am wondering what I should do with all I have found. What should come from all God has allowed me to witness?

As I ponder and draw in my own dirt, clarity comes. All I've seen builds inside me like a roaring wave, and I pray for Jesus to lead me into His plan.

After my time in Congo, Sudan, and Uganda, I was not the person I used to be. I came back from those initial trips with a new perspective and spiritual clarity. Suddenly things such as cellulite, bank accounts, and letters after my name didn't mean much. I had stepped into the pain of children who, in their slavery, had endured more horror than we can imagine in our worst nightmares. But almost

If the world could learn forgiveness, resiliency, and joy to this level, the world would change. And these young survivors could be our greatest teachers.

as astounding as the extent of the horror was the resilience and strength in their smiles. How do you dance after the LRA has forced you to kill your mother? How do you sing praises to Jesus with abandon after being tortured in captivity? I thought about a quote by Frank Warren, "It's the children the world almost breaks who grow up to save it."

If the world could learn forgiveness, resiliency, and joy to this level, the world would change, I thought. *And these young survivors could be our greatest teachers.*

Who better to become leaders for peace than those children who have been wounded by war? Thinking about the powerful life stories of Nelson Mandela, Mother Teresa, and Martin Luther King Jr., I envisioned a new generation of leaders—once-broken children who would rise to overcome suffering and step out to lead others in peace.

During the months following my return, I began work on a new program for war-affected children. The art therapy and trauma care workshop I had used with the children was deeply healing for them, but I realized that they also needed weekly group counseling and consistent care to heal from years of war-filled memories. They needed someone to walk with them through the slow process of mending and finding their childhood again. I called the program the Hope Initiative, and it was designed to be led by local African leaders during weekly group meetings. (We now sometimes refer to the group meetings as Peace Clubs.) The program would walk former child soldiers and war-affected children through three focus areas: (1) trauma-focused art therapy and forgiveness; (2) peace-building and conflict resolution skills; and (3) leadership skills training. My dream was that this program would one day spread through eastern and central Africa, reaching hundreds of thousands of children who had been emotionally wounded by war.

I also started doing something I never dreamed I would do: political activism. Never having had a passion for politics, this was foreign to me—and a bit uncomfortable. My only training was when I took a few policy classes in my master of social work program, but I must confess that I sometimes fell asleep in those classes, finding them quite boring. However, any intimidation I felt was quickly ousted by a laser-focused mission—to do all I could to stop the rebel groups and the warlords who were enslaving, maiming, and kidnapping children.

Before leaving Gloria and the other children, I promised myself that I would share their stories of survival. The honor of hearing details that wrenched my heart also came with a responsibility. The children could not take their stories to members of the US Congress, but I could. Their stories needed to be shared with influencers who could help stop the warlords responsible for torturing them. In order for the cycles of destruction to end, the voices of these survivors had to be heard. Advocacy and awareness became part of our mission. I started connecting with activists and influencers in Washington, DC, and our small team began meeting with members of Congress.

> *The children could not take their stories to members of the US Congress, but I could.*

As Gary Haugen, CEO and president of International Justice Mission, stated, "History teaches that the struggle for justice is not a sprint; it's a marathon."[1] We were ready to run the race.

To change the course of war, I thought, *we must stop the bleeding*

and mend the wounds of trauma. In addition to providing emotional
care, we must advocate for these children in Washington, DC. Their
stories must be told to those with political influence, to those who can
help to stop this madness.

In the meantime, friends started asking how they could help, and
with the partnership of a few dedicated, tireless teammates, Exile International began to establish roots as a nonprofit organization. When
I wasn't working on Exile-related activities or seeing clients in my
counseling practice, I shared Exile's vision with whoever would listen.

During this time, our volunteers worked countless hours to raise
funds. Musical artists gave of their talents and used their platforms to
amplify the voices of people across the world they had never met.
Old friends and acquaintances with whom I had been out of touch
for years began donating what they could, and most important, they
began praying and providing timely encouragement. Women from
local churches spent hours making dresses for the girls at the orphanage. We started selling "Believe" T-shirts; each shirt purchased
provided another "Believe" T-shirt for a child in Exile's programs as a
tangible reminder that we believed in them and that God believed in
them.

Exile also started selling beautiful jewelry handmade by women
and children who had survived war in Uganda. My nieces and
nephew "gave away" their birthdays; instead of presents, they asked
for art therapy supplies and donations to help bring restoration to
children who had been enslaved. Churches wanted to be part of our
mission, so I started speaking to groups who began praying for our
work. I was humbled at the responses of so many. At one point

during a fund-raising event I looked around and marveled: *They really care. They care as much as I do.* It was a strange and glorious feeling to know that I wasn't alone in this fight and that others had caught God's vision of redemption.

In my full-circle journey, I saw other lives changed as well. Young mothers who thought they had lost their passion began volunteering and hosting house parties for Exile. Teenagers who were searching for purpose told others about the children we work with and wore "Believe" T-shirts—using their voices to amplify the voice of others. God's work of redemption was crossing borders.

One of my favorite stories involves an elderly lady from the church where my father was a minister. She had never traveled very far outside Kentucky, where she was born. One day I received a note in her feeble handwriting, with a check for thirty dollars: "Here's a little extra money I have left over this month, please use it to help the children." I still have the note. The loving sacrifice of this elderly woman continues to leave me teary.

During this time of discovery, God, in His patience and kindness, showed me the healing side of suffering. By taking step after uncomfortable step into war-affected communities across the world, something happened to me. The eyes of my heart began to see the spiritual *wealth* of my new friends in Africa and the spiritual *poverty* that so characterized the place I called home. And I found something else in the lives of my new friends: purpose. Much like the scene in *The Wizard of Oz* where Dorothy and her friends follow the yellow brick road through fear and danger, only to find what they long for already living inside them. So it was with me: my purpose and calling were already within me; I didn't have to search for them; I just had to start walking and living for something bigger than myself. When I did, I gained an intimacy with God that I had never known.

My egocentric prayers slowly transformed into petitions of surrender. Instead of asking Him to do something *for* me, give something *to* me, or grant the desires of *my* heart, I began to ask Him to do something *with* me. I craved being used by God more than I craved my own needs being met. Not because I was special, but because God had so graciously redeemed my life. I wanted to use this "second life," this gift, completely for Him. Slowly, beautiful things began to unfold.

I don't claim that my new journey brought complete emotional and spiritual healing. It didn't. In fact, it brought a world of heartache of a different kind. I neglected relationships. I experienced the fatigue of burnout, and I still battled my demons. Even now, depression and anxiety sometimes rear their ugly heads, but my arsenal of coping skills is much stronger than it once was. I have learned that answers are not found in hiding, and I've learned that those I once felt I needed to save have much to teach me about resilience and gratitude for life.

I think some people thought I was a little over the top; looking back, I can understand why. But I remember a UN ambassador who, when referring to bringing attention to the more than one million lives lost in the 1994 Rwandan genocide, said, "I swore to myself that if I ever faced such a crisis again, I would come down on the side of dramatic action, going down in flames if that was required." The ambassador also recalled a phrase used by a colleague: "having to run naked through the West Wing of the White House to raise attention and to get action on something that one believes to be urgent."[2] Why? Because she valued human life and knew that the embarrassment of appearing to be over the top was worthwhile if it saved even one. Some things are worth shouting about, and if we wait for someone else to do the shouting, we run the risk of allowing silence to win. Edmund Burke, a politician and statesman, is quoted as saying, "The only thing necessary for the triumph of evil is for good men to do nothing." We can no longer do nothing.

When I thought about the children I'd met who had returned from battlefields, struggling to survive, I could not be silent. These children are valuable, and if given the opportunity, they could teach the world beautiful things—the very things they were already teaching me.

I remember two little girls I spotted in Congo. They were holding hands when our team drove past them. They were covered in dirt and wore tattered dresses, and their feet were bare. Behind them stood a massive volcano that had erupted six years earlier and destroyed 40 percent of their city of Goma.[3] Less than twenty kilometers to their left, warring rebel groups were fighting and people were dying in the crossfire.

And what were these little girls doing? They were dancing. They were laughing and singing and radiating *joy*.

Why? Because they had no idea they weren't supposed to dance. They did not know they were supposed to be sad or unhappy. God was living inside them, amid all the destruction, and He was beaming from the inside out.

In my experiences, I have yet to see much self-pity in developing nations. I see as many dancing children as I see hungry ones. I see far less blaming God and far more praising Him. Less God-directed anger and more God-directed dependence. Rarely, if ever, have I witnessed a sense of entitlement.

I think of people such as Robert, a guide in Kenya who was the only African man I have ever heard speak with a lisp, adding to his eclectic personality. Of seven siblings, he was one of only four who were still living. He told me that at night, in his childhood home, his mother would take off her dress and lay it on the floor for her children to use as a bed mat.

"Robert, in America, if we had experienced such hardship, we might blame God. We might even be angry with Him. But in Africa I rarely hear of anger toward God. I rarely hear about Africans blaming Him for allowing such heartache to happen. Why do you think that is?"

I could barely complete my sentence before he replied in his sweet, lisped Kenyan accent.

"Ooooooh, nooooo. How could we blame God when He is the one who helps us? He is the reason we are living, the reason we are breathing. When we are harmed, it is because man has harmed us. Not God."

> *"How could we blame God when He is the one who helps us? When we are harmed, it is because man has harmed us. Not God."*

I thought at that moment, *That sounds so simple. Can it really be so hard to understand?*

Yes, it *is* hard for many of us to understand. But I think the answer may go something like this: God is love. Life is hard. People

cause pain, and people fall victim to that pain. Yet Christ offers redemption and offers us the hope of an eternity beyond heartaches.
In some parts of the world, people believe in a God of "give me." But
in the countries I have visited that struggle in poverty or war, their
belief is in a God of "hold me," "guide me," or "save me." Yet we are
praying to the same God.

We often seem to shake our fists at a God who has to dodge our
flailing arms as He attempts to wipe our tears. We fight the very One
who desires to hold us.

Life is imperfect. In an imperfect world, there are unfortunate circumstances that are nobody's "fault." And all the angry finger-pointing
in the world won't make them any less real.

Anger has its place, but we only hurt ourselves when we allow
anger to turn into bitterness. "Shooting ourselves in the foot" takes
on a different meaning when we understand that bitterness creates a
distance from the very One who gives us the ability to walk.

When we credit God for "God things" such as life, love, redemption, and hope, and we credit human beings for "human things" such
as abuse, killing, crimes against humanity, and betrayal, we no longer
distance ourselves from the Creator Who gave us life. And when we
are no longer pushing away from Him, we can draw closer to His
heart.

And when we draw closer to God's heart, we can be instruments
of His change. I was ready to advocate for peace, for hope, for a new
life for these children. I was ready to bring their stories to the world.

Reflections from My Journal...

I Believe in You

I think a tiny part of me has always believed in the Easter Bunny and Santa Claus—and, well, maybe even the Tooth Fairy. But not really. I mean, not really the Tooth Fairy.... I feel I am called to believe in the unbelievable and to have hope for those who have none. This has simultaneously caused me much pain and given me tremendous joy. It's a blessing and a curse.

Many clients come into the office without it— hope, I mean. They have given up on life, on their marriages, on their dreams, on finding "the one," on having children, or on being happy. My job is not only to believe in them, but to hope for them when they can't muster any hope on their own.

Some people say we lose hope. I disagree. I think we give our hope away. When holding on to hope begins to hurt, we loosen our grip on it. We confuse blind hope with false hope, and we can't see how anything can or will ever be any different than it is in the present moment.

But it will be. It will be different.

If we want something we have never had, we have to do something we have never done. We have to find a way to change—to change either what we are or who we are becoming, our environment, or our perspective. People word this idea in lots of different ways, but the meaning is the same. If we want something different, we have to do something different. So why don't we?

We stop believing in ourselves or in life. And we give our hope away.

My mind wanders back to one of the displacement camps we visited while in Uganda. We were there in the middle of the land that the LRA had torn from its core. Children orphaned by Joseph Kony's rampage surrounded us. Dancing. Living. Some of these children are called "forced orphans," meaning they were orphaned when forced to kill their own parents in horrific ways. Many of the children came from "child-headed households," which means children orphaned at eleven or twelve were taking care of their younger siblings because they had no caregiver. But no one would have known it, at least not by observing them on that day.

The children greeted us with joy, but they also greeted us with pain. After the dancing stopped and after the singing ceased, I saw such pain behind their big, brown eyes.

Seated on a tree stump with my bare feet in red, Ugandan dirt, resting from the hour of dancing the traditional dances with the children in the blazing sun, I was asked to give a few words to the group.

Soaking in the awe of these beautiful survivors

and feeling the freshness of their heartache as
though it were my own, I knelt to look into their
eyes. About fifty faces looked back at me as I
remembered the instruction: "Give them a word." I
looked at the translator, and without thinking, the
following words came: "Tell them I am sorry for their
pain. Tell them that they are strong. Tell them
we believe in them. We believe they can overcome
their pain. We believe they can be the future
peace leaders for this community and change their
nation for the glory of God."

She did. All was quiet and still. I have realized
that there are four words that may hold more power
than the most eloquent of greeting cards or all the
length of Tennyson's poetry:

"I believe in you."

Thinking about that day, I remembered one of
my secrets. The number of people who know this
about me could be counted on one hand. During the
darkest time in my life I did something odd during
my escape to Boulder, Colorado: I bought greeting
cards for myself.

When I walked by the greeting card sections
in stores, I would stop to read the cards. I often
chose the one I thought God would give me; I would
buy it, sign His name, and carry it around with me.

Looking back, this practice spoke to a desperate
need to be encouraged, to feel loved, to somehow
hear Him whisper, "My daughter, I believe in you."

Even when I didn't believe in myself, I knew that if anyone believed in me, my Creator did. My Beloved. My God. It was then I realized the power of those four words:

"I believe in you."

Those four words kept me alive. And it's those four words I wish to whisper to the dear children I now hold in my heart.

SECTION FOUR

The Simplicity of Madness

Blessed are the peacemakers,
for they shall be called sons of God.

—Jesus

CHAPTER TEN

Grace Comes Full Circle

*There is no passion to be found playing small—in settling for
a life that is less than the one you are capable of living.*

—NELSON MANDELA

Victor Frankl was a prisoner. He was a psychiatrist held captive in a Nazi concentration camp for Jews. During his time of torture, holding on to life in this death camp, he discovered the importance of living life with meaning and in a way that was worthy of his sufferings. As a prisoner, he found that treasures lie in finding purpose in pain. In his book *Man's Search for Meaning*, he explains that a life lived with intentional purpose (even during intense suffering) is a life most fulfilling. His wisdom forever changed me. In his book, Frankl writes:

> The way in which a man accepts his fate and all the suffer-
> ing it entails, the way in which he takes up his cross, gives
> him ample opportunity—even under the most difficult cir-

cumstances—to add a deeper meaning to his life. It may remain brave, dignified and unselfish. Or in the bitter fight for self-preservation, he may forget his human dignity and become no more than an animal. Here lies the chance for a man either to make use of or to forgo the opportunities of attaining the moral values that a difficult situation may afford him. And this decides whether he is worthy of his sufferings or not.[1]

Worthy of his sufferings. Could it be that suffering is a gift, a gift of which we need to prove ourselves worthy? He then says:

A man [in the concentration camps] who let himself decline because he could not see any future goal found himself occupied with retrospective thought. . . . Such people forgot that often it is just such an exceptionally difficult external situation which gives man the opportunity to grow spiritually beyond himself. Instead of taking the camps' difficulties as a test of their inner strength, they did not take their lives seriously and despised it as something of no consequence. They preferred to close their eyes and to live in the past. Lives of such people became meaningless. In some ways suffering ceases to be suffering at the moment it finds a meaning.

God planted Frankl's words in my spirit and, without my knowledge, began watering them. Suffering was gaining meaning not only in my own life, but also in the lives of those whom I was growing to love. There was no sudden realization that my hardships were being used to bring hope and life to others. But the miracle of grace slowly and surely took shape within and around me. Grace often works this way—falling like a slow rain. First there are just sprinkles, but as we allow ourselves to embrace the gift of its refreshing newness, it slowly gives life to our dry bones. But it cannot be forced. Grace is a gift, and it must be embraced if we are to discover the new breath it offers.

> *Grace is a gift, and it must be embraced if we are to discover the new breath it offers.*

It was 2011, and my heart raced when I thought about my upcoming return trip to Congo and Uganda. I could hardly wait to get back and begin the long-term rehabilitative care programs with the children there. Reviewing all my journals of notes and ideas and the program planning I had written on napkins and random pieces of paper, I was elated to know that God was pulling it all together. It was happening! Dreams of giving hope to these beautiful faces danced within me. I found myself on my knees with gratitude. My life was far from typical, but it was deep and wide and full of undeserved grace.

Sure, I had moments of envying couples holding hands and mothers pushing strollers. I longed for a family, but the path God had placed me on felt so far from "settling down." Although I occasionally dated, I continued to wear the ring on my left hand. Still feeling married to the Lord in many ways, I often quipped that I was a protestant nun. The few dates I'd gone on hadn't revealed a partner who could join me on this adventure of loving and serving children across the ocean. When others casually talked about a new show on television, I would be contemplating how to stop rebel leaders in war zones. I would be a hard match to make. So I decided to trust the Lord Who had given new life to me—even in those moments of envy or desire.

I had gone from the depths of despair and depression to truly finding deep joy in God's call on my life. Yes, the life I knew had crumbled to pieces, but God had given me a second chance, and I knew He'd done this for a reason. By the kindness of God, I did not lose myself in depression. By His grace, I had tasted and received new life. Because of His tender mercy, my own selfishness and fleshly desires were forgiven.

My climb out of that emotional pit had a purpose. My pain had meaning. None of it was to be wasted. Instead, it was being redeemed. Jesus could and would use it all.

Because I have so thoroughly experienced heartache, I often say, "When your greatest heartache becomes your greatest ministry, grace comes full circle." As I followed God's lead in my life, I stepped into that circle. The situations I once thought I could not survive were the very things that bound me to these strong souls I now had the privilege to serve. My own survival of heartbreak and trauma had ignited a passion to fight for justice and to bring healing to children of war.

During the months prior to my next trip to Congo and Uganda, I made several visits to Washington, DC. My purpose was to meet with US senators and representatives, to tell the first-hand stories of children such as Nelson and Joyce, and to raise awareness regarding the plight of former child soldiers and child survivors of war. I lobbied alongside like-minded organizations for a bill that would help disarm the LRA—an army whose crimes against humanity had landed Joseph Kony at the top of the International Criminal Court's most wanted list.

On one trip to Washington, DC, I brought along some of the children's heartache drawings—some on handkerchiefs and some on construction paper—hoping and praying for the opportunity to give them to the right person who would value them and be moved to advocate. The pictures portrayed guns, children running from bullets, and trails of blood.

How could such small hands draw such evil? I thought as I looked at them.

I was given the opportunity to hand them to the director of the Office of Public Engagement of the White House after he spoke at a meeting concerning international areas of armed conflict. The plan was for one of his assistants to get his attention and arrange a few seconds for me to hand him the drawings as he exited the stage. But something went wrong and I noticed him making his way to the door, and no one was stopping him! He was just a few steps from the door, and I was faced with only one solution: to stand in his way. I stepped in his path and quickly said, "I made a promise to some children to pass along these drawings, and I wondered if I could give these to you." When he looked at me in confusion, I wished I had worded my plea more articulately.

"These drawings are from child survivors of war and depict their time in captivity after being abducted by Joseph Kony's Lord's Resistance Army. I wondered if you would be willing to look at them and, possibly, pass them along to the president." He looked down at the details in the drawings, and compassion touched his face. Thanking me sincerely for passing them along, he ended our short conversation with, "I will make sure these get into the hands of the president."

The stubborn spirit in me rose again. Before thinking, I boldly replied, "Will you really?" As I asked, I looked him square in the eyes. "Yes," he said with a smile. "Absolutely."

Moving hearts in our nation's capital was a big dream for a little woman in a big world with no consistent funding. But God spoke the world into existence by His breath, and I believed in a Lord of miracles.

> *How do you solve a problem so massive? You begin with the smallest children and empower them to lead a different way of life.*

How do you solve a problem so massive? I wondered. Almost as quickly as the question formed in my mind, so did the answer: *You begin with the smallest children and empower them to lead a different way of life. You give them the opportunity to heal from their wounds while also raising them to become the next generation of peace leaders.* This was the vision I wanted those in positions of power to adopt.

Soon it was time to depart from America once again, and this time for one month—the longest amount of time I had ever been in Africa. Two teams would spend two weeks in each country. The first team would be in Uganda, working alongside Rose and Cindy with a select group of children at Village of Hope Uganda to provide group counseling. The second team would go to Congo to lead the one-day art therapy workshop with the girls and boys we had visited on the first trip.

When I left Congo on the first trip, I never dreamed I would get to see these children's faces again. When the boys at the orphanage had asked me to be their "father," I had no idea I would ever be reunited with them. When I left Uganda after so much research, I never could have imagined the ways God would turn those hours of listening and learning into programs that would bring LRA child survivors life and honor again. Before my very eyes, I witnessed what God could do if we just put one foot in front of the other and dedicate the outcome to His glory—surrendering all. He is a God of mystery. More than I imagined.

Reflections from My Journal...

I Will Be Brave

In more than fifteen years of counseling work, I've cried maybe three times in session with a client. In therapy, it's normally not hard for me to keep my emotions in check. My role is that of supporter, encourager, and listener. But last week, I cried. The "can I get you a tissue?" kind of crying. It came over me before I could stop it or even think about it.

Sitting across from me, a woman talked about the wisdom she had gained in her suffering, processing what God could do with her pain. At that moment, I felt a rush of purpose and knew I was there, present with her at that very second, to tell her to hold on, to tell her there was something better around the corner. And so I cried with her. It felt strange to me. It felt weak. It felt wonderful.

Wisdom in suffering. Purpose through pain. Beauty in brokenness. Can we find the hope? Can we hear the voice of God calling us out of the darkness and into His arms?

"Come then, my beloved, my lovely one, come. For see, winter is past, the rains are over and gone. Flowers are appearing on earth. The season of glad songs has come" (Song of Solomon 2:10b–12a, NJB).

Redemption seems to follow me, even in the dark:

A patient on the brink of suicide. A loved one who has lost a job. A sexually abused four-year-old. A marriage meant to change the world now shattered in a million pieces. Children across the globe dying of something we could fix with a small purchase from a corner drugstore.

Fear. Weakness. Hatred. Evil. Good. Light. Dark. Suffering. So much suffering—yet so much love. So much hope—if we could only see it in the midst of our suffering.

I told a friend last year that most days I feel as if God puts a cape around my neck and kisses me on the forehead to say, "Go get 'em, girl!" Then on other days, I am on the ground, feeling alone and broken into a million pieces. But there is one thing I will not do: I will not stay down.

Why? I am in a battle. I believe we all are.

A few weeks ago, we received some good news about a bill that would call the United States to orchestrate a plan for the disarmament of the LRA, which was responsible for torturing the children we work with. It was a good day. A full day.

The day ended with something I had wanted to do for a while: go to a movie theater by myself. I watched Alice in Wonderland and adored it. Top to bottom. Beginning to end. Why? Because, at that moment, I was Alice. As cheesy as it may sound, it felt as though I had that sword in my hand, fighting the Jabberwocky in the biggest battle of my life. I have to fight. I have to believe. The only other option is not believing, and I am not ready to give up.

Swing. Stab. Twirl. Fall down. Get back up.

As Alice fights the Jabberwocky, she reminds herself, "My dad used to say he believed in six impossible things before breakfast.

"The last one? 'There is a place called Wonderland.'"

How did Alice defeat the Jabberwocky? She believed she could.

One of the things we tell the children we serve is that man can burn their homes, kill their families, force them to do things they would never normally do. But man can never steal the power that lives inside them—the power of their creator who gives them strength. The One who gave them breath can also give them Life. Abundant Life. True Life. Hopeful Life.

In these children, there is a strength that is bigger than their suffering and larger than life. There are moments when their eyes dance as they realize they are more than what they have been forced to do. God has a redemptive purpose for their pain, and for that moment, for that child—I will be brave.

CHAPTER ELEVEN

With Story Comes Song

Unless you be as a little child, you will not enter the kingdom of God.
—JESUS

Closing my eyes, I slowly breathed in the African air as I stepped off the plane in Uganda. It smelled like home. In the few weeks leading up to a trip, I am often on my knees in prayer. Before this trip, my knees were a bit more worn than usual. I was praying to be poured out for every child God would bring across our path and for each hand we would hold.

Plans were in place to use the art therapy workshop with children we had previously met at Village of Hope Uganda. Rose and Cindy, from Village of Hope, had gone to great lengths to arrange for our team to bring this workshop to twenty-three children in their program. Each of these young, brave hearts—ranging in age from eleven to fifteen—had experienced deep trauma at the hands of the LRA. All of them had been orphaned.

My friends Amanda, Britt, and Jake came along to help lead the workshop. Amanda was my roommate and, over the past few years, had played a vital role in helping me see God's heart for the orphaned child. She had worked with orphaned children in several African countries. Britt was a contemporary Christian music artist who was passionately in love with Jesus and spoke life into those around her. These women are two of the most life-giving souls I know. Jake is like a brother to me. He, his brother, and his dear family supported the work of Exile International since the very first trip to Congo and they were the first friends with whom I processed my broken heart upon my return—listening, caring, loving, and standing by my "bigger than me" dreams to see child survivors healed and restored.

After landing in Uganda, we all hopped into a dusty van that took us five hours north down broken and bumpy roads to the remote location of Village of Hope Uganda. We were filled with excitement, and I could hardly wait to see the children again! Gloria, Molly, Nelson, Robert, and so many more. The next few days were going to include rice and beans, head lamps, cup baths, and concrete "squatty potties," but I didn't care. I loved it, actually, and I was ready for all God had in store.

The first day, we spent hours around the campfire, singing, dancing, and simply being with the children. The kids needed to bond with our team to develop some rapport before starting the emotionally difficult portions of the art therapy workshop. Watching them beam as they performed their traditional dances, I could hardly imagine the reality of the emotional scars that hid behind their laughter and joy. The African sky that night was captivating. But I couldn't help but remember that just a few years earlier, this very land teemed with thousands of LRA rebel soldiers—perhaps even in the very place we were standing.

When we awoke the next day, we began the expressive art therapy work with the children. The sun was shining brightly, and the sky was perfect. The smell of fresh dirt from the huts reminded me of playing in the woods of Kentucky when I was younger, and the mosquito nets felt like magical canopies over my bed. We were far away from any town, which also meant we were far away from electricity and running water. In their simplicity, this place and these children were beautiful.

I wasn't sure what to expect from our time together. This would be the first time many would share details of their personal stories of abduction, rape, torture, or being forced to kill their family members. I anticipated that this would be deeply painful for them, and we were praying for God to give them—and us—strength.

> *Secrets that are locked inside us—especially painful, dark, or shame-filled secrets—soon become cancerous and bring multiplying pain.*

Secrets that are locked inside us—especially painful, dark, or shame-filled secrets—soon become cancerous and bring multiplying pain. Our wounds become deeper when we hide our scars, and freedom comes when we dare to be vulnerable. Sharing those wounds creates opportunities for healing, acceptance, and victory. In my practice in Nashville, I'd seen both children and adults who shared their painful memories and weighty burdens of shame leave our sessions with a lightness in their step and a wider smile. After embracing the unconditional love of God, they leave knowing they are not, never were, and never will be alone. The God of redemption suddenly feels as close as their next breath.

Here, on this bright, sunny day, I was nervous, as though I sensed something wonderful or awful were about to happen, and I wasn't sure which. As we gathered together, children started singing praise songs to Jesus, one by one. No one prompted them; they just started singing, because that's what they do.

The next three hours seemed timeless.

Children plopped down on the concrete floor of the open-air room. Britt, Amanda, Cindy, and Rose were at the front of the room. Praying before we started, I asked God to use me, to choose my words and guide my thoughts. Even with a master's degree in social work, a PhD in psychology, and years of experience in counseling, I felt like a nervous student. Feelings of incompetence swept over me as I asked myself, *Do you realize what they have been through, Beth? Do you understand the pain they have experienced? Who are you to talk to them about hope? Who are you to talk to these children about healing and forgiveness?*

But at that moment, I got it. Yes, I was incompetent, but I wasn't there for me. Our team was there to serve God and His children, like an instrument or pencil serving the will of its master. He was and is their Shepherd. He is their *forever Father*, unchanging and ever-present. I felt very strongly that He wanted us to love and hold these children, as extensions of His fingertips. It wasn't about us. It was about loving them through the love we had been given from God. While He was not physically or tangibly there, we were. We could embody and incarnate His love for them.

What happened next spun a web of healing. I was thankful for Rose, who was translating for me, to assure what I said was both culturally appropriate and therapeutically on point for the group. We talked with the children about hope—its true definition. We discussed God's promises that, while there will be trouble in the world, He will be with us through it. I told them that if God were visibly and audibly present there with them, I felt He would tell them He loved them dearly and He was proud of them for being so brave through their trials. Their beautiful faces did not leave mine for a second. They hung on to each word of encouragement.

To lighten the mood, we played a "feelings game" to help them identify their emotions. We whispered a feeling word in the ear of someone who volunteered, and that child would act the feeling out dramatically. The children laughed loudly as they yelled out their guesses. Feelings aren't talked about freely in the Ugandan culture, so this was an icebreaker for them.

Their eyes widened when I began to explain that other children around the world had also gone through trauma. Other children had even been through war. Looking around at each other, they reacted as if I had spoken a secret they had never heard before. I explained that these other children possibly shared some of their feelings, and they were not alone in their pain. When I shared that I had also gone through a dark time, the room became quiet. In that moment, I was no longer just a woman who had come to visit from across the world. I was a fellow sufferer, even though my scratches were tiny compared to their gaping wounds.

Post-traumatic stress disorder (PTSD) is common in children involved in armed conflict. In some countries, 90 percent of child soldiers show evidence of PTSD.[1] Personally, I don't often find it helpful for children to be told they have a trauma "disorder." I do, however, find it helpful for children to know that other children have similar struggles as a result of trauma. Sharing that truth provides a means of normalizing their symptoms and emotional pain.

I shared with the children that many who have experienced trauma in the world had struggles (symptoms) similar to theirs. I explained that I was going to name some of the struggles (in a way they could understand them) and, if anyone in the group had experienced these, they were invited to raise their hands if they felt comfortable doing so. I explained that I might raise my hand too. Even with my awareness of their levels of trauma, I was still taken aback by the response.

"Nightmares or very bad dreams." Almost every hand went up.

"Times where you feel you are reliving something very bad that feels as though it is happening again and again." Almost every hand went up.

"Trouble concentrating."

"Being confused in your mind."

"Having difficulty sleeping."

"Feeling as though you are in a daze."

One by one, we went through the clinical symptoms of PTSD for children. Hand after hand held still in the air.

The room was quiet again.

"Keep your hands up and look around you," I said.

The looks on their faces told me they were as shocked as I was when they looked into the eyes of their brothers and sisters, their fellow survivors of war.

Bending down so I could see their faces, I intentionally looked them deeply in the eyes. "You are not alone," I told them. "Your brothers and your sisters around you have also gone through war. Many here were forced to perform acts they would have never participated in on their own. You ran from the rebels together. You have seen the pain caused by the LRA together. You have survived together. Now you can grieve together. Now you can heal together."

> *"You have survived together. Now you can grieve together. Now you can heal together."*

Their faces began to relax, and their hands came down. Some were even smiling at each other—as if they could feel at ease with their memories because their burden was no longer theirs alone.

There is a balance to grieving: we must allow ourselves to feel the pain but not live in the pain. We must not stay there. Letting ourselves dream and understand that there is life beyond our pain empowers us to transcend the grief.

The children stood together, and Britt led them in song. Their voices blended like the threads of a tapestry, and I tasted what heaven might sound like. After Amanda read Jeremiah 29:11–12 aloud (a key set of scriptures we use in the workshop), the team gave each child two white handkerchiefs and a set of markers.

Though their minds contained memories that were too horrible for words, drawing their stories was a safe way for them to communicate their pain.

The Bible tells us that God "captures our tears in His bottle" (Psalm 56:8, NKJV). "Our sad tears and our happy tears," I said. "These two handkerchiefs represent God capturing your tears. If you wish, on one handkerchief you may draw your heartache or a sad time in your life. On the other handkerchief, you may draw what you dream for your life after war—what your happy tears would draw if they could." Some of the children giggled at the thought of their tears drawing on a handkerchief.

"Now I am going to share with you the most important part of the drawing exercise," I explained. "In the middle of our times of suffering and our times of joy, God is with us. Sometimes we feel Him there. Sometimes we don't. But He promises us He is there. As a reminder of that promise, I want to invite you to draw Jesus in the center of both of your drawings, as a reminder that He was beside you in your darkest and happiest times."

The room fell silent. They drew slowly at first, looking around to see what their friends were doing. A gentle breeze came and flipped up the edges of their handkerchiefs as they held them down on the concrete floor. Their eyes became fixed and determined. You could tell that the details they drew were etched into their hearts, and they needed to release them. Their drawings were specific and detailed—

helicopters, soldiers, guns, blood, bullets, dead bodies (some muti-lated). When the drawings were complete, it was time to share.

One by one, the children who volunteered to share the story of their drawing bravely stood before their peers. Holding their drawings up, they explained in detail those things they had held in secret—memories of war, flashbacks of killings, nightmares that had come to life.

Thomas: "We heard a loud scream when we were sleeping. We awoke and our hut was on fire. The rebels were there, and they made me to watch as the knife came across my mother's neck. But God saved me to live. He saved me to dance.

"The rebels made me to watch as the knife came across my mother's neck. But God saved me to live. He saved me to dance."

"I dream of being a doctor one day by the grace of Jesus Christ. I wish to help other children who suf-fered like me."

Robert: "The rebels came and kicked in the door. They abducted my parents and cut my brother into pieces. . . . When I was in captivity, the rebels made me to kill one of the other boys with a machete who tried to escape. He was my brother and my friend.

"My hope is to one day be the president of Uganda and give the good news of peace to our country."

Grace: "The rebels came into my school and took me. There was loud fighting and fire. They tied my friends and me together with a rope. I was made to carry heavy loads on my head. If I said a word, I was given more loads to carry or was beaten one hundred strokes. . . .

"My dream is to finish school and one day be a teacher of children by the grace of God."

Story after story. And then it came. The weeping. Dennis started crying. Then Grace. Then Barbara. Tears of pain started to flow like rivers of life. Silent tears. Raging tears. Tears held back for years by dams of strength. The sound of the sobbing was almost unbearable. Some children ran out of the room. Some ran to their beds to weep privately. Some could go nowhere except where they were, covering their faces with their handkerchief drawings, which were *literally* capturing their tears. The colors of their art mixed with their tears on the cloth, and Jesus was right there in the center of it all.

The team divided up to sit with the children, to be present with them, and to pray. Each was given as much space as needed for his or her grieving. Everyone was silent for some time, with only the sound of children lamenting before the Lord. And He was there, weeping with them. Holding their hands. Wiping away their tears and collecting them in His bottle for safekeeping—to remind them how precious they were to Him.

Slowly everyone trickled back to the group. A circle was formed, and everyone stood as they held hands. There were no dry eyes. Not one. There were only broken hearts that had started the process of being mended. Each and every child was still holding both handkerchiefs as they held hands.

"The enemy would want you to see yourself as what you have done or what has been done to you," I said. "He would want you to live in your past and be held down by your pain forever. Just like a broken bone, your heart can and will heal slowly. Day by day, God will turn your mourning into dancing. But today, the enemy will not win. God has beautiful plans for your lives!"

As we shared with the children how God can use their pain to help other children, the expression on their faces began to shift. They were coming to understand that what they had gone through was not just for evil. They began to believe that God could use their heartache for good. If they desired, they could be Uganda's next generation of peace ambassadors. The next Nelson Mandelas of Africa.

Still in a circular formation around the room, *all* of us began throwing our heartache drawings into the center of the room—some with anger, some with timid pain. But we all threw them with intention, refusing to be defined by our past and longing to live in the hopes of our futures.

The children began praying and singing softly. Unrehearsed, they began to kneel. Not in any order, just as their hearts led them. Amanda and Cindy prayed gracious prayers. Britt led them in a song to their Savior. The angels in heaven rejoiced. Hands outstretched. Eyes closed. It was abandonment. It was beautiful. It was the worship of grateful children whose lives had been spared and saved by their Father. This raw, pure dependence on God was such as I had never seen in children before and had rarely seen in adults.

With the drawings of their dreams still in their hands, we asked them to choose a small stone from outside the room. We placed a cross made of branches just around the corner from the meeting place. Explaining that these stones were to symbolize the many burdens of their hearts, I invited them to leave the stones at the cross as they left the room.

It was a somber time. One by one, young hands released the burden stones and left their wounds, hurts, and pain at the cross. Then something magical happened. The mourning literally turned into dancing before our eyes! One of the children started singing a song of redemption and joy. Soon everyone joined in, and they began waving their handkerchiefs of hopes and dreams above their heads. Some were jumping, others dancing! Sweet sounds of praise rising high! As the sun was setting, there were twenty-three burden stones at the foot of the cross and twenty-three healing hearts dancing toward their dreams of redemption.

On that day, hope became mingled with peace. After processing that remarkable day with the children, saying good-bye was difficult. It was also not easy to leave Britt, Amanda, Cindy, and Rose after what we had experienced together. Jake and I were staying behind a few extra days to meet with community leaders in Gulu to share plans of partnerships and program development. In light of the past few days, I was ready to dive in deeply.

Reflections from My Journal...

Chain around My Heart

Sitting down for the first time to write since leaving Uganda, I'm not sure where to begin. I have a chain around my heart—and my arm. As I write, I look down at my right wrist. I can't stop looking at it. The chain was given to me by the most wounded and bravest boy I know. He had been abducted by the LRA at about the age of nine. The very day he was abducted, Joseph Kony's soldiers forced him to kill his parents. It does not stop there. He was then forced to hack them into pieces. It does not stop there, but for the sake of mindfulness, I will.

Nelson rarely smiles. He is often found off by himself, away from the other orphaned children. He is tall, and he is strong. He speaks little English, and he rarely looks people in the eye. But he gave me the greatest gift I have ever been given.

Britt, Amanda, Jake, and I spent three nights with the children of Village of Hope Uganda—but that short time seemed like ten days. Most of the children there were formerly abducted, having watched their parents be killed or having been forced to kill their parents. We prayed with them, sang with them, and cried with them.

Nelson, this boy whom I have grown to love, not only drew, but he and his brother were brave enough to share their stories with the group—the first time they had ever voiced their pain in front of others. After they shared, they wept. They wept so much that the stories drawn on their handkerchiefs with markers began to blend with their tears and became, in many ways, a rainbow of pain, hope, and healing on cloth.

After the day ended, I was walking back to the hut and felt something touch my arm. I turned to my right to see Nelson quickly placing something around my wrist. In a flash it was there, almost as if he hadn't put it on my wrist at all. No words were exchanged as we walked beside each other. I smiled and he smiled, and I grabbed his hand.

What did he put on my arm? A chain—a thick chain link, to be exact. It's a silver chain link that fits perfectly on my wrist. Here is the magical part. It has no beginning and no end, and it has no clasp. How did he place it on my wrist so quickly? I wonder how he placed it on my wrist at all!

The moment was as magical as the chain itself, and I knew there had to be a meaning behind it. Tonight I realized what the meaning was.

Chained. I am chained. I am happily chained to these beautiful survivors for life—to tell their stories, to hold their hands, and to believe in them with every ounce of my being. They are becoming my greatest teachers.

SECTION FIVE

Life Is War

Fairy tales are more than true, not because they tell us that dragons exist, but because they tell us that dragons can be beaten.

—G. K. Chesterton

CHAPTER TWELVE

To Come Back to Life

The light shines in the darkness, and the darkness can never extinguish it.
—JOHN THE APOSTLE

Those next few days in Gulu, Uganda, were filled with questions, answers, and stories—much like my first trip there in 2008. We hopped on and off bodas and met with wise men and women who had not only experienced the bloodshed of Kony's LRA but also the forgiveness and reconciliation of the community.

We heard stories of LRA victims forgiving rebels who had maimed family members, and we sat with village elders as they described a tribal ritual of reconciliation. The value of cultural kinship was evident. One seasoned and elderly chief said to us, "Our Acholi tribe is one people. We must forgive. It is the only way to peace."

With each conversation and interview, I saw differences between this culture and the culture I knew in America. Resilience was richer.

Community was deeper, and forgiveness was offered more freely. Tucking away each detail in my heart, God continued to teach and change me.

Getting in the van and preparing for the long drive to the airport (in typical "my head is full of thoughts I must get out" mode), I scribbled words on paper along the way. Later they came out in my journal:

> *Child slaves now dancing in freedom. It is simply not of this world.*

I am full. Filled to overflowing.... The memories of sights, sounds, smells, and lives surround me as I ride through this green, beautiful bush—the place where so many died not long ago. Young and old. Bosco, our driver, is my new friend. He loves listening to the Grease sound track and laughs at me as I belt out every word. "I love this so much!" he says. "Have you seen the movie?" I ask. "The movie? No? There is a movie?!" "Yes!" I reply. "It's great." I smile and look out the window again.

As I watched the children at Village of Hope dance in the dirt this past week and beat their drums, I grew in my respect of their deep traditions. These traditions bring them together. They unify them. I also loved watching them find life when we told them God was with them in their deepest pain.

Child slaves now dancing in freedom. It is simply not of this world.

As we drive, I think about my other new friend, Justin, whom I met yesterday. He teaches farming to those who are unable to feed their families. Driven, articulate, and intelligent, he tells me about his dreams for his people. He is missing his right ear. I know how he lost it. I don't have to ask—nor would I. The LRA is known for chopping off body parts. But he lives on. He lives in hope. He lives in color—the color of grace.

"Even I am war-affected," he shares. "You know, they would come into my school and take you. They would chop the children into bits and force the others to kill their teachers. Even they would make you eat her flesh."

"I am so sorry, Justin," I whisper. I could feel my heart break.

I am humbled that he would trust me with his story of pain and amazed at how God has taken his pain and turned it into purpose.

Riding along, Bosco asks me if I am hungry. No. No— I am not hungry. I am sad. I am hopeful. I am full. Remembering young Robert as he stood before his friends and held up his "dream drawing," telling us that he hopes to be president of Uganda one day. A forced orphaned person because of LRA tactics, he is tall and bright. I believe in him.

I have fallen asleep, dreaming of many things. I open my eyes, and the sunset is enchanting. It captures my heart and I smile. I pray: "Your love is as faithful as the sunrise and as soothing as the

sunset. I will not fear. I will hope. I will believe.
Just as powerful as are these stories of evil are
the stories of forgiveness and resilience. What the
enemy intended for evil, You will turn into good. I
stand in that truth."

On the plane from Uganda, I started preparing mentally for our time in Congo. I would meet a new team—Jennifer and Adria, who were friends of Exile International—in Rwanda, and we would travel to Congo in a few short days. This would be my first trip back since Exile International was founded. I had left there in 2008 with a broken heart, but I was returning a year and a half later with a soulful anticipation of what could be.

We had arranged meetings with the UN peacekeeping sector (called MONUSCO, an acronym of its French name,[1] in the Democratic Republic of the Congo) and with the only transit center in the area. Transit centers take in children who have been rescued or who have escaped the rebel army. These transit centers provide much-needed initial crisis intervention for one to three months. But beyond this initial care, these recently rescued children need several months of rehabilitative care. Just as exciting, we were going to return to the boys' and girls' orphanages I visited on my first trip. This time, I brought plenty of art supplies, and we would have ample time to provide art therapy. I also brought them new shoes, donated by some of Exile's supporters. I was in awe of God's fingerprints of redemption as I realized He was bringing me back to the very children

I had sang and blown bubbles with just a little over a year ago. God had truly gone before us and paved the way.

After meeting the team in Rwanda, we started the drive to the Congolese border. Rwanda is often called "the land of a thousand hills," and it certainly lives up to its name—it was simply breathtaking. This was my first visit to that beautiful country, and the drive took us through a wonderland of lush, green beauty. As we rode up and down Rwanda's thousand hills, I reflected on the genocide that had happened there some twenty years earlier. I grieved for the one million lives lost in 1994—all while the world stood on the sidelines and ignored the atrocities.

The same beautiful Rwandan road on which we traveled would lead us over the Congolese border, directly into the heart of a war that had taken more lives since 1996 than all of World War II. More than five million people have died in eastern Congo as a result of ethnic rivalries and competition for the region's deposits of gold, diamonds, copper, and cobalt.[2] Two words came to my mind: *never again*.

This phrase has strong significance to the Rwandan people. It represents their dedication to never again allow the type of brutality that raged during the genocide to ravage their beautiful country. As I thought about the genocide, the war, and all

> *Awareness without action is an empty breath to a dying man.*

the lives lost, I thought, *Never again—the power behind these words are in the action. Awareness without action is an empty breath to a dying man. Our task is not simply to trumpet bold and fearless words. We must rise to action.*

Ask most people who cross the border into Congo from Rwanda, and they will tell you they hold their breath. Each time I cross, I feel a tinge of tension in the air, hoping all goes well and that we receive permission to enter. No pictures can be taken, at the risk of being arrested. Men with guns and solemn faces are as normal as the multiple volcanoes surrounding the town of Goma. If you are driving a car, you must park it on the Rwandan side of the border and then walk to the other side. You then hand over your passport at the visa window, step back, and pray that no one requests a bribe. I once had to pay a bribe because my bags were too large—bags carrying shirts and shoes for the orphaned children just a kilometer away. After some negotiation, explaining firmly that there was no such law against having large bags, and praying with one of the border officials who was ready to deliver her baby at any day, I was able to cross by paying only twenty dollars (down from a hundred). I even made friends with the border patrol and waved good-bye.

With a sigh of relief, our American team greeted our Congolese friends and brothers who had come to welcome us and take us to the guesthouse. It was getting late. We were told we could not be out after dark for reasons of safety, so we had just enough time to stop by the girls' orphanage to say hello. My heart was racing as we waited for the gate to open. The girls ran toward the car and welcomed us with screams of glee and giggles. After a short greeting and prayer, we were off to settle in at the guesthouse.

Diligently praying for our time with the sweet girls we would see tomorrow, I felt overwhelmingly honored to be a tool in God's hand and to speak love and life into their lives. I yearned to hear their stories and to learn their names. Jennifer, Adria, and I led the girls at the orphanage through the art therapy workshop. Through tears of sorrow and smiles of joy, these precious children were helped just by knowing they were not alone.

Later, we were privileged and humbled to share the Hope Initiative program with local teachers and leaders so they could provide long-term trauma care to children in their communities. Some of the people we trained were themselves former child soldiers. They had left the army and were now working with children who were recently rescued or found in the bush. During our time of explaining symptoms of trauma and how to help the children they served, a man raised his hand and stood up.

> *"He had seen five men being burned alive on a fire. What should I say to him when he begins to cry?"*

"How can we help these children when we, ourselves, have been traumatized? There was a boy who told me he had seen five men being burned alive on a fire. What should I say to him when he begins to cry? What is the answer?"

That question and *many* others helped me see that this land was immersed in pain and that its healing was going to be anything but quick and easy. It would be a long, hard, heart-breaking road. But it was going to be absolutely worth the journey.

One afternoon while serving the boys and girls at the orphanages we engaged in one of my favorite activities. At the end of our time of drawing, counseling, sharing, dancing, praying, and singing, we asked the girls and boys if they would allow us to wash their feet before we gave them new shoes.

The children were restless with anticipation. Some were very timid and quiet—not knowing exactly what to do with this act of love; others were excited to be receiving new shoes on their clean feet. We read the gospel account of when Jesus washed the disciples' feet to show them "the fullness of His love." We explained that this was a special day, a day of renewal, and we were also doing this to show them the fullness of our love and God's love for them.

The children giggled and laughed and loved having every inch of their feet washed! Too embarrassed of their dirty toes, some of the girls went to wash their own feet before they got in line for us to wash them. Not one of them had ever had anyone wash their feet before, and we were honored to be the first.

That night I wrote this prayer in my journal:

> Father God, It isn't often that I have no words. I am in my bed tonight, beneath my mosquito net. I sit here in darkness with no electricity—only my flashlight and my journal. Stomach growling, but not caring. I am in a daze of drowning in new knowledge and need—a need for your grace and peace in this place. Grace and peace for these boys and these girls, who are trapped in the bush. But I am more determined than ever to help them find this peace. They are worth it. I think of Emerson, my little

nephew. So tiny. Barely able to make sentences
that you can understand. What if Emerson were in
their place? What if Haley, Julia, or Emma had been
taken and used as a slave or wife for the rebel
commanders? Would I fight for them? So hard! Thank
you for leading us to these wonderful men and women
who believe in them as much as we do. Open the
doors of support for them and for sponsoring these
children. Show me the way, Lord.

I remember observing how tiny their feet were, and my mind went back to the last time I had a conversation with one of our Congolese teammates.

"These girls—will they ever marry?" I asked. "After they are older, if someone finds out they have been sexually violated by rebels at such young ages—will they still marry?"

"No. For these girls to marry here, they must never tell that they have been raped. They must not tell the community."

My heart sank at the thought, yet I immediately thanked God for leading us to Janelle. This compassionate, gifted Congolese counselor would soon begin restoring and empowering these young girls through weekly counseling groups through Exile. No longer would they have to keep their secrets hidden in their hearts. Little did I realize (or dream, for that matter) that over the next three years thousands more children would experience physical, emotional, and spiritual healing as a result of this first step.

I had been diligently praying for Jesus to cross my path with Africans who shared my heart's cry for emotional restoration of children of war. And so it was that on this trip I first met Jacob, David, and Janelle.

These great men and women had recently started to care for former child soldiers they found on the streets, young survivors of gender-based violence, and children who had been orphaned by war. In time, these three (and other local counselors) would become part of Exile International's team in Congo. We simply loved being together—sharing our heart for war-affected children, dreaming about programs that enable children to bring peace to their communities. The more we talked, the more our dreams and visions aligned. It was clear that God's hand had brought us together to provide holistic, rehabilitative care to hundreds of children in this area—raising up peace leaders in this nation.

We set aside the last full day in Congo to meet with the leaders of a center who worked with child soldiers when they were first rescued from the bush. Our team—along with my new Congolese kindred spirits Jacob and David—sat down in the office of the center's chief. Thankful for translators, I had a pen and paper ready. Perhaps they wondered why this little American lady cared so much. But I did care. Much more than they yet knew.

In my attempts to understand as much as possible, I saturated the air with as many questions as it could hold. I was hungry to know more about this country, these rebels, these children. Without wearying, the managers of the center outlined complex answers to difficult questions. But in my naïveté I was not prepared for the answers I would hear.

"How many rebel groups are in Congo?" I asked. Immediately they all started laughing.

"There are many. In North Kivu there are many. In South Kivu there are many," the chief answered, looking at his bookshelf in search of something.

He pulled a book from the shelf and turned to a page that listed the rebel groups. He started turning the pages. One. Two. Three. Four. Then he showed it to me.

The list: FDLR, PARECO, CNDP, LRA, Mai Mai (many different sects of them). Then I noticed the numbers to the left.

"These numbers—are they the phone numbers of the rebel leaders?" I asked.

"Yes. They are there."

I shook my head. I couldn't help but laugh.

They have the actual *phone numbers of rebel leaders?* I thought. Sometimes I had to shake my head when realizing my new life included casual conversations about "rebel militia" and sitting with grown men who had the mobile numbers of warlords. They laughed with me. Sometimes you just have to.

"Seriously . . . you have the mobile numbers of the rebel leaders?"

"Yes, but they change often," he said.

I would imagine they do, I thought.

So close and yet so far. But on occasion, the phone numbers— when they are current—help facilitate meetings to negotiate rescuing children.

The more questions I asked, the deeper my immersion became,

and the more I understood. Question. Answer. Question. Answer.

What did we find out? Much. Much that I knew. Much more that I didn't. We were told:

- Children too young to carry large guns are given pistols.

- Children forced to fight in battles are sometimes forcibly given drugs and told the drugs will make them bullet-proof.

- In battle, the smaller boys and girls are placed on the front line as human shields.

- Both girls and boys are kidnapped and used as forced soldiers. Along with being made to participate in gunfights and war, both sexes are used to cook and to fetch wood. Both are also used as spies and slaves.

- Between fifty and two hundred boys are rescued and brought to the transit center each month in the Goma area. I say "boys" because the girls are rarely rescued. They quickly become slaves or "wives" of the rebel soldiers and are hidden when the UN (MONUSCO) or the Red Cross tries to rescue them. They are taken at young ages (often below age ten) and rarely return.

- The girls who *are* rescued or somehow escape are often stigmatized as prostitutes, even by their own families. Many have been abused as sex slaves, and some come back with babies needing medical attention and nutrition.

- The children are sometimes branded with an "S" for "soldier" on their arms so that, if they do escape, the rebel militia can identify them again and force them to return.

- After they leave the transit center, many do not return home for fear of being abducted again or rejected by their families. Many become street children or return to the rebel groups because in the rebel army there is food and they have a gun. "With guns there is power," the chief clarifies.

- The war is fueled by many different factors. The primary ones are tribal conflicts, territorial disputes, grabs for power, and the fight for minerals.

"Where there are minerals, you will find the rebels; where there are rebels, you will find the minerals," the chief said.

In one day, we visited three facilities that provided crisis care to children rescued from an armed group, and all the answers pointed to the same conclusion: more must be done.

Girls are rarely rescued. They quickly become slaves or "wives" of the rebel soldiers and are hidden.

On our last visit, the program director pulled me aside, looked intently into my eyes, and said, "There is a great need for care of the spirit, and our children need you to help them. The rebels try to kill the minds of the children. They try to kill the spirit for the good of their mission. There is a great need to help them come back to life."

Reflections from My Journal...

Scars on My Heart

I washed the feet of a former child soldier today.
They were scarred and scraped and dirty and
beautiful. Beautiful because of the story they told.
Not a story of hopelessness. Not a story of pity.
They told a story of strength. They told a story of
newness.

"What is your name?"

His feet were the most wounded I had seen.

"Paul. My name is Paul," he said. A huge smile
spread across his face when he brightened up—and
a look of solemn intimidation spread across it when
he didn't.

When we wash the feet of the children, I always
try to look into their eyes and ask them their
names. They are more than just feet and faces.
They are spirits and eyes and hearts and souls.
They are children.

But they are also not children.

"Many of the child soldiers have never known how
to be a child because they were taught to be
an animal. I try to teach them how to play. They
need to know how to play," said one of the program
leaders.

One of the boys had said to him a few weeks

before, "You treat me like I am a child. I am not a child. I have cut off the head of a man. I have held his heart in my hands. I am not a child."

But they are children.

Returning to the present moment, I said quietly, "Paul. Of course your name is Paul." He smiled at me. I smiled with him. I continued washing his feet as I prayed for him to know healing and restoration, to know hope and a bright future, to know Jesus as his Savior, as his Redeemer.

I thought about another Paul, the Paul of the Bible—a man whose past consisted of persecuting others, but whose present became a testimony of God's turning evil into good.

Looking up at the Paul in front of me, I said, "I believe you can be a great leader for your people. You are a strong young man, and God can use you in great ways. Do you know that?"

Gazing deeply into his eyes because I wanted him to know that. To know that!

"Yes," he said, "I know."

I said another prayer, and he was off with his new shoes. Smiling.

From my time in Africa, my heart has been seared. Scarred, really. But I welcome every scar. Because of them, I will be a voice for these wounded hearts, as will Jen, Adria, Britt, Jake, and Amanda. We have all been changed.

My mind remembers these words of Khalil Gibran: "Out of suffering have emerged the strongest souls; the most massive characters are seared with scars."[3]

CHAPTER THIRTEEN

The Mercy Fast

A small body of determined spirits fired by an unquenchable
faith in their mission can alter the course of history.

—GANDHI

My spirit was weary. I felt I had been happily poured out for a little more than a month on this visit to Uganda and Congo. The nonstop schedule, the difficult truths I learned, and the feeling of urgency to do more to help the children produced a wonderful weariness, a weariness I welcomed.

On most of my plane rides back to America, I like to sit in quiet. I write in my journal; I process; I pray. On my way home from this trip I wrote:

My heart is sore. Sometimes I think I laugh so
loudly because I hurt so deeply. This work is not
for the faint of heart; it is for the strong in

spirit. God was kind to dim what my physical eyes saw and allow me to see through spiritual eyes. With every sunset in Africa, He showed me more of the spiritual wealth that surrounded me. For that, I am so thankful. For the opportunity to wash the feet of children who were once slaves, I am humbled. For all the information I have been given, I am responsible.

I am honored to have stepped into the children's story of healing. They are not what has been done to them. They are not what they were forced to do. They are beautiful, dreaming children in the hands of a redemptive God.

What is greater than their stories of pain? Their stories of survival, forgiveness, and strength. One thing I know: the power seen in the children's ability to forgive and to dream is stronger than the force of evil that stole their innocence.

I do not live in their pain. I cannot; I will not. I will live in their future. Their future of peace. Their hope of healing. I will tell their stories and then retell and tell them again, helping the world see what true resilience looks like. Bringing the nations a glimpse of true forgiveness. Showing the world a picture of true joy. Not from me—from them. From You, Lord.

Father, God of heaven and of all the earth. I come to you with a sore heart, and I am thankful. I desperately wish for Your heart, and yet I know that with Your heart comes hurting. And I am *hurting. But my hope is bigger than my hurt, and the warmth of sharing a part of Your love with them outweighs it all.*

Our first landing place outside Africa was Amsterdam. After I connected to the free wireless in the airport, emails started coming into my phone. One in particular caught my eye. It was from our advocacy partners Michael and Lisa at Resolve, an organization in Washington, DC, that works through research, advocacy campaigns, and lobbying efforts to end atrocities perpetrated by the LRA. The message was an update on the bill for which Exile's team had previously advocated under the leadership of Resolve, the Lord's Resistance Army Disarmament and Northern Uganda Recovery Act. This bill, as I mentioned earlier, called on the United States to work with multilateral partners to develop a viable path to disarming the LRA.

It's important to note that only 4 percent of bills submitted to the US Congress are ever passed into law.[1] Because of the groundbreaking work of Resolve's team, support from Invisible Children, and a group of dedicated, tenacious young people who refused to stop caring, this legislation was defying the odds.

The email read:

> After thousands of us rallied, spoke, wrote, and lobbied for peace this past year, legislation aimed at ending Joseph Kony's reign of terror stands on the precipice of passing Congress. But one senator is using procedural rules in the Senate to single-handedly block the bill's passage.

The email went on to explain that, during the very month I had been in Uganda and Congo, Kony's fighters had attacked a remote village in Congo and abducted more than three hundred people. If the hold that the senator placed on the bill was successful, the bill would die. Along with many others, I was going to do everything within my power not to let that happen.

Let me stop here and explain something: I don't like politics. Before I got involved in advocacy work, I voted only because I felt guilty if I didn't. My television was on to watch University of Kentucky basketball games, and I rarely watched the news. But during the previous few years, I had become actively involved in understanding the legislative system and connecting with political organizations that specialized in advocating for children in armed conflict for one reason: These children need others to stand for justice on their behalf. Someone needs to stand for the children who have been murdered and for the children who've been kidnapped and used as slaves in the bush. Someone must amplify the voices of the children who had been orphaned—children who bore emotional and physical scars created by evil. Because our work involved the rare opportunity to provide one-on-one emotional care to LRA child survivors, former child soldiers, and children orphaned by war, we had a responsibility to bring their stories to others.

I rarely become angry, but when I do, I am passionate, and it usually has to do with respect or justice. I remembered that my sinless Savior once turned over some tables when sellers at the temple dishonored His Father (Matthew 21:12–13). Sitting in the Amsterdam airport, with dirt from Africa still under my fingernails, I reviewed drawings from LRA child survivors. One heart-wrenching drawing detailed (in color) the image of LRA soldiers forcing a child to cut a baby from a woman who was pregnant. As I brushed over the art therapy drawing with my fingertips and blinked back tears, I decided I was ready to turn over a few tables.

I immediately emailed Lisa and Michael. "I have some ideas. When is the deadline for the vote? *How long do we have to change his mind?*"

Over the next five weeks, our determined and impassioned friends at Resolve led a campaign to unite thousands of people through phone calls, letters, and petitions.

> *One heart-wrenching drawing detailed (in color) the image of LRA soldiers forcing a child to cut a baby from a woman who was pregnant.*

Still seeing the faces of the children we had left only weeks before, our small team from Exile International came together to send emails to the office of the senator who was blocking the vote on the Lord's Resistance Army Disarmament and Northern Uganda Recovery Act. Attached to these emails were scans of the children's vivid drawings. We rallied our supporters to rise to the occasion and join with us in emailing the senator. I also did something that seemed a bit radical at the time.

Resolve and Invisible Children had invited people to camp outside this senator's office until he lifted the hold on the bill. Planning to speak at a press conference regarding the hold, I was prepared to spend one night. But I had appointments with clients in Nashville, and I could not be gone for more than a few days. Wanting to support our friends who were sacrificing so much by sleeping outside in thirty-degree weather, and knowing something radical must be done, I prayed. I prayed for God's guidance and mercy.

> *"The rebels came and abducted my parents. They cut my brother and killed him in pieces."*

His mercy, I thought. *That's it!* My mind went back to Dennis. The first boy who started to weep when telling the story of his handkerchief drawing in Uganda. I remembered his words:

The rebels came and abducted my parents. They cut my brother and killed him in pieces. My brothers and sisters ran into the bush. We had nothing to cover ourselves, and we had nothing to eat. We continued to run, and the rebels continued to come. We fasted for God to have mercy on us. As we were fasting, we managed to escape. When we came back, we continued to fast for God's deliverance. I thank God we were saved. I thank God for that.

In the bush, naked, after losing their parents and their brother to the atrocities of the LRA, they fasted. They fasted from food they did not have, asking God for mercy.

Children such as Dennis could not come to Washington, DC, and tell their stories, but we could. Only the senator could release the hold on the bill, but we could fast for mercy and ask others to join us. We could fast for Gloria, Solomon, Grace, Nelson, Scovia, Fida, Dennis, and the more than thirty-five thousand children who had been abducted or killed by the LRA.[2] If Dennis, hungry for food with no means to obtain it, could intentionally fast at age eleven, we could fast from our abundance in his honor. Praying for softened hearts and for justice, we called our fast "The Mercy Fast."

Announcing a public fast felt strange, but we knew that making it known was the only way to invite others to pray and fast with us. One by one, others joined. Even my dear friend Katie Davis, who lives in Uganda, caring for her thirteen children, started praying and fasting with the team. I'm sure the senator was surprised to receive her call from Uganda, but this was personal for her, and she was dedicated. One of her adopted daughters had been orphaned as a result of the LRA's brutality, so she knew the emotional wounds firsthand. For her and her daughter, this was more than a bill. This was a real chance to stop a real horror that was part of her real life.

We were honored to stand in solidarity with so many others who were standing up for justice. It was beautiful to see all these hearts coming together for something bigger than themselves, amplifying the voices of hundreds of thousands of LRA-affected communities and villages.

Honored to speak at a press conference connected to the "hold-out," I asked those listening not to see me as I spoke, but to look behind me and imagine the tens of thousands of children who had lost their lives or who had been abducted by the LRA.

I explained, "Ending crimes against humanity calls us to stand as a collective group, walking as one in the same direction. It calls us to see a man living across the ocean as our brother. It calls us to see a child living as a slave in the bush of Africa as our son or daughter. It calls us to see humanity as *us* rather than *them*. What would we do if this were happening in America in our towns? To our neighbors? To what measure would we go to protect our own children?"

After I returned home, I received numerous messages and emails about the Mercy Fast from others around the country, committing to join the fast on behalf of the children. I called the senator's office and left this message: "This is Dr. Bethany Haley. I just returned from Africa after working with children who have been abducted by the LRA." Calling a specific child by name, I would tell one of the children's stories. I would go on to explain that many of us were still fasting from solid foods until the hold on the bill was lifted, and that we were praying for the senator. Then I called again the next day and did the same thing.

Exile made T-shirts reflecting the slogan of the brave young people who founded the White Rose Society, a nonviolent resistance group against the Nazis during the Holocaust: "We will not be silent." Their mission included creating leaflets that quoted scripture, sermons, and renowned intellects and leaving them in telephone booths, books, or mailing them to academics throughout much of Germany and Austria. In their protest against the atrocities that were happening to the Jewish population, five words echoed throughout their message. These five words—*We will not be silent*—were repeated until many of the protesters were beheaded in 1943. Exile took that slogan and placed it on the front of black T-shirts in simple white lettering. We wore these shirts as a commitment to amplify the voices of the vulnerable and to answer the call of Proverbs 31:8 to "speak up for those who cannot speak for themselves."

After nine days of fasting, ten thousand petition signatures, hundreds of phone calls, and nine days of dozens of dedicated "concrete sleepers" bundled up outside the senator's office, the hold on the bill was lifted.

Resolve continued its efforts, and less than a week later, the Lord's Resistance Army Disarmament and Northern Uganda Recovery Act passed the US Senate with more bipartisan cosponsors than any Africa-focused legislation in at least three decades.

Because of that experience, I am forever convinced that together we can do more. I know and believe that the word "impossible" is just a word made up of ten letters. I know now that those ten letters are no match for the force of the Almighty.

Reflections from My Journal...

The Power of Believing

I stand in awe. Speechless. I stand tall. Not because of my own strength, but because I have had the privilege of standing next to strong souls, strong hearts, stubborn spirits. On this day, the Senate passed a bill that could begin to end the heart of the madness of Kony's LRA.

I simply feel in awe of God tonight, and I'm in wonderment of the good found in the human spirit. In a strange way, I am less and less surprised when I see God's hand in this work—not because He is less amazing, but because I've learned to actually expect His hand around every corner. The more I believe, the more I see His fingerprints. His gracious love for these children is a testimony to the beauty that can be found in suffering.

A year ago I didn't know a constituent from a barbiturate. Now I find myself practically begging people to call their senators, speaking at press conferences, writing letters to politicians I don't know, and lobbying for children I do know. I know these children and I love them in my innermost heart. I cry for them because I have cried with them, and I will never stop fighting for them until my dying breath.

Why? Why have I gone from avoiding political conversations to sleeping on a sidewalk outside a senator's office with some of the finest people around? Why have I gone from thinking that my voice makes little difference in this great big web of Washington to refusing solid foods for nine days to change the mind of one senator?

I am alive, and I believe that through passionate living we can bring life to others. I believe when we choose to hope, our hope becomes contagious. When I flew in to speak at the press conference, my visit was less than twenty-four hours, and yet I saw the life that God can bring to others through us when we choose to act. I could feel it—the power of believing.

This power was seen in grown men who joined the young, peaceful protesters because they started to believe in the cause. It was seen in the quiet strength of a deli worker who bought food out of his own pocket for those "concrete sleepers" because he saw democracy in their eyes. It was seen in the bond that wove more than fifty people together in community.

The passion of living for something bigger than yourself is undeniably larger than life. Finding your voice. Finding your purpose. That's what makes a person come to life.

And I wonder... what makes us lose our passion

for life? Do we lose it when the rat race begins?
When the scars and disappointments of life leave us
facedown in the dirt?

When do we stop dreaming and believing? I am in
my thirties. Single. No children. Living alone. And I
ask myself, "If I had a family, a husband, children—
would I still have passion? Would I still breathe in
life as I do now?"

I believe I could. I believe we can have both.

I am thankful for all of the concrete sleepers,
mercy fasters, silent soldiers, long-suffering,
showerless wonders. Together we can do more. This
week was a beautiful testimony of tenacity and
resilience. And democracy.

The power of believing.

I wish those children across the world could have
seen us fighting for them. I think they would have
been proud.

SECTION SIX

Beautiful Scars

Never be ashamed of a scar.
It simply means you were stronger
than whatever tried to hurt you.

—Author unknown

CHAPTER FOURTEEN

Dancing in Their Darkest Hour

In the midst of winter,
I found there was within me an invincible summer.

—ALBERT CAMUS

It seemed God was calling me into the most broken, most dangerous places on Earth to serve His most vulnerable children. Yet somehow, I felt at home in these environments. Strangely, they felt comfortable. But "comfortable" is not fertile ground for growth. So God put another opportunity in front of me: a chance to travel into a different heart of sorrow.

On January 12, 2010, as the team and I were serving children in Africa, a 7.0 magnitude earthquake hit the country of Haiti. Soon after I returned home, Exile International started receiving phone calls asking us to provide emotional care to children traumatized by this natural disaster.

Having traveled on a mission trip to Haiti in 2005, I loved the country and I hurt deeply for her people. On that first trip to Haiti, I drove through the countryside, passed multiple witch doctors' quarters, and gave care packages to children living in poverty-stricken villages. Now, on television, I was watching orphaned children walk aimlessly through the streets, surrounded by rubble.

These are not child soldiers, I thought. *These are not war-affected children.* But they were hurting children, and we were being asked to help.

The day I returned from Africa, the newspaper headline spoke of the devastation from Haiti's earthquake. The front-page photo showed Haitian survivors dancing, singing, and praying in the debris-filled streets. Amazing. The article spoke of a people who refused to give up even though they were surrounded by great devastation, in a country with one of the highest levels of poverty in the world. The image captivated me, and I could not get it out of my mind.

As I reached down to pick up that newspaper to look at the photo again, I received another call asking if we could help. They asked us to provide counseling to children in the tent camps, train faith-based leaders in providing trauma care, and lead the art therapy workshop at an orphanage that had doubled in size since the earthquake. I said yes. We would accompany a medical team, and in addition to working with the orphanage and in tent camps, we would provide trauma-care training to assist ministers in the Port-au-Prince area in caring for survivors.

Driving from the airport to the guesthouse, we watched as crews continued to dig out bodies from the rubble. Our driver told stories of children sleeping outside the house where their parents had died. They refused to go in for fear that an aftershock would collapse their home completely, but they also refused to go elsewhere because they wanted to be as close to their parents' bodies as possible.

The day after we landed, our team started the trauma-care training. Standing in front of two hundred strong Haitian survivors, I remember telling them how amazed

> *The children refused to go elsewhere because they wanted to be as close to their parents' bodies as possible.*

I was when reading about them dancing in the middle of their darkest hour, singing in the streets surrounded by rubble. Holding up the newspaper that had touched me so deeply, I shared with them how much their strength inspired me and let them know that the rest of the world was watching hope come to life through them. The look on their faces was priceless as they realized that people outside of Haiti actually knew what was happening in their world.

"Our streets were turned into churches," our host Dr. Jeudy explained.

This wise, joyful man was also a great surgeon, minister, and Haitian theologian. He told stories of the people coming together in the streets as brothers and sisters on the night of the earthquake. Singing to a God they still trusted. Crying out to a Creator to put their broken world—and their broken streets—back together. Dancing together as a people of pure strength. He told stories of how the people of Haiti had turned to God during deep crisis instead of shaking their fists at Him in blame.

"This sidewalk was lined with corpses. Women. Men. Children. Lined up for days. One on top of another," he said.

How do you find wisdom in suffering and rejoicing in the face of despair? How do you look into the dust created from ashes and see a reflection of beauty? I had seen this same kind of hope rising from pain while in Africa. And I had come to understand that this wisdom and rejoicing was much more alive in countries that had experienced great pain and sorrow than in countries of great wealth. They had a spiritual richness I did not see in my land of plenty. Perhaps having no gadgets and i-distractions to numb their pain compelled them to face their sorrows head-on. And perhaps by truly sitting with their brokenness, they recognized a universal truth, regardless of hardship or income: we are small and God is great and we are not in control. And in some strange way, grasping our smallness and learning to embrace hardship (whatever that may be) with a surrendered spirit that refuses to let go of hope can deeply change us.

Dr. Jeudy continued, "Women were dancing in the streets singing 'Haiti is alive!' after the earthquake killed more than two hundred thousand of our people. There were orphans marching in white, singing songs of hope after losing everything—parents, homes, limbs."

It was as though God had taken His chisel and carved a pathway in the deepest places of pain, then gently taken my hand and led me into them—into the hearts of His most broken people, His most wounded children. And through it, I was taught where true beauty could be found.

The character of C. S. Lewis in the movie *Shadowlands* says, "We think our childish toys bring us all the happiness there is and our nursery is the whole wide world—but something must draw us out of the nursery into the world of others. That something is suffering."

Suffering. Despair. Heartache. I believe these are the very places Jesus lives in His fullest form. Holding us. Loving us. Mending us. In broken desperateness—the place where we think we cannot breathe or stand anymore, the place we never dreamed we would be and would never wish on our greatest enemy—that place is where we can find the heart of God.

It was also in Haiti that I first felt afraid in a foreign land. That may sound strange after the time I had spent in Congo (one of the most dangerous places in the world), surrounded by UN planes and handheld missile launchers. But I had not felt afraid there.

One day in Port-au-Prince, however, I was afraid for my life. After the team left, I stayed an extra day by myself. I loved the dear people of Haiti; I gained strength from them; and I wanted one day with no agenda so God's Spirit could lead me as He wished. Sylvestre, our new Haitian friend, was our trustworthy guide and translator during this trip. His personality was vibrant and compassionate, and he loved the Lord with passion. He was not a believer in God until the earthquake came. He explained, "I could not understand all the things of God, so I did not believe. Then I saw how He saved so many of our people, and how we cried out to Him in our time of sorrow. He brought comfort, and I saw Him bring the dying person life again. When I was escaping as the house was falling down around me, I prayed for Him to save me, and He allowed me to live. He is a great God!"

On that last day, Sylvestre and I started walking into remote locations in Port-au-Prince to see how we could be of help. Knowing so many people were in desperate need, I prayed for God to lead us to those He wanted us to serve. So, literally, we just started walking. Before long we found a camp of survivors who had taken the sheets and mattresses out of their fallen homes and were sleeping on them in an open field. There were about 120 people living in this place, mostly women and small children. These resilient people had tied one bedsheet to four long sticks, forming a canopy to protect them from the sun. They called their camp a "sheet camp." Sylvestre and I went from family to family, praying for them and asking how we could help. Some were very sick—and they were excited to hear that they could receive free health care at the nearby clinic where we had been working. They were just as thrilled to know that someone cared, that they were not forgotten.

Looking around, I remembered a friend in America who had a connection with an organization that provided tents to the homeless in Haiti. After making some phone calls and getting the best directions possible to this remote location, the organization told us these wonderful people would receive tents a few weeks later. I was thrilled! Everyone in the field began cheering and thanking God for their new tent homes, which would soon arrive. They were overflowing with thankfulness, and I was humbled to see God's hand at work.

Excited about this answered prayer, Sylvestre and I said good-bye to our new friends and left to return to the clinic. As we walked away, I heard someone yelling in a disturbed tone. This shouting, in French, seemed to be getting closer, so I looked over my shoulder to see what was happening. As I turned, I saw a man running toward me at full speed—with a machete in his hand.

The only thought that went through my head was, *I think he's going to kill me.* And before I even realized what I was doing, I stuck out my hand to greet him, smiled the biggest smile I could muster up, and said, *"Je m'appelle* Bethany!" (French for "My name is Bethany!")

I guess I thought if he saw me as friendly, maybe he wouldn't kill me. In small-town Kentucky, we were raised to be friendly. That gesture

> **As I turned, I saw a man running toward me at full speed—with a machete in his hand.**

might have been what saved my life. The expression on his face changed in seconds. As if he knew me, he immediately put down his machete and smiled! He even stuck out his now empty hand to shake mine!

After a quick translated conversation, I found out that my new friend was upset because he thought we were giving out free food to the sheet camp, and he had not received any food for his family. We explained that tents would soon be coming for them. He was thankful, and we waved to each other as we departed.

Flying back home, I welcomed that time of silent prayer and contemplation. I realized God was pulling my heart into different places. He was giving me opportunities to live out the Gospel in ways that stretched me. But I welcomed this, and I prayed for more. With each glimpse behind the veil of physical pain and poverty, I saw more and more spiritual beauty and strength. I was learning the greatest lessons from those for whom I once felt pity. With each step into the stories of the world's broken, I realized that I was there to be taught even more than I was there to serve.

Reflections from My Journal...

One Day. One Crayon. One Earthquake.

Survival. Suffering. Strength.

There are certain wisdoms and understandings that can only be learned in suffering. There are songs that can only be heard in the pits of despair. There are lights that will never seem so radiant as when we are covered in darkness. I only know this because I have seen it.

I saw it this past week in the eyes of an orphaned child.

I was sitting on the rocky ground at an orphanage, surrounded by a group of about twenty children, all orphaned as a result of Haiti's earthquake. They were sharing their memories of the earthquake with me.

"The ground came alive and started swallowing my home," one remembered.

"I fell to the ground when the world started shaking, and I prayed for it to stop," said another.

"When my father died, I died, too. The earthquake killed my father. I am now alone. God is my father now," one boy told me. His words didn't break my heart as much as the smile covering his face as he said it—a smile he used to hide his pain.

The strength of these children humbled me. The Haitian people are survivors.

On another occasion, a beautiful, elderly Haitian woman, whose weathered skin could tell centuries of stories, shared with me, "We have survived poverty. We have survived typhoons. And now we have survived the earthquake. This will make us stronger."

Yes, this will make them stronger. I believe that. I saw it in the eyes of that recently orphaned boy. His smile was as alive as his pain, and today God used him to teach me this: There is a richness in the core of pain that can only be found in the pit. There is a sweetness in the first food eaten after being starved for days that can never be tasted again. The breath taken just seconds before suffocation is the most precious air that could ever cross a person's lips. A dying man understands the treasure of life when given a second chance at living—a treasure that those who have never looked death in the eye can't grasp.

This is the gift of suffering. We can be broken but not desperate. And we can be desperate but not broken. When we allow ourselves to be desperate for God out of our brokenness, we find true surrender in Him.

In my own time of surrender, I learned that when you have nothing else to hold on to but God, all of a sudden, God is all you need. You treasure Him. Like breath. Either that, or you blame Him. But healing cannot be found in blame, and I chose life.

One day I asked this question of a man at a

trauma-care training session: "Do you not blame God for what has happened? For your loved ones who died in the earthquake?"

He shook his head, as though he almost pitied me for asking such a question. I think I even saw him smirk at me.

"I have never heard of this. He is God. He is good. He can do what He wants, when He wants, how He wants. He is God, and He gives life."

The heart of Jesus is found in the middle of suffering. This is the core of the cross. In the midst of the thorns and tears of sorrow, we find a deeper communion with the heart of Christ.

I saw this today: We were standing in front of at least a hundred children; they were sitting on dry, rocky ground in a tent camp under a scorching sun with a heat index of 115 degrees. The children were dirty and hungry, and we were surrounded by what seemed to be a thousand people—just watching. I felt small and inadequate.

We had given the children paper on which to draw their heartaches and stories of the earthquake. As we began to hand out crayons one by one, a mob of little Haitian hands quickly reached out to us. Poking us. Prodding us. The children grew louder and came closer, pushing, shoving, and beginning to yell. For what?

For one crayon.

I handed them out as quickly as I could, and the

children grabbed them even quicker. All I could feel were little fingers all around me.

"Blanc! Blanc!" ("White person! White person!") they cried.

Sweet fingers poked at every inch of me. Mothers shoved their children closer and closer to me. My heart raced faster. The sun beat harder. No space to even move.

Poke. Prod. Shove.

One prod, one poke was more intense than the others. Poke. Prod. Poke. Irritating, actually. Fed up, I looked down.

It wasn't a hand asking to receive a crayon at all. It was a hand begging me to take what was in it. A picture, a picture of her heartache. As I looked into her eyes, the hundreds of children faded away for that one moment, and I took her gift. Her smiled beamed of life.

Her drawing? It was her mother lying down. She had died after the earthquake, and, above her mother, there seemed to be a spirit or an angel in the room. This little girl wanted desperately to show me. She wanted to tell her story. And soon there were more.

Giving out crayons quickly gave way to grasping drawings as fast as we could. They wanted to give us the drawings of their heartaches as much as or more than they wanted a crayon. One crayon. One heartache. One day. One earthquake.

In that tent camp, I was surrounded by hundreds of broken Haitian hearts that still reached out in hope. Many of us would have stopped reaching. But not the people I've met here.

"Many have come to God from the earthquake," said one of our translators. "Out of their suffering they have found wisdom. They have found hope."

All of this brings me to a question: can we say we welcome suffering if at the end of the journey of pain we look more like the heart of a Savior on a cross?

I can't say yes. Not yet. God is showing me a new world of spiritual wealth and is sitting with me as I ponder it. I'm realizing in my country of physical wealth, we are actually living in spiritual poverty. We are surrounded by "things" that keep us from being desperate for God. But it's in the cry of the desperate that glorious spiritual riches can be found.

Father, I pray You are patient with me in my wrestling, and I ask that You give me Your eyes with which to see this world. If we walk by faith and not by sight, Lord, then may we be blind and led only by Your hand. In full surrender I am Yours.

CHAPTER FIFTEEN

Peace Lives

*Start by doing what's necessary, then what's possible;
and suddenly you are doing the impossible.*

—St. Francis of Assisi

"Is it dangerous where you are going next week?"

I lay beside my niece in her bed, having just finished a peaceful bedtime story. Her eyes were big and bold as she asked me. She loves adventure.

What do I say? I wondered.

The answer is yes. Usually when people ask me if where I am going is dangerous, I say, "Dangerous is relative, and we are always careful."

But I looked at my niece and remembered the two aid workers killed not long ago in Congo. Rumors of increased violence were flying, and we had already canceled the trip once.

"Not *so* very much!" I said, and tickled her.

After I put my nieces to bed, the night became quiet and I wrote:

> Sometimes I feel like a girl with a dream. Sometimes I feel like a woman with a burden. Much of the time I feel as though all that surrounds me and is inside me is too much to carry, and I crave to be normal. But I know that is not what I was created for. A normal life isn't always possible. But that doesn't mean life can't be beautiful. More than beautiful.
>
> I am surrounded by beauty. I see in these children the power of the redemptive love of Jesus. I see hope for the future of this world. This hope for the future is much more than being rescued from the bush or learning to believe in themselves again. It is even more than changing the course of a generation by empowering them to pursue peace, healing, and leadership at young ages. This hope is for us, too.
>
> There is much we can learn from them. If a little girl who was raped by soldiers at age five can be a leader in her community—and if a boy of ten who was forced to kill in unspeakable ways can later return to his village to teach his community about forgiveness—then there is hope. There is hope that each of us who has been wounded can be transformed into something beautiful. We can do more together, and when we walk in the "we" rather than the "them"— the world is changed.

It was January 2011, and Exile International was growing. The previous year had brought a whirlwind of wonder: a second trip to Haiti to work with more children. Exile International partnered with Mercy Ships to take art therapy to children in West Africa. After the hold on the LRA bill had been lifted, the bill continued to move forward and (best of all) Exile International's child-sponsorship program was started. If these war-affected children were going to change their generation, they needed more than counseling; they also needed education, food, medical attention, and physical care. When you bring education to girls and boys, you empower them to move beyond their circumstances and into an opportunity to redefine their futures.

> *These children needed more than counseling; they also needed education, food, medical attention, and physical care.*

On my last birthday, my only wish was for some of the children we'd been working with to be sponsored. We set up a simple sponsorship page on our website explaining that sponsorship would help provide education (pay for school fees), food, and medical care for the children and that 100 percent of the funds would be sent for care overseas. By the end of the day, five children had sponsors! It may sound small, but it was one of the best birthday presents I have ever received. Over the years, five turned into twenty, and twenty turned into more than a hundred. I continually pray for more.

Still feeling my way through running a nonprofit organization and learning as I went along, I did a lot wrong, and (thankfully) God did a lot right. Funding was limited, but somehow He always provided. Some days we looked at our bank account and weren't sure how we would make it through the next month. Then, on that same day, we would receive a donation for the *exact* amount we needed!

The night before I left on our 2011 trip to visit our programs in Congo, my wonderful parents came to my home to help me pack. That had become their tradition. Dad helped pack the art therapy supplies and T-shirts for the children, and Mom helped pack protein bars and bug spray. In previous years, my family questioned my decisions and wondered if I had gone a little crazy. I was putting so much time, money, and energy into something they didn't quite understand. They had seen me walk through struggles, and they wanted a peaceful life for me.

Going into war-torn countries wasn't exactly the "peace" they had in mind. They knew there was financial security in the professional life of a successful psychologist, but they saw little security in the life I was beginning to lead. Even though I continued my counseling practice part-time, I had chosen to greatly decrease my annual income. Slowly I saw God shifting the hearts of those within my family. My sister and her family hosted a house party to raise money for Exile; my brother and his family sponsored a child; and my sweet nieces and nephew gave me toys from their own rooms to take to our children in Africa. We had all come full circle. Grace was coloring us all.

My parents now say, "We knew we either had to stand behind her or get out of her way!" So they, along with my entire family—cousins, uncle, aunts, siblings—decided to stand with us. I was and am very thankful for their love and encouragement.

On this trip, when I crossed the border into Congo, I noticed more UN trucks and soldiers than I had previously seen. Truckloads of blue helmets were everywhere, and government soldiers were around every corner. The tension in the air was as thick as the volcanic, dusty streets. Along with more men carrying ammunition and artillery than I had ever witnessed, I was also greeted by those who had become some of my dearest friends, including David, Jacob, and Janelle. Despite our differences in culture, skin, and accents, we shared the same deep passion to see children find healing from their wounds of war. They were like family to me.

"Welcome home," Janelle said when I first saw her.

Her smile lit up the room. Janelle is short but assured, and her laugh is even louder than mine. Ask anyone who knows me, and they'll tell you this is quite impressive!

On this trip, I met former child soldiers whom I now consider my sons and daughters.

"Three of the demobilized boys are sleeping in one small bed," David explained. They were living in a small wooden shack, with cardboard covering the holes in the wooden slabs on the walls. I looked at the bed; it was smaller than the twin bed I slept in at home—and it wasn't even a bed. It was a bamboo mat on top of a slab of wood on four legs. David and Jacob had taken in more boy soldiers who had recently been rescued, and they were trying to provide for them as best as possible.

"How can they fit on one bed?" I asked in amazement.

"You know, they love each other! They are brothers! They do not care if they are crowded. They are used to sleeping in the forest," David said as he laughed.

Having recently returned from the bush, these children were unable to return to their homes—some because they had been orphaned by the war and others because the rebel militias were near their homes and it would be unsafe to return for fear of being kidnapped again, which was not uncommon. They had no caregivers except David and Jacob—mighty men with servants' hearts trying to provide security for these children, many of whom were found living on the street.

"We first welcomed them into the church," they explained. "They begin learning about the love of God. Then they begin singing the hope songs in the choir. We tell them Jesus loves them and you can see life return to them."

They both spoke with great passion and bright smiles. Anyone could tell they loved these boys and girls as their own.

> *"Because they have been in war, they love peace even more. They dream of being peacemakers in their country."*

One of my most special memories came when David, Jacob, and I sat together beside Lake Kivu, dreaming of a restoration center for former child soldiers—a place where art, dance, song, and drama would be used as catalysts for healing. A place where the love of God would be poured out and peace shared. We sat for hours praying, planning, laughing, and sharing like-minded visions.

"Some of these youth," David said, "have been kidnapped three different times by three different militia groups. Because they have been in war, they love peace even more. They dream of being peacemakers in their country."

"What do you think we should call the center?" Jacob asked me.

"It is not my center," I said. "It will be the center for the boys and the girls. I think we should ask them!"

The name they chose spoke to a truth that rose high above the war surrounding them: the Peace Lives Center. If anyone would have told me three years earlier that I would be leading a nonprofit organization for former child soldiers that would run a rehabilitation center for war-affected children, I would have told them they had clearly confused me with someone else. This was never in my wildest dreams and certainly much too large to think possible. But when God said with Him all things are possible, I think He was serious. Especially about the "all" part.

I not only experienced abundant joy on that visit to Congo; I also experienced fear.

Following church one Sunday, a group of boys gathered around me to kindly introduce themselves.

"These are the new former child soldiers," David whispered to me.

They captured my full attention as they told me their names.

"My name is Shadrach."

"My name is Blessed."

Suddenly, there was a great commotion. Chaos and loud yelling ensured. Outside the church, a man had reached into the car we were using that week and stolen my phone from the seat. Several of the boys immediately took off to find him, and a restless crowd gathered around us.

"They are chasing the thief!" I heard.

Within a forever-long three minutes, they found the man and

dragged him back around into view. Wanting to prove their loyalty and show me they were going to punish him for his dishonest actions, they started beating him on the ground. All I could see was them kicking and hitting and stomping his head into a rock, then more kicking and hitting.

"Stop! Make them stop! It's enough! You have to stop!" I yelled.

At about that time, a man came around the corner with a handsaw. I froze. He looked at me. I immediately looked away as though I didn't see him. Apparently he had come to saw off the thief's hand, which is not uncommon in some cultures. It certainly gave a literal meaning to "If your right hand causes you to sin, cut if off" (Matthew 5:30, NKJV).

"Let him go. Just let him go," I pleaded, as calmly as I could.

Finally they released the man, and everyone was silent as they watched for my reaction. The man slowly pulled himself to his feet and looked in my direction. Raising his shirt to reveal his thin body, he tapped his stomach. Bleeding. Wounded. Scraped and tattered from the beating. In that moment, he told me, in his own way, "I am hungry." Before I could respond, someone pushed me into the car for safety, and we drove away, with the crowd of onlookers chasing after us.

At the end of the day, I lay in the quiet before bed. I thought of the man. Praying for him, grieving that I could do nothing more at the time than stare in shock. Realizing that I might have done the same thing in similar circumstances, I asked myself, "If my family or my baby were dying of hunger, would I steal?" I didn't know, but I was more thankful than ever that I had never known starvation. The thought challenged me.

When we understand the stories behind someone's actions, we often stop judging them and start relating to them, realizing that we are all capable of the same sin given the right situation. I knew that all too well in my own personal story. The one who judged became the judged and rejected. Given the right, vulnerable situation, we are all capable of almost anything.

> *When we understand the stories behind someone's actions, we realize that we are all capable of the same sin given the right situation.*

Later that day, I saw the boys who'd witnessed the thief that morning after church. I asked them what they had learned from the morning's event. Many of them were angry about this man's crime and, understandably, wanted justice. We took time, however, to process how our anger or hurt can turn into understanding—even forgiveness—when we take the time to understand another human's story.

"What about when you were with the rebels? Did you ever have to fight or hurt anyone to get food?" I inquired.

Many of the boys nodded their heads. We were able to connect our humanity to those whom we want punished for their sins. We are all, ultimately, one step away from the sins we judge in others.

Before we ended the night, we all joined hands and prayed for the man. We prayed he would find food and that, if he did not already, that he would know Jesus. "Peace lives only if we choose mercy, kindness, and forgiveness," I told them. In a strange way, this initially tumultuous day turned out to be a day of peace. A beautiful day of *pamoja*.

Reflections from My Journal...

Beautiful Scars

"I am going to tell you the most important part of your handkerchief drawing now," I said to the children. "The most important part is drawing God in the middle of your heartache. Perhaps drawing Him beside you when you were crying your sad tears. Even when we don't feel Him, He is there, because He promises us He will never leave us or forsake us."

I looked into their eyes, and I wondered what they had seen. I watched the markers in their hands, and I knew if their hands could tell stories, they would be of bloodshed.

If their scars could speak, they would scream.

But the children don't scream at all. They stand. Boldly. As if to say, "I am here, and I am strong."

I see these young men now, and I can't fathom what they have been through. But I must do more than fathom it. I must hear their truth.

Before my eyes, I see them dance and rejoice. Before my eyes, I see life and redemption. They beat their drums, play their ragged guitars, clap their hands, and praise the God who gave them new life.

The last time I was with these boys, they allowed me to wash their feet as a sign of renewal—

washing away an old life of pain and a former
identity and embracing a new life of grace. Today
I watched these thirty former child soldiers—once
forced to kill and to steal—wash the feet of thirty
more recently rescued child soldiers. Sitting to
the side as I dried their damp feet, we shared
a celebration of redemption. In the past, some
of them may have fought each other. Considered
each other as enemies. Some came from different
tribes and rebel groups. But now all of them were
demonstrating love and the unity of newfound
brothers.

I watched them as they prayed for their fellow
survivors, and this ceremony of peace was serene.
And they didn't even know each other.

But they did not need to know each other. They
were already brothers. The bond of life that now
connected them is stronger than the killing that
was once their common story. The peace that
surrounded them that day was greater than the
war they had lived through.

I watched as they gave their brothers their
first Bibles, and I was taken aback at the rejoicing.
I could feel their prayers for each other. Hearing
their songs of reconciliation, I could sense their
newfound love of God.

If the world could taste and see this, what could
we learn?

My mind goes back to our time with the girls who

had survived sexual violence during the war. I told them, "When God looks at you, He does not see what has been done to you. He does not see your scars. He sees the newness and beauty He has given you. Clean and pure. He sees you as beautiful. He has great plans for you."

I watched one girl as I said these words aloud. She is thirteen. She had been abducted when she was about eleven. She became pregnant after militia soldiers raped her, and months later she escaped with her baby.

For two days, she walked trying to find her home, but never found it. She was picked up and taken to the orphanage, where she still lives with her baby—her only family now. Our eyes connect and she smiles at me, a million-dollar beaming smile. She looks down at her baby, and the love on her face is the love of Jesus. A mother of only thirteen years bestowing love on her baby girl.

My heart breaks. Silently.

My spirit swells. Loudly.

Because I am witnessing a miracle. I am witnessing pure love.

I often stand before these children—these young men and young women—feeling like a tiny child who needs to be taught rather than a woman who is there to teach; like one who needs to be mended rather than one who is here to mend.

I remember what Gerald May writes in The

Dark Night of the Soul: "Suffering arises from the simple circumstance of life itself. Sometimes human suffering is dramatic and horrifying. More often it is ordinary, humble, and quiet."[1]

Throughout this journey into the dark places of the world, I have realized that by not saving us from pain, Jesus may be extending a great kindness. It is by not rescuing us that He may be saying: "I honor you. I want you to grow and live in fullness more than I want you to be comfortable. I want more for you because I love you too much to let you live in weakness or mere comforts. I believe in you too much to give up on you."

Whether the pain is the loss of a loved one or the loss of innocence, it is all a reminder of how imperfect our world is and how perfect His love is as He whispers these sweet sentiments to us: "I do not see you for what you have done. I do not see you for what has been done to you. I see the newness and beauty I have given you. I see you as My beautiful one."

If it's possible to gain strength from our scars—and I believe it is—then these children will hold the world on their shoulders. And I will be at their feet. They will change their nations. They can change this world. It is up to us to see them. Hear them. Learn from them. Believe in them.

Bless them, Lord. Put within their hearts a stirring for peace, a peace that passes the understanding of the world they live in. I passionately desire for them to show the world that you can turn mourning into dancing. Let the world see them dance. More important, let the world learn how to dance from them. Fervently. In freedom and joy.

CHAPTER SIXTEEN

It's Worth It All

He is no fool who gives up what he cannot keep
to gain what he cannot lose.

—JIM ELLIOT

"**I**s it worth it?" the nurse asked as she anesthetized my skin with the needle and started to take tiny pieces out of my body for the biopsies.

"What's worth it?" I asked.

"All of this. You are here because you spend time in Africa, where you were exposed to this serious disease. You have seen many doctors trying to find out what is wrong with you, fearful that you may go blind. This . . ." she said as she completed a stitch.

The biopsies would be sent to one of the few men in America whom the Centers for Disease Control and Prevention have authorized to test for onchocerciasis, also called river blindness.

I had returned from Congo a year earlier with a number of intense symptoms: severe itching on my arms and legs causing open wounds and scarring, extreme fatigue, and loss of appetite, to name a few. I had a seemingly undiagnosable illness. After initial assessments, a doctor said it was scabies. The next doctor decided it must be an allergic reaction to a bug bite. I kept getting rediagnosed until finally, nine doctors later, I heard the words "We are pretty sure you have something called river blindness."

"I do?" I exclaimed. *No, I don't*, I thought. *That sounds crazy. I'm fine.*

But I wasn't exactly fine. On that last visit to Congo, a black fly bit me. Seeing blind people in Goma is not all that uncommon. Many blind men or women move about guided by children holding ropes tied around their waists, leading them from place to place. I had never stopped to question how these individuals became blind. Until now.

The doctor's voice interrupted my thoughts. "Fortunately, you can get the medication you need here. You will take the pills three times a year for five years. But if you plan to return to Africa regularly, you need to take the medication for fifteen years—just in case you are bitten again."

"And what if I didn't have access to the medication?" I asked.

"Then you could go blind," she responded. I thought about the hundreds of thousands of people around the globe who do not have access to this medication. It is the second-leading infectious cause of blindness in the world, and on occasion almost entire villages have gone blind. The realization hit me hard: without this medication or health care, I could lose my sight.

Back to the nurse's question: "Is it worth it?"

I sat on the table as she completed the tedious procedure of removing eight tissue samples for biopsies from different parts of my body. Memories of the past three years rushed through my mind. I remembered when the girls at the orphanage were given their very first Bibles by Exile International. Having never owned a Bible before, they shouted and sang praises to God for almost an hour! The next time I saw them, they couldn't wait to share the scripture they had memorized about forgiveness and kindness. Simply through the words of Jesus, they found deeper freedom from their shame. I recalled the hundreds of leaders and ministers who had been trained in trauma-care programs, which they would use to bring healing to thousands.

My memories drifted back to the moment when Joyce lifted her face to whisper in my ear, "Last night, for the first time in many months, I slept without nightmares of the rebels coming to take me."

Her smile was priceless.

Then there was the drive up into the mountains of Congo. Two flat tires and four hours later, we reached a small village that had once been home to seven children from the Peace Lives Center. They were returning to encourage other newly rescued boy soldiers. There, at the very place of their painful and guilt-filled memories, they performed dramas about peace, reconciliation, and forgiveness for the villagers. Some had spent years fighting within the ranks of various rebel armies. Now they were soldiers for peace. They ended their time by washing the feet of other recently rescued boy soldiers and praying for them. Grace had come full circle yet again.

Tumaini stood next to me as we waited for one of the tires to be changed. "Mum," he said in his soft voice, "do you remember when you first met us? Do you remember how tired we were and how you encouraged us? You helped us find peace in our hearts. Now we will tell our brothers about peace, so they can find their way to God."

As the nurse continued to poke and prod, I also remembered an afternoon in Uganda. Young Rebecca was one of the brave children who returned to the site of her deepest pain. We helped her find her way to the remnants of the place she once called home. I felt her strength in my spirit as we looked at the charred ruins of her family's hut, now remembered as the place where the rebels had forced her—as an innocent seven-year-old—to participate in killing her mother. She shared her story with pain and courage.

> "Bring me twenty breasts. Bring back fourteen ears. Bring back ten penises." If she failed to deliver them on time, she and the other children would be tortured.

Rebecca had been taken by the LRA and spent two years in captivity. During that time she was forced to remove and collect the body parts of victims. The rebel commanders often assigned quotas of body parts to the children, and Rebecca was no exception: "Bring me twenty breasts.

Bring back fourteen ears. Bring back ten penises." If she failed to deliver them on time, she and the other children would be tortured. Her guilt was deep and her tears were cleansing.

"Rebecca," I said, "since we are here, at this place where your guilt began, I wonder if you think you could say a prayer to God, inviting Him to help you in your healing."

The sky was growing dark. I was there with Kari, a wonderful counselor from the United States, then serving as an Exile teammate in Uganda. We stood beside Rebecca as she looked up at the stars.

"Let us pray," she said hesitantly. "I thank you, my God, for giving me such a beautiful mother. I ask for forgiveness for what I was forced to do to her. I ask that You give me a new life."

When Rebecca first entered the sponsorship program and joined the Peace Clubs, she could barely speak without crying. Now she is healing. She is dreaming. Recently, when drawing her hopes on her handkerchief, she drew herself as a psychiatric doctor. She said she wants to help others who have gone through emotional pain.

When asked what, if anything, she would want to communicate to Kony and her other captors, she said, "I would tell them to come back home so we can forgive them."

Walking together back home that night, I asked her, "Rebecca, how are you able to forgive Joseph Kony and the other rebels after all the pain they have caused?"

"Because the Bible says to forgive. God tells us to, so we must forgive our enemies," she replied, with no hesitation and the sincerity of a child.

I recall another hot Uganda day when we shared a small classroom with more than forty LRA child survivors. "There is another group of children we work with at Exile International who have also been rescued from or have escaped rebel militia," we told them. "They live in Congo. They are much like you, and they love Jesus so much! The war is still happening there, and I wonder if you would like to give them encouragement during this hard time."

Their faces started to shine, their eyes widened, and they blurted out their questions: "Are they also in school? Are they going through the Peace Clubs program and learning about trauma healing? Do they also love to sing and dance like we do?"

"Yes" to all.

Matthew, one of Exile's team members, read 2 Corinthians 1:4 aloud: "He comforts us in all our troubles so that we can comfort others. When they are troubled, we will be able to give them the same comfort God has given us." And we asked if they would like to write letters of encouragement to their fellow brothers and sisters. The words of their letters brought a new kind of reality to their stories, and young hearts started to unite across borders.

Dear child of war in Congo,

We are children orphaned by the LRA in Uganda. Be encouraged. Jesus is with you even in your time of suffering. Do not be afraid because He will give you life. He will rescue you just as He has rescued us.

Drifting on in my memories while I sat contemplating the nurse's question, I felt my heart swell when I thought of Brenda. She watched the brutal murder of her parents at the hands of the LRA. Because her infant sister was crying, the rebels picked up her tiny body and threw her against a tree to silence her. Forever. Fifteen-year-old Brenda is now the eldest member of her family and caregiver for her two surviving sisters. All three are now in Exile's sponsorship program, attending school, and receiving emotional healing for their pain.

When asked about Joseph Kony, she responded, "I have forgiven him and the rebels. If I refuse to forgive, it will not bring my family back. So I must forgive to have peace in my own heart."

Gabriel's songs always fill my heart when I see him at the Peace

> *Because Brenda's infant sister was crying, the rebels picked up her tiny body and threw her against a tree to silence her. Forever.*

Lives Center. He has been orphaned and often feels alone in his pain. Gabriel spent several years witnessing and being forced to participate in horrendous acts of violence in the rebel group. When he was baptized, he surrendered his life completely to Jesus.

Gabriel shared, "Now I have given up my gun for a guitar."

He turned to music and songwriting as a critical part of his healing. Watching him teach the lyrics of his songs to his peers and direct the choir of the orphaned children awes me.

"We lay down our guns, for it is not the way. Join us in peace—Christ is the way," he sings. When he closes his eyes and raises his head toward the heavens, anyone listening can see and feel his desperate love for God. He praises Him as the One who has given him new life. I am so proud of him.

Bahati's gentle spirit also comes to mind.

"Momma Bethany, do you remember my name?" he asked.

"Of course, Bahati. Of course I remember your name," I said, holding his hand and smiling back at him. He loves reading his favorite scripture passages to me and talking about how Jesus has changed his life. Since we gave the boys their first Bibles, they have fed off its words. Even writing scripture by hand above their beds at night.

Bahati read aloud, "Blessed are the peacemakers, for they shall be called sons of God." My heart burst with pride for him. He has grown into a servant and a leader. "This one is my favorite," he whispered. I smiled and tried to hide my teary eyes.

I think of Solomon. During Solomon's abduction, his father and grandparents were murdered by the LRA. His younger siblings were left, and the rebels instructed his mother to "raise them well. One day we will return to take them, too."

He was trained in the bush to be a medic and was removing bullets from LRA members and child soldiers at the young age of ten. He was personally with Joseph Kony on occasion. Today this well-kept, handsome young man proudly shows off his notebooks full of songs, some expressing hurtful memories from his time in the bush. But vastly outnumbering his lamentations are his songs of redemption and hope for the future. He dreams of being a peace leader for his country and is learning each week in the Peace Clubs about conflict resolution, forgiveness, and emotional strength.

"I am a child of the sun. I am a child of the sun. I am no more a child soldier. My Bible is now my gun," he sings.

Finally, I recall Samuel, a former boy soldier with the LRA. With a scar on his forehead where a bullet was removed and a limp in his walk from the time he was shot in the knee during battle, he looks at me and says, "Forgiveness is the only way to peace. We must forgive. We will never find the peace without it."

Is it worth it? I thought as I weighed the changes in my life and contemplated the sacrifices.

"Absolutely," I answered her, smiling. "Yes, it's worth it all."

If God can use a broken, selfish woman such as me to be part of these beautiful stories of healing and redemption, He can use anyone.

Reflections from My Journal...

"My Name Is Bill. I Have No Legs. I Am Just Fine."

Sitting in the quiet. Nieces are in bed. Warm coffee by my side. Music wafts through the air, putting them to sleep. I treasure time with them. I often wonder what normal life would look like for me had my path been different. "Normal" life could easily have led me into marriage again. Quickly. Years ago.

Children. House. Dogs. Homework. Late nights with sick children, rocking them. The feel of a baby snuggled up next to me. I crave that sometimes. I'm not convinced it's not in my future. And I'm not convinced it is. That's the tricky part about surrender. It's not up to me. What "normal" woman wouldn't want all of that?

Some people envy my life. But would they envy it if they lived it? Would they make the sacrifices it would take for them to have it?

Sometimes I envy their lives. Sometimes I don't. Somehow I believe there is room for both: the life of the mission field and the life of the family. Is that normal? No. Not even remotely. But it doesn't mean it's not possible. It just means it's harder.

There is a homeless man in Nashville who has no legs. He is about sixty years old. The night before I went to Haiti last year, it was raining hard. Driving

to the bank for a last-minute ATM cash run for
travel needs, I saw him. Barely able to see out of
my window, I caught a glimpse of him. He was at the
corner of an old abandoned building, under an awning.
Soaking wet. I was drawn to him. Turning around,
I drove up next to him and rolled down my window,
asking, "Are you okay? Do you need anything?"

"No, honey!" Big, sweet grin. "I am just fine. Just
trying to stay out of the rain a little bit." He was
there in his wheelchair. Pant legs as ghosts below
his knees.

"Are you sure? Maybe I can take you somewhere
or call someone who can take you somewhere dry and
safe."

"No, honey! I am just fine." I left knowing that
maybe he was fine. But I wasn't.

I returned from the Democratic Republic of
the Congo last week. The trip was more than
two saturated weeks of hearing stories of child
abductions and the injustice of child rape. I was
overwhelmed at the need we found there and
bursting at the seams to put things in place.
Wonderful weariness, I call it. But it is wearying
nonetheless. I had been very sick after returning
from Africa. Jet lag sprinkled with an intense skin
allergic reaction to an "African something" left me
pretty much in a bed of misery for a week.

On my first day back, behind at work, I dropped
by Redbox at McDonald's on my way home to rent a

movie as I caught up on things at home. It had been
a long day, and I was tired.

I looked to my right. He was there. Same man.
Same wheelchair. Same smile. Taking my movie, I
walked over. It was cold.

"Do you need anything? Can I help you with
anything?"

"No, honey! I am fine! Might use a cup of coffee.
It's forty-nine cents inside. It may warm me up."

"That's all you need? No food? You aren't hungry?"

"No, honey! I am fine! Just a cup of coffee
might be good to warm me up. It's forty-nine cents
inside."

I got him the largest cup of black coffee they
had and took it to him. Hands miserably chapped, he
put his beer can down to grab the coffee. Face
chapped and red. Disheveled. Joyful. Truly.

"Thank you, ma'am!"

I smiled at him in adoration.

"What is your name?" I asked.

"Bill, my name is Bill. What's yours?"

"It's Beth... or Bethany. Either is fine."

"Oh, that 'Bethany' may be hard for me. But I can
call you Beth."

"I would love that." I gave him a "God bless you"
and went back to my Jeep, taking a few minutes to
soak in what just happened.

I had just returned from one of the most
dangerous places on Earth; I had gone to bring life

to hundreds of children of war. But when I came home, I saw Bill. Where? Right in front of me. Where was he the night before I flew to Haiti? Right in front of me.

I looked down at my hands as I sat in the Jeep and I noticed that, strangely, they were...

Right in front of me.

I understood the Good Samaritan that night as never before. One message from that story screams out to me: the wounded one was right in front of the passersby.

They did not have to search for their purpose or calling or passion in life. They just had to start with what was right there. Staring them in the face.

But only one person picked him up, bandaged his wounds, and led him to safety. The Good Samaritan didn't have to fly across oceans or battle customs or fear gunshots in the middle of the night. He just had to begin—right where he was. He just had to help the man right in front of him. One person at a time.

The reason we don't? For me, it's either because I am looking past them to get where I am going or because I doubt that I can make a real difference.

Until we have been to Vietnam and our legs are amputated in the war, the addiction to painkillers comes upon us like a thief in the night, and alcohol becomes our only friend because few people want to take care of a crippled man—until we find ourselves outside McDonald's asking for a simple cup of coffee to keep us warm—until then, we can't really understand.

If we cannot completely and perfectly fix the broken pieces, should we just let the chips fall where they may? And if we do, where will they fall?

I believe the answer is not even remotely found in making all things fit together perfectly. Perhaps it isn't our job to make it all better, and it may not be possible. I _do_ believe the answer is found in looking at the one right in front of us. The lonely lady in the elevator who is a single mom. The refugee who needs someone to teach her English. The wife whose day would be made new if her husband handed her a single flower. The child who longs for one second of your attention and the words he so needs to hear: "You are important to me." Does it fix everything? Not a chance. But perhaps fixing isn't what we are called to do.

Maybe serving doesn't have to look like making everything better. Maybe it's more about the mending. And perhaps it is in the momentary mending that Jesus' love is heard the loudest and seen in the most radiant of colors.

"My name is Bill. I don't know if I will remember yours or not, ma'am."

"You don't have to," I said, smiling. The cup of coffee he allowed me to give him was much more of a treasure to me than it was to him. It's not easy going back and forth to Africa as a single woman, I thought. Cravings for family and a ministry partner and some sense of normalcy run deep. Even though it's not easy, it is one thing above any other.

It's worth it all.

SECTION SEVEN

Out of Exile

God's revolution is big enough
to set both the oppressed and the oppressor free.

—Desmond Tutu

CHAPTER SEVENTEEN

The Voices of Survival

The world is a dangerous place, not because of those who do
evil, but because of those who look on and do nothing.
—ALBERT EINSTEIN

The famed and beloved Mother Teresa has taught the world—and me—much about love. In a way, she has been a mentor to me. In this one heartbreaking picture, I see my mission:

Some people talk about hunger, but they don't come and say, "Mother, here are five rupees. Buy food for these people." But they can give a most beautiful lecture on hunger.

I had the most extraordinary experience once in Bombay. There was a big conference about hunger. I was supposed to go to that meeting and I lost the way. Suddenly I came to that place, and right in front of the door to where hundreds of people were talking about food and hunger, I found a dying man. I took him out and I took him home.

He died there. He died of hunger.

And the people inside were talking about how in fifteen years we will have so much food, so much this, so much that, and that man died. See the difference? I never look at the masses as my responsibility. I look at the individual. I can love only one person at a time. I can feed only one person at a time. Just One. One. One.

You get closer to Christ by coming closer to each other. As Jesus said, "Whatever you do to the least of my brethren, you do to me." So you begin . . . and I begin.[1]

This story cut deep into my heart, as Mother Teresa's words resonated in my soul. I thought about the man who died of hunger on the doorstep of the great conference room. I thought about those inside who saw the man and walked past him. I thought about Mother Teresa. *What made her different from the others? What caused her to stop?*

Perhaps she saw humanity in this man. She valued him and knew he had a voice, a story.

A desire of my heart has always been that the actual child survivors' voices be heard as the priceless individuals they are. My heart's desire is that their stories be given a voice and brought to life through their letters, their drawings of war, their songs of peace, and their dramas of being captured and set free. These children are not voiceless. They are not helpless or hopeless. But they need us to honor their stories of survival and give dignity to the hope that lives inside them.

In 2010, I began inviting the children in Uganda to write personal letters to the president of the United States. I explained that this was their opportunity to share their feelings about their time in captivity, what it felt like to be orphaned by the LRA and to be a child survivor of war. I believed that if he, and other change agents in the world, heard their words, knew their names, and understood their stories of torture and potential, more would be done. When we asked the children if they would like to write letters to the president, the response was huge!

> *These children are not voiceless. They are not helpless or hopeless. But they need us to honor their stories of survival and give dignity to the hope that lives inside them.*

In the words of Matthew Williams, our director of operations and the trauma counselor who collected additional letters the following year, "A core experience of trauma is the feeling of powerlessness. But when these children wrote letters sharing their story, they cheered. They raised their voices. They were empowered."

When Matthew returned to the United States from Uganda, he carried with him two hundred letters from LRA child survivors.

Sometimes it is best to step out of the way, and let those who have a voice and have survived war tell their own stories in their own words. So we did. Following are excerpts from the actual letters written by some of these children. Because the writing may be difficult to read, we've retyped the excerpts, but I wanted the children's own handwriting to be represented. Seeing their personal handwriting touches my heart.

I got a bullet shot at my cheak near my eye and indeed it damaged my eye (left eye). Now I'm using only one eye (left eye). Now I'm using only one eye. When my friend tried to escaped, they were killed before us or cut using a panga before us or even they picked some of us to killed him/her to discourage us from escaping. Since we were young we fear it so much hence not escaping.

Some times we walk for 2 days and nights without food, or rest.

I got a bullet shot at my cheak near my eye and indeed it damaged my eye (left eye). Now I'm using only one eye. When my friend tried to escaped, they were killed before us or cut using a panga before us or even they picked some of us to killed him/her to discourage us from escaping. Since we were young we fear it so much hence not escaping.

Some times we walk for 2 days and nights without food, or rest.

When I was abducted, I was made to walked very long distances even in rain. Not only that, we were made to carried heavy loads and this has caused cheast pain to me upto now. I was also made to kill innocent civilions by the used of rock, I too was forced to kill my fellow friends whom were caught escaping. I was also given a gun to fight against the government of Uganda. We were made to ambush people on the way and kill them.

So this war affected my life a lot by delayed me in education. Not only that but also affected me mentally, when I came back home, I was not that very kind to my friends from home but the only thing that helped me was prayer.

When I was abducted, I was made to walked very long distances even in rain. Not only that, we were made to carried heavy loads and this has caused cheast pain to me upto now. I was also made to kill innocent civilions by the used of rock. I too was forced to kill my fellow friends whom were caught escaping. I was also given a gun to fight against the government of Uganda. We were made to ambush people on the way and kill them.

So this war affected my life a lot by delayed me in education. Not only that but also affected me mentally. When I came back home, I was not that very kind to my friends from home but the only thing that helped me was prayer.

I was abducted in 2002 when I was 9 year old and stayed for two and half year in captivity. What hurt me most from the bush is forcing us to fight, carry heavy loads, killing peoples and heavy punishment. They said that to make us become real soliders and we had to know how to use a gun and sometime they would force you to kill your real parents, guardians or relative which is not good and setting people's property on fire including human being and their animals. The L.R.A Leaders forced young girls to stay with them as their wive.e.

I was abducted in 2002 when I was 9 years old and stayed for two and half years in captivity. What hurt me most from the bush is forcing us to fight, carry heavy loads, killing peoples and heavy punishment. They said that to make us become real soliders and we had to know how to use a gun and sometime they would force you to kill your real parents, guardians or relative which is not good and setting people's property on fire including human being and their animals. The LRA Leaders forced young girls to stay with them as their wives.

I was abducted in 2002 when I was 9 years old and I come back in 2004 and this is how I was treated when in captivity. I was made to carry heavy loads, they rebels beat me with a panger and the worst of it was when they made me carry the head of my brother they had cut off and my brothers blood was all over my clothes, This still disturbs me upto now.

We as children of northern Uganda don't want this war to continue, we don't want the children of D.R - congo and central Africa Republic to suffer like us in northern Uganda.

I Thank you for the great work towards peace in Uganda,

I was abducted in 2002 when I was 9 years old and I come back in 2004 and this is how I was treated when in captivity. I was made to carry heavy loads, they rebels beat me with a panger and the worst of it was when they made me carry the head of my brother they had cut off and my brothers blood was all over my clothes. This still disturbs me upto now.

We as children of northern Uganda don't want this war to continue, we don't want the children of D.R. Congo and Central Africa Republic to suffer like us in northern Uganda.

I thank you for the great work towards peace in Uganda.

Collecting these letters was just one step; the next step was praying for the opportunity to deliver the children's words to the White House and to have additional opportunities to amplify their voices. It was a big prayer, but we have a big God, and He is trustworthy. Part of God's answer led me down totally unexpected pathways. In the summer of 2010 I was introduced to Bryan Single, filmmaker of *Children of War*, and Jane Ekayu, a Ugandan counselor who founded the organization Children of Peace Uganda. Jane and I had a shared passion for seeing children of war returned from captivity and given opportunities for education and emotional healing. We have shared many moments on our knees, in prayer together for that dream, and today we are partnering to bring holistic care to many children in Uganda. Bryan and Jane quickly became dear friends and teammates in the fight to increase international awareness of child soldiering.

As a result of that introduction, they extended an invitation for me to join them on a panel advocating for child soldiers worldwide at the International Criminal Court in The Hague, Netherlands. The symposium, titled Understanding Child Soldiers and the Need for Education, was held in August 2011, in conjunction with the trial of Thomas Lubanga, a former rebel leader in Congo charged with conscripting, enlisting, and using child soldiers. Leaders from around the world who worked in research and rehabilitative care of children in armed conflict were also invited to attend. (Note: Thomas Lubanga was found guilty on March 14, 2012. He faced a maximum sentence of thirty years. On July 10, 2012, he was sentenced to a total period of fourteen years of imprisonment.)

Also attending the 2011 symposium were Ishmael Beah and Emmanuel Jal—both former child soldiers, now leading international peace efforts. They were living the very dream we had for our children, the dream they also had for themselves: to lead their countries in choosing peace over war by using their painful pasts as catalysts for forgiveness and reconciliation. As honored as I was to have this opportunity to be part of the symposium, I was equally excited to sit down with and learn from these two young men.

As I boarded the airplane to The Hague, framed drawings from two children named Shalom and Rebecca were carefully tucked into my suitcase—both articulating their stories of survival in striking color, both boldly declaring their hopes and dreams for the future. I was not going alone; I was traveling to The Hague with many children in my heart and many of their stories in my spirit.

Sitting in the courtroom, my stomach turned as I watched Thomas Lubanga during the trial. I knew what he had done and what he was capable of. This large, broad-shouldered man sat emotionless as he listened to the stories of children he was responsible for capturing and forcing to kill. A few times I thought he caught my eye as I stared at him. *What is he thinking?* I pondered. *Is he feeling remorse? Is he feeling anything?* I imagined Joseph Kony (who is number one on the most-wanted list of the International Criminal Court for crimes against humanity) and the other warlords responsible for the torture of many of our children sitting in that same courtroom. I prayed for their capture. I prayed for justice.

During the three-day trial and the symposium, I had the opportunity to ask Ishmael and Emmanuel two questions: "What helped you most when you were in the rehabilitation center? How best can we help the former child soldiers we work with?"

But there was one question I wanted to ask them above all others, the most important one: "What has made the greatest difference between who you were as a child soldier and who you are today?"

> *I will never forget Ishmael's answer: "My adopted mother saw within me my humanity. She did not see what I had done; she saw what I could become."*

I will never forget Ishmael's answer: "I had someone to believe in me. My adopted mother saw within me my humanity. She did not see what I had done; she saw what I could become."

Emmanuel answered similarly. He told me about Emma, a British aid worker, who helped him escape to Kenya. "She changed my life. Because of her, I am alive," he said.

Pondering those words, I was convinced once again that believing in people—especially our children—brings power and hope into their lives. They need someone to look at them and see more than what they had been forced to do—more than what had been done to them. They needed someone to see them in the reflection of their Creator's eyes, living out a beautiful plan of redemption. And they needed someone to remind them of their potential.

Reflections from My Journal...

Do You See Them?

Below is a portion of the speech I wrote and delivered at the ICC symposium Understanding Child Soldiers and the Need for Education, in The Hague on August 24, 2011.

You are ten years old. You are asleep on the floor of your hut and the sounds of bullets wake you. You open your eyes and a rebel commander is shining a light in your face. He grabs you and beats you as two other soldiers take your mother and father and tie them up in front of you. You have difficulty seeing because there is blood in your eyes and the light from the burning huts is blinding you.

You are terrified.

Terrified because of the stories you have heard of the LRA. Terrified because of what you think may happen next. The rebel commander is screaming something at you, but you can't hear him over the screams of the women around you, the screams of women being raped and children crying. The rebel commander puts a machete in your hand. He is screaming at you that you must now kill your parents. That you must "chop them." You shake your head and begin to cry. And you are beaten more and more until you can barely move. They begin shooting bullets over your head, and you shake with fear. Now you can hear nothing. Your younger brother is watching you, and he begins to cry harder.

The rebel commander pushes you closer, kicking you. He forces the machete in your hands and begins to cut your parents with it. He tells you that if you do not finish this, then he will kill your brother in the same way. You are beaten again and again.

He is screaming at you: "Chop or you will all die. Chop or you will all die."

You see nothing because of the blood and tears in your eyes, but you close them anyway as you move the machete up and down. Up and down. You feel blood splatter your face, and it mixes with your tears. You keep your eyes closed, and you hear the screaming.

The screaming of the rebel commander. The screaming of your mother. The screaming of your baby brother. The screaming in your head.

You vomit because of the smells around you and the thought of what you have just done. You wipe the tears and blood off your face and open your eyes for the first time.

You are ten years old. You are a boy.

You are in a daze and the only thing you can think is, I am an orphan now. I am an orphan now.

You look down and you have blood on your hands.

You are ten years old. You are a boy. You have blood on your hands.

I, ladies and gentlemen, have blood on my hands.

We, ladies and gentlemen, have blood on our hands.

This international community has blood on its hands and a grave responsibility to save and rehabilitate these children.

In order to change the course of war, we must stop the bleeding of violence and start mending the wounds of trauma. With a problem so massive, we must start with children and teach them a different way—to teach them about peace, to believe in them, to see them as the future peacemakers of their countries. Our dream for them is not only that they survive war, but that they grow into leaders of peace in their communities.

That is redemption. That is rehabilitation—rehabilitation that is needed and restoration that is deserved.

I would like to ask you to take a moment

and picture this room filled with well over three hundred thousand children of war whose spirits, bodies, and minds have been ripped apart because of a type of torture that, even as a psychologist, I cannot begin to understand. I have not been in war. I have not been forced to tear my brother apart with my teeth. I am not a six-year-old girl who has been raped so severely that she bears the scars of the surgery that put her body back together.

Do not see me. I ask you to see them.

Some of them died in the bush. Some young girls were killed after guns were placed inside their vaginas—and fired. Some of the boys were killed as other children were forced to kill them for attempting to escape. Some of them are still alive. Some of them are in the bush right now. As we sit here in our black-and-white dresses and our suits, and as the world goes on, and as the sun sets, and as the moon shines tonight. They are there. They are here.

Do you, ladies and gentlemen, see them? Can you hear them? We stood back and watched the genocide unfold in Rwanda. Day after day after a hundred days. And when it was over, the world shook its head in pity

and false penitence and said, "Never again."
And here we are searching for Joseph Kony,
twenty-five years and more than thirty
thousand precious children later.

I would like to commend the prosecutor
and the International Criminal Court for your
diligence and passionate commitment to this
issue. I look forward to seeing what comes
from this day.

Ladies and gentlemen, the reality is this:
Each day that little is done becomes a day
another mother is forced to decide whether
she will kill her seven-year-old son or if he
will kill her. It is another day that a young
girl's brother is forced to slice off pieces
of her face until she bleeds to death. I
could fill the room with stories, but if nothing
is done, there will be just as many or more
stories this time next year.

Each day of doing nothing is another day of
the world utterly and undeniably failing these
children. These children who could easily be
our own.

After I first returned from Congo and
Uganda three years ago, I remember being
unable to sleep one night. And I sat up in
bed thinking, They don't know. There is no
way the world knows. They can't. I refuse

to believe that the rest of the world knows of the horrific tragedies committed against these children and is doing so little.

I have since discovered two things: Most people in the world do not know. And the ones who do know become the individuals with opportunities to be change agents—elevating their voices and pursuing justice for the oppressed. So we come to the question: What will we do?

Will I wash the blood from my hands because it is messy or because it may leave a stain on my very soul so that I can sleep better tonight—or will I see them? Will I hear them? Will I honor them as though they were our very own? Because they are. They are not someone else's children. They are my children. They are your children.

I ask you to see them, because they deserve to be seen.

I wear around my wrist a chain given to me by a teenage boy who was forced by the LRA to chop his parents into pieces and eat their flesh when he was about ten years old. I wear around my neck the scarf we used to wash and dry the feet of 150 young girls in Goma, Congo—girls whose bodies bear the scars of rape and sexual violence. I wear around my heart a burden that I place before the feet of the world. And I boldly ask, as I look into the eyes of the world: What will we do with it? With this burden?

Will we go to sleep tonight after we place it under our beds, believing this problem is too messy and believing we can't make a difference?

Or will we say, "Enough. It is enough now"?

Frank Warren said, "It is the children the world almost breaks who grow up to save it."[2]

You have heard brave and courageous testimonies today from our brothers and sisters who are survivors of war.

As we end, I would ask that we be silent for a few seconds. I ask that you picture these children filling up this room, laying down their weapons, and whispering, "Enough. It is enough now. We are tired."

If they are to experience such torture, can we not be brave enough to do whatever is in our power to stop it and to use whatever influence we have to give them the opportunity to live again?

CHAPTER EIGHTEEN

Storming the Heavens

*When a train goes through a tunnel and it gets dark, you don't throw
away the ticket and jump off. You sit still and trust the engineer.*

—CORRIE TEN BOOM

There are some days that words cannot describe. There are some
miracles that stories cannot capture. November 19, 2012, was one of
those unbelievable days—and, a few days later, we would see one of
those powerful miracles.

The rebel group M23 had, for some time, been threatening to
take over the city of Goma, where the Peace Lives Center and eighty
young peacemakers (fifty-two former child soldiers and twenty-eight
children orphaned by war) resided. But few people thought they
could actually do it. For nearly eight months there had been ad-
vances, threats, retreats, and declarations by M23, a group known to

be raping women, killing, and recruiting child soldiers, but the fighting remained outside the city of Goma.

Many children we worked with in the villages outside Goma had been forced to flee in the fighting. Most were found; some were not. More than five hundred thousand people had been displaced since the previous April and lived in exile from their homes and communities. During the preceding weeks, we had been in close contact with our Congolese teammates, receiving updates, praying with them, and praying for them. Fear was ever-present and very real. I felt as though my children were in the pathway of a life-destroying storm—a storm I had no power to stop.

But stronger than the fear in our hearts was the faith of our children and Exile's teammates in Congo.

Trying to prepare for the worst and create a possible evacuation plan, I asked David by phone, "What do you *think* will happen? Do you think the rebels will come, or do you think Goma will be spared?"

He responded, without hesitation and with complete trust, "We do not know. We have prayed to God, and now we will have to wait to see what He decides." Often, when I called David in the evening, he did not answer the phone because he was with his family in prayer—for hours. Prayer can be your sustenance, especially when you are fearing for your life and the safety of your family. It is a priceless, utter dependence on God that we, in the West, rarely taste.

Matthew and I were in Washington, DC. Coincidentally, we were meeting with members of Congress to advocate for some of the very children we were holding up in prayer. It was on this trip that we hoped to deliver the children's letters to the White House. The previous day, I had sent an email to a connection at the White House. We prayed that God would make a way for the two hundred letters to be delivered to the president and for a meeting to be approved. As we ended our day in DC, the dawn brought bullets and bombs to our family in Congo.

I woke the next morning to the following text from David: "War is around Goma. Camps are destroyed. Our soldiers are running. We are at home with nowhere to go. Send texts for any info. Will tell you when to call."

My heart stopped. My breath left me. Even as I write these words and recall this story, my heart races and tears fall. I got on my knees, offered a tearful, pleading prayer to God, then

> *I woke the next morning to the following text: "War is around Goma. Camps are destroyed. Our soldiers are running. We are at home with nowhere to go."*

immediately responded with texts of questions. "Are the children safe? Should we try to move them? Would it be helpful to call the United Nations to see if they can send someone?" Praying. Waiting. Checking news sources.

I sent emails to friends at the United Nations base in Congo asking for protection and contacted other friends in Goma to better understand the situation. Then more texts, more prayers, more waiting.

Our flight back to Nashville was the following morning, so this was our only day in Washington to deliver the letters. If the White House emailed or contacted us, we needed to be ready to go. This was our chance. The original plan was to purchase a beautiful gift box in which to place the letters and drawings. In the event that we received a green light, I wanted to present the letters as though they were a treasure—a gift to the president—because they were.

At about noon, Matthew and I taxied to a store to purchase what we needed. He was checking out, and I was walking outside to make another phone call when I received another text from our teammates in Congo: "Bombs and much guns. They are fighting at the airport. We are under the bed. Much guns."

"We love you all so much. We are praying. We are with you," I responded.

But we weren't actually with them. I wanted to be there, beside them, to pray and comfort the crying little ones at the center. I longed to be there dodging bullets with them, holding their hands. But instead I was some sixty-five hundred miles away, weeping on the sidewalk in Washington, DC. I felt utterly helpless.

Trying to push back every emotion, I called our contact at the United Nations.

"Philip, this is Bethany Haley in America. I texted and emailed you about our children at the Peace Lives Center. I'm wondering if someone can go to them. They are near the worst part of the fighting."

"I am sorry, sister. We are evacuating our office at this very moment. Please send me the phone numbers I need, and I will contact David. I will do everything I can," he said.

Everything I can, I thought. I *have to do everything I can.* During the next several minutes, I called and texted everyone I could think of who had connections in Goma as well as anyone living nearby who could help. In my desperateness, I even contacted some-one who had unique connections to black ops contractors in the area. Nothing. If I had had a plane at that moment, I think I would have attempted to fly it into Congo to try to get the children to safety. (Not that I can fly a plane, nor would I recommend this to anyone.)

Between sobs, I said, "There has to be a way. There has to be a way to help them."

"We have done everything we can," Matthew said as he tried to comfort me. "All we have now is prayer."

So we prayed. *Desperately.* Because the lives of our loved ones depended on the One who heard our prayers. We also asked others to pray—thousands of others. Five words were repeated in every email, every post, every text message: "Storm the heavens with your prayers."

And people did—families, friends, people we didn't know, entire churches.

At about three that afternoon, my phone rang. The caller was our contact at the White House.

"I received your email about delivering the letters today," she said. "I'm wondering if you could meet us at 5:00 p.m. We don't have clearance to meet with you inside because it's so late in the day, but we can meet you at the security gate."

I had cried off all my makeup, my eyes were swollen, and every possible emotion ran through my body at once. I took a long, deep breath.

"Absolutely," I said. And we were off.

Matthew and I went straight to the Resolve office to prepare the letters and write a letter of explanation about this gift to the president. Would he actually see them? I didn't know. But just in case, I was not going to miss the opportunity.

We prepared the gift box and were on our way. Walking as quickly as possible, I checked my phone every two seconds as I waited on updates from our team in Congo. And I prayed with every step. Because my body was walking to the White House, my spirit was overjoyed; because our children and friends were facing such terror, my heart was in pieces. It was nighttime in Goma, and the evening had brought a bit of calm to the fighting.

"Thank you for taking the time to deliver these to us," the White House contact said, smiling. "There are members of the National Security Council upstairs and ready to read some of these letters now."

"Will the president see these letters?" Matthew asked.

"Heavy shooting now. We can see their faces. The area around the center is covered by M23 rebels."

"His staff will read the letters and select some for the president. He will definitely see a few of these," she responded.

Delivering the children's letters felt sacred. Having their voices heard by the president and his staff added a new chapter to their stories of redemption. The moment was filled with glory.

Walking away, I realized what walking on cloud nine felt like. God had been, as always, faithful. From the day those tender hands wrote their letters, He knew. He made a way. I had no doubt.

Joy was overflowing, but reality grounded me quickly. Before bed, more text messages from our Congolese brothers came: "Heavy shooting now. We can see their faces. The area around the center is covered by M23 rebels."

"We are praying on our knees. We pray to a God bigger than war. How are the children? Are they safe?" I asked.

The response was remarkable. "They are singing the hope songs and the songs of peace. Your prayers are keeping us safe and strong. We thank you for your prayers. The children greet you. We know we have a great Provider."

In the middle of war, in the midst of bullets, surrounded by rebels, strong voices and sweet spirits were singing songs of hope and peace to calm their fears.

The next few days, more people than I knew forwarded our messages and joined us in prayer. What I also didn't know at the time was that a miracle was happening around the Peace Lives Center in Goma. The youngest children were lying on the ground during the fighting with mattresses over their bodies to protect them in case bombs landed inside the house. Bullets were flying overhead, and mortar bombs were falling around the center. After the fighting stopped and the guns went silent for a time, we found out just how faithful the Lord had been.

Not a single bullet harmed a child.

Not one bomb fell in the center.

Other civilians lost their lives, and our staff told us there were several dead bodies around the center and many tragically lost their lives in the conflict. Rebels had surrounded the area, but not one came to the door to take boys who were already trained to fight. *Not one.*

Reflections from My Journal...

At the Foot of a Volcano

I'm remembering a scene in the movie Mother Teresa; she is riding through the roads of Calcutta. It's like she begins to see her surroundings through a different set of eyes as she travels the streets and looks out the window. The cries of the hurting seem louder than normal. Those begging in the streets seem to call her name—the empty, the lonely, the poor, the physically distorted. All begin to call to her heart and at one point she says, "I have lived here for many years, but it is like I am seeing it for the first time." It changed her.

I'm also remembering a day that transformed my soul. That gave me a new vision of the suffering in Congo. A new heart.

Wrapping up trauma training for more than a hundred local leaders at HEAL Africa, the rest of the team left for the Rwandan border. I was staying a few more days to work with our new programs and was excited to have some time alone. The driver and I played a delightful game of charades as I attempted to explain where I would be staying (I was getting good at this game—plus it's quite humorous). Knowing just enough Swahili and French to get me into trouble, I tried to keep my mouth shut. After a good laugh, we pulled out to start the journey.

Driving in quiet. Windows down. Sunset to the left. I soaked in the city of Goma. Starting to take a few shots with my camera, I am gently reprimanded.

"No photo. Not good. Police and then the jail. It is Congo, you know. It is terrible."

Putting my camera to my side, I knew I would be using it again. Unfortunately, I'm stubborn like that. Slowly, I began to see that tiny part of Congo as I have never seen it before. Nothing to distract me. Just me. And Congo. The empty seemed to cry to me. The lost were desperate to be found. The wounded screamed to my heart. Black dirt streets. Black volcanic rock walls. Black lava-stained city.

And then I see a figure moving across the road.

At first I can't make out what I am seeing. It looks like an animal, but as we approach, I see more clearly. It is not an animal at all. It is a man. He is a young man in the heart of Goma traffic ... crawling across the road.

This is not just any road. The ash-covered roads in Goma were "repaved" by a volcano a few years back. The 2002 eruption of Mount Nyiragongo had wiped out 70 percent of the city and destroyed forty-five hundred houses and buildings. The aftereffects are everywhere. Houses built with lava rock. Walls constructed with lava rock. And the roads, well, they are simply broken lava rock. Driving or riding in a car is like driving or riding up the side of a rocky mountain.

As we get closer, I see that the young man's hands have flip-flops on them. He is using them as shoes. On his hands. With two hands down, he lifts the rest of his distorted body and drags himself a few feet at a time. He lifts and scoots. Lifts and scoots.

Cars pass him. Motorbikes dodge him. Black dirt covers him.

As we pass him, time morphs into slow motion. Our eyes meet. He is to the right of the car. I look out the window and toward the ground at him. I smile. He returns the smile, so brightly. I wave. He waves back with a beaming smile. And we drive on. In the middle of the street. Using his hands as his feet. Mangled legs that must have been bruised and calloused. Covered with the black dirt of Congo. He smiles.

But that was just the beginning of the drive. We pass person after person who is maimed or handicapped. We see children walking on homemade crutches. We watch men and women riding makeshift tricycle-like wheelchairs, with pedals and gears at hand level so they can "pedal" the three-wheeled contraptions.

One man has no legs at all and only one small arm,

which he uses to steer a three-wheeled chair
as two friends help push. Hundreds of people line
the sides of the roads and we are in stop-and-go
traffic. We keep passing the man in the three-
wheeled chair, then we catch up to him and pass
him again. His head is larger than the rest of his
body and he has one limb where two legs were
supposed to be. But he is smiling. Laughing, actually,
along with his friends who are pushing from behind.

We pass child after child carrying six or seven
jugs of water. Some empty, some full. We see women
carrying charcoal and bundles of wood that seem
triple their body size. I feel as though we are
driving through the blackest darkness.

A few nights before, I had very intense and evil
nightmares. I could feel it somehow—the heaviness.
But what I felt more than anything was that these
people of resilience didn't view their burdens as
being as heavy as I did. As horrific as they were,
they carried their burdens with a courage our
culture can't imagine. Our culture, which some
consider easier or more inviting than this one, lacks
the inner strength I witnessed here.

My heart was heavy and my mind spinning from all
I had seen. I kept going back to the young man
crawling across the street. What is his name? What
is his story? How does one begin to make a drop in
this ocean?

I drive through neighborhoods in America and see

houses that engulf those who live within their walls. The cost of food that we (I) throw away in one month could feed hundreds here. And it's not okay. There should be an answer. Or at least we should not settle; we cannot give up. There is an answer. There has to be.

We finally pulled up to the guesthouse where I was staying. It felt like a piece of heaven in the midst of an abyss of anguish. I couldn't get into my room soon enough. I immediately took the cover off the bed, placed it on the cold concrete floor, and fell prostrate on the ground in a prayer position of surrender. Face to the floor. Hands out, palms up in surrender. Facing Lake Kivu, the volcano was to my right and the sunset faded in front of me. And I wept. Praying that God would take my heart and make it His. That He would show me my role. My heart ached for the injustice here, for those who suffer in the streets, for the women pedaling their makeshift wheelchairs. For the man crawling across the road.

And then I stopped.

I looked up, out over the lake, toward the sunset. I stopped and stood still. Wait!

He had smiled at me. He smiled! How was that possible? Crossing a volcanic road covered with remnants of ash, wearing flip-flops on his hands, which he used as feet. He smiled at me.

It was a moment that transported me to a new

perspective. I could see the truth more clearly. I felt the pain more acutely. Maybe, just maybe, that man has more within himself than I will ever hold in my wealth-filled hands. Maybe he has found more joy in the limitations in his life than we "privileged" will ever find in our bounty. Maybe it is not he who needs saving. And maybe, just maybe, he is the teacher and we are the students.

And maybe—I have found my Calcutta.

I remember another quote from Mother Teresa that brings me pause: "The greatest disease in the West today is not TB or leprosy; it is being unwanted, unloved, and uncared for. We can cure physical diseases with medicine, but the only cure for loneliness, despair, and hopelessness is love. There are many in the world who are dying for a piece of bread, but there are many more dying for a little love. The poverty in the West is a different kind of poverty—it is not only a poverty of loneliness but also of spirituality. There's a hunger for love, as there is a hunger for God."

Father God, I ask nothing more tonight than that You help me see life through spiritual eyes. Teach me. I am Your student. You are my Lord. I am Yours.

CHAPTER NINETEEN

I Have Been Set Free

I saw the angel in the marble,
and I carved until I set him free.

—MICHELANGELO

Most of the time, I stand in front of the children—giving them a word of encouragement, leading a time of group counseling, or reading and acting out a Bible story. But this day was different. This day the children asked me to sit.

Andrew, who had been in the Congo program for years, spoke for the group: "Momma Bethany, we have drawn our stories of pain and dreams before, but today we have decided to share our stories in a drama."

Walking out of the tent, about twenty boys soon returned with AK-47s made of corn shuck and bamboo, and with walkie-talkies they had carved out of wood. They had bandaged their heads with cloth as if they were injured, spattered red paint on their bandages to represent blood spots, and rolled small pieces of paper to mimic cigarettes. In minutes, as they reenacted their nightmares, their horror came to life. Some boys played the roles of rebel leaders and some played the roles of children. In the drama, they acted out being at school and being abducted, then went on to reenact being beaten, captured, taken to training camp, and taught to use guns for the first time. Next, the commanders taught the boys how to kill someone with a machete.

"Now you are a man!" the rebel commander shouted.

When the boys reenacted an ambush, the designated abductors shot imaginary guns—and the abductees dodged bullets, hid behind trees, or acted out being killed.

It was so real that, at one moment, I found myself hiding behind a bench in the tent! I felt as though I were in the middle of the Congolese bush, and in those few minutes I tasted a tiny fraction of the world from which they had been saved.

Finally, they reenacted being rescued by MONUSCO and being taken back to safety. Everyone cheered and clapped.

> *"I give glory to God for saving me until this day. Even me."*

After they finished, they sat down, and a young man named Shalom stood before the group.

"I want to give God glory today," he said.

He told a story about the rebel commanders getting on the backs of the child soldiers to cross a river because it was too deep for these men to cross by themselves. The commanders rode on the young boys' backs until they got close enough to the other side that they could swim to land. But, in the process, many boys drowned under the weight of the commanders.

He finished with these words: "And I give glory to God for saving me until this day. Even me. I did not drown with the others, and I thank Jesus for saving my life."

Shalom. His name fits him perfectly. His smile is bold, but his spirit is gentle. Two years after he said these words, he graduated from secondary school and finished the Young Peacemaker program at the Peace Lives Center. At the center, we do not call the boys and girls "former child soldiers." They are given a new name: "young peacemaker." They love their new identity and live it out each day. Using expressive art, song, and dramas, Exile's counselor at the center leads the children through the Hope Initiative program twice a week, where they process their trauma, learn the power of forgiveness, and are taught conflict resolution and leadership skills. The change we see in these children is remarkable—especially in Shalom.

When the time came for Shalom to return home, all the children and youths gathered outside the center and formed a circle—singing for their brave brother, praying for him, dancing together, rejoicing as a family over what God had done in his life.

Shalom's dream had been to return to his village and begin the first Village Peace Club, taking the tools he had been given involving trauma healing, forgiveness, and conflict resolution and sharing them with his peers back home. Once a boy soldier, he was now a young peacemaker returning to the very village from which he had been kidnapped. Now reintegrated into his community, he is teaching his peers and a younger generation about peace, forgiveness, and a new way of life following Christ. After a year of leading the Village Peace Club, investing life and hope in his peers, working and saving money for school, Shalom will begin university next month, as of this writing.

Sitting beside him as we drove into the mountains to his home was one of the greatest honors of my life. Not being used to riding in a car, he became carsick, so we stopped a few times along the way. He took this opportunity to show us where he once fought as a boy soldier. Sharing these stories was healing for him. With each one, the sense of freedom he seemed to feel in his heart became stronger and stronger as he released memories of a past life and an old identity. After getting as close as possible by car, we began the walk toward his home, with Shalom carrying a pack on his back and a new mattress on his head.

"It is just there," he said with a radiant smile. "My home is right around the corner!"

> *"When your greatest heartache becomes your greatest ministry, grace comes full circle."*

He was filled with joy, and I was beaming as I thought of this boy soldier whom we had watched grow into a young man of peace. We arrived at his small home and shared hugs with his family and the village chief. We ate with them, laughed with them, and, finally, prayed with them. Before leaving, I looked down at my right hand to see the bracelet I was wearing—a simple cord with a metal circle attached. I remembered that Exile International had begun using these bracelets as reminders that "when your greatest heartache becomes your greatest ministry, grace comes full circle." I smiled.

Yes, he should have it, I thought.

"Shalom, I want to tell you the meaning of this bracelet," I said. "It is a circle and it represents redemption in Christ."

Explaining the saying, I told him, "Today your greatest heartache is becoming your greatest gift to others. You are taking the healing you received back to your community, to your people, to your country. The very thing that caused you the most pain in life has been turned into strength, and because of that pain you have grown to be a great leader. I have watched you grow into a strong and capable man of God, and I am so very proud of you!"

I put the bracelet on his wrist.

Almost before I could place it there, he gave me a huge bear hug, exclaiming with joy, "I will never take it off my wrist, Mum. I will never take it off!"

Walking out to the van, his last words to me were, "Greet the people in your village. Tell them thank you for praying for me all of these years." Assuming the "people in my village" were my friends, family, and Exile prayer supporters, I gladly passed along his request.

A few days later, I asked the children a big question: "If you could write a letter to the world, what would it say?"

There were many answers.

"We would tell them we love them and thank them for praying for us."

"I would tell them to love each other and forgive their neighbor."

"I would ask them to come and dance with us!"

Through this journey, God has granted me the opportunity to be in the presence of children who teach me the greatest lessons in life. Much of the time, I feel I am in the presence of prophets. The truths these children believe and embody astound me, and I long for my country and other developed nations to pull back its curtain of plenty and glimpse the reality of their world. A sacred beauty resides in the hearts of these children who courageously impart wisdom to their elders. To me. They teach us of forgiveness, reconciliation, faith, hope, and healing. I am in awe.

So in an attempt to bring their voices to others, I invited them to write actual letters to the world so we could glean from their wisdom. They wholeheartedly accepted. I pray that the world can learn these truths we so desperately need to invite into our humanity. May the voices of these great teachers—these prophets for peace—be heard by the rest of the world, and may their Savior be seen and glorified in all things.

"Forgiveness is an act of trust and choice... a choice not to harm those who brought us heartache.... It is an act that brings us freedom."

—Rebecca, Democratic Republic of the Congo

"What helps me trust God in the middle of war is because I saw His hand of mercy when He saved me from death" (Psalm 23:1-6).

—Molly, Uganda

"I know God will use my heartache to help others... as I serve in the church, when I sing God's songs.

Those who would consider joining the army will see
that God has changed me and they will not become
a rebel."

—Fidel, Democratic Republic of the Congo

"Before you can forgive, you first must know
yourself and forgive yourself."

—Patrick, Democratic Republic of the Congo

"I forgive myself because it was not my will and
choice to kill."

—Gloria, Uganda

"In all the hardships I have survived, I see that
it was only God who could have saved me."

—Virginia, Uganda

"In spite of war in Congo, I know that I live
today because of the grace of God; He is the first
and the last. He is my refuge. I know that God
loves me and will use my heartaches to help others."

—Andres, Democratic Republic of the Congo

"I forgive the rebels because forgiveness comes first
from God, and it helps us to be free when we have
heartache."

—Shalom, Democratic Republic of the Congo

"Forgiveness is very important in life, because if you don't know how to forgive, you will not be forgiven."

—Andrew, Democratic Republic of the Congo

"As for me, I forgive the rebels as they are my brothers and sisters created by the same Father, but only they are taken by earthly desires. I take them as they are and choose to forgive."

—Timothy, Uganda

"As children must be protected, educated, and assisted... we become the first victims of the war."

—Gloria, Uganda

"I have forgiven the rebels because the Bible says that you should not repay bad things for the bad things you experienced."

—Benjamin, Uganda

"As Christians, we need to take forgiveness as the medication for misunderstanding."

—David, Uganda

"For me, I want to say I have forgiven the LRA rebels from the bottom of my heart."

—John, Uganda

"Forgiveness is a choice not to stay negative toward someone. It is a gift given even if it's not deserved.

This does not mean to excuse someone; it doesn't mean to forget what happened."

—Christian, Democratic Republic of the Congo

"Forgiveness is not something that can be won. It's one of the ways we can bring peace."

—Justus, Democratic Republic of the Congo

"I've been able to forgive the rebels because of many lessons about peace and forgiveness I've enjoyed from the Holy Bible."

—Alice, Democratic Republic of the Congo

"Forgiveness is important. Even LRA soldiers are human beings and, like us, they were created by God."

—Richard, Uganda

Reflections from My Journal...

"There Is Not Enough Room Here"

I look into the eyes of a young man. What have they seen? I wonder.

I look down at his hands. What was he made to do? I ask myself. I look at the scars, and I wonder what stories they could tell.

The things he was forced to do and experience at the hands of the LRA are unspeakable to anyone other than a chosen few. To repeat them to most individuals would be traumatizing. But he, and many other children, experienced them. They have lived through these things, and many have already forgiven the very men who forced them to kill their own families.

Unimaginable.

I say to the young man, "Here are two handkerchiefs. Both representing tear catchers. Both reminding us that Our Creator collects and remembers all of our tears—our happy tears of hopes and dreams as well as our sad tears of pain. They are both equally important to Him. He has not forgotten your tears."

I had invited him to draw memories of his pain on one handkerchief and to draw his dreams on the other. He stared at them blankly, and then looked up at me as his words came slowly. "There is not

enough room here for me to draw all of my pain."
This young man is a wise teacher. Love pours out of
him, and his very life sings like a poem—speaking
with the wisdom of Solomon and the rhyme of David.
I watch as he sits in extended moments of silence,
thanking his savior for small morsels of food.

Once a commander in Joseph Kony's LRA, now a
tender giver of the grace that has been gifted
to him, he was saved for a reason—perhaps, and in
part, as a testimony to the power of redemption. He
is a peacemaker.

"I will sacrifice myself," he says. "I will sacrifice
myself to take care of her."

I look in near disbelief at the extent to which
he believes in and lives out sacrificial love. I watch
as he lightly beats his chest over his heart, and he
says again with diligence, "I will sacrifice myself."

He spoke these words about Florence, a woman
who was tortured by the LRA so severely that she
travels into and out of mental instability. That day
we had found Florence lying in the dirt outside her
home, catatonic.

What horrors and brutality did she live through to
leave her in this state? I wonder.

But I don't want to know. Not today. So many
stories of torture this week; I'm not sure I can
hold any more details and still be able to sleep.

I do know this: The LRA attempted to gouge
out her left eye, and now it is shaded over with

gray and blue and blindness. Her five children have raised themselves and been ostracized by the community because their mother is known as "the crazy woman."

Fortunately, her four youngest children are now sponsored; they have food, education, a safe place to live, and social support. The youngest was born just days after her mother returned from the bush, hemorrhaging. She is a miracle child, and her smile is breathtaking! I thank God that she is healthy, strong, and full of hope and potential. And I believe with all my heart that her mother will be healed of her torment. She will be freed from this residue of brutality.

I believe that.

Richard, a former child soldier, said, "Yes. I sat with Kony. He has a witch doctor who tells him what to do. Then he will go and tell the commanders the number of people who need to be killed. Sometimes it is like the witch doctor is a ghost. I saw Kony disappear one time when we were being attacked. He was beside me and, suddenly, he transformed himself into an antelope. I saw it with my own eyes." Stories like these from the youth and older escapees from the LRA are not uncommon. We have heard similar stories from many who don't even know each other. Part of me wants to believe it is impossible. Another part knows that witch doctors and witchcraft open a different realm of reality that few know about.

Richard continues, "'We need forty-two ears,' he may say, or 'We need this many body parts.' Then we were forced to go and collect them. It didn't matter if the people were dead or alive. If we did not bring back the right number, we were punished severely and others were killed. But we were just children."

I am in the presence of giants. To hear what they have experienced, to witness their peace and forgiveness, to hold their hands and know what those hands were forced to do—it is beyond words.

But there are words. Their stories must be told. Not just their stories of survival, but their stories of abundant life.

I believe these children can and will change the world with their stories of forgiveness and dreams for peace. They not only survived the torture of rebels, but they are testimonies of peace. I believe that their forgiveness, their love for peace, and the redemption lived out in their lives transcend the evils they have experienced.

I believe Kony will be stopped and that his victims—these survivors—will sing of being saved. I believe that the children the world almost breaks can and will grow up to save it.

And I will not stop believing.

Final Thoughts

Blood on My Hands

I have come to love some very small things in this life of mine. Like how the shadow of my pen prances in the sunlight on the page where I write these words. How the dense moisture of the morning air causes the ink to seep a little deeper into the paper of my journal. How the dull eyes of an older gentleman suddenly dance when I ask him his very favorite memory. How a small child sees magic in a story that isn't magical at all, simply because she's never heard it before. Why? Because she is able to *dream* and *imagine* impossibilities we grown-ups usually cannot. Story becomes *life*.

Sitting with some of the world's most wounded souls and hearing their pain, their stories become a part of my own. Sometimes I can almost feel the pain . . . and the joy. I am burdened almost daily by the pull to write down all of their stories. There are so many—trapped inside my heart and dancing inside my mind. They need to be told.

Being gifted with their stories, I feel as if I have blood on my hands, and I imagine God whispering over my shoulder, "What are you to do with it?"

Should I wash it off because it makes me weep? Should I wipe my hands because I am uncomfortable or because of what others may say? Should I pretend it isn't there because I don't know what to do with it or how to make it go away? No, I should not. And I will not.

Today I stopped to think of my own path. How my own steps and story of woundedness walked me into their stories. It was no accident.

Having recently been forced to once again look my own past darkness in the eye, I realize I am a walking testimony to His re-demption. Looking into my soul, I see a wondrous, colorful image, not of my own doing or creation. It is a tapestry woven with the remnants of my spirit's broken past and knitted together by the threads from others' stories—enveloped by the hands of a healing Savior and a merciful God. It is the color of grace. When your greatest heartache becomes your greatest ministry, grace comes full circle. I believe if scars could sing, their songs would be of triumph.

> *If scars could sing, their songs would be of triumph.*

I am not my own. And neither are these stories.

My memories of the world's broken and the stories of redeemed suffering are stories for all of us to share. The scars on my heart and on the hearts of others whom I have been honored to touch were the beginnings of beauty and not the end of life. No matter what the story is—your story, their story, my story—with Jesus as our Rabbi, the ending is *beautiful* because the ending is always *redemption*. Even if that does not come until heaven.

"Leave your hearts here, and take ours with you." These were the words of a gentle, resilient pastor in Congo, who, after losing many extended family members, had been forced to flee into exile, along with his immediate family. His life—his story—spoke of strength.

"Now that you have seen, go and tell, I ask of all of you," he said. "Now that you have seen, go and tell."

An untold story cannot continue living. Lessons unlearned steal opportunities to experience the beauty and wisdom God has prepared for us. Donald Miller knows about stories:

> I don't know why there are dark forces in the world, but there are . . . there is a force in this world that does not want us to tell [our] stories. It doesn't want us to face our issues, to face our fear, and bring something beautiful into the world . . . I believe God wants us to create beautiful stories.[1]

Our lives are our stories. When we live them out loud and with purpose, we not only abide in a story of adventure, but we also abide within the hands of a trustworthy God, giving Him glory for each step. When we see another person's scars and hear the stories of the pain that created them, then we get to step into their stories as well. And when we begin to love them—simply love them—we begin to walk into the story of redemption. Not of our own strength, but through the heart and soul of a crucified Creator whose suffering bonds us to Him for eternity. It is only in being broken that can we be mended. It is only in being mended that we can be whole. That is what makes the ending of all suffering beautiful.

Afterword

"When can we read your book, Mum? When can we read the stories you have written about us?" Prince asked. He is tall and quiet. He doesn't usually ask many questions in group settings, but today he raised his hand high in the middle of the 115 kids at the Peace Lives Center in DR Congo who were gathered together.

It was the day before we would head back to America, and we had gathered all of the children to tell them I had written a book. I wanted to make certain each understood that their stories of survival and strength would be read, along with portions of their letters to the world about forgiveness. They began cheering as soon as the words were out of my mouth! Looking up at me as I stood before them, their eyes danced with excitement and awe. I was, again, full circle.

"You have told the world about *us*?" one of the girls asked, as if they were not worthy to be mentioned.

"Oh yes! We always tell others in America and everywhere we go about you! You have inspired them with your strength and hope. You teach them how to forgive and how God can use the pain of our past for purpose and beauty." More dancing eyes. Bigger smiles.

Do they know they are the light of the world? Do they grasp the power of their stories . . . their lives? The power in their joy, hope, re-silience, and forgiveness? I thought.

These young peacemakers, in the heart of a war, dared to dream of leading their communities and nation toward peace. My heart yearned for the world to be radically changed by their stories of faith.

Still gathered together in giddy excitement, Denis, the PLC counselor, began to sing in a soft, sweet tone, "The color of grace . . . the color grace . . ." It was spontaneous, yet in a matter of seconds, all 115 boys and girls were singing those four words in unison, over and over. Their voices were quiet and then slowly became louder. It took my breath away. I am reminded how singing is like breath to them.

Even at such a young age, they understand that it's not all about them, I thought. *It's all about Him and His love for them. His plan for them . . . for all of us. A plan to give us a hope and a future. A plan for beauty and not for disaster.*

Grace comes in colors too otherworldly for words, but, if it could be seen, it would have been radiating all around them as they sang their song of grace.

Later, once the group had begun to disperse, Bahati came and stood beside me. He and Shalom had ridden four hours, down from their village in the mountains, to see us. Just six months prior, Bahati had graduated the rehabilitation program and had been reunified with his mother and young brother. He was finding his way in his new life. Each time I see the scar on his face, given to him during his time in captivity, I am reminded that Jesus can transform our broken stories into pathways of redemption and unexpected joys.

"How are you, Bahati?" I asked.

"I am doing well, Mum. But I need a Bible," he responded.

"What happened to your Bible?"

"I was reading the Bible with one of the rebels, and he wanted to take it so he could learn more about love and forgiveness. So I gave it to him. I am teaching the rebels about forgiveness and hope. I am teaching them about Jesus."

He was beaming with the smile of one who had joyously found his calling in life. It was like his heart was getting ready to explode. He had been waiting for this moment for months. To tell "Mum" his good news and celebrate together.

> *"I gave my Bible to one of the rebels. I am teaching the rebels about forgiveness and hope. I am teaching them about Jesus."*

Bahati went on to explain that he was now visiting the rebel compound three days a week to study the Bible with anyone who would come. Not only was he teaching from the Bible, he was using what he had learned from the trauma care and forgiveness curriculum

Exile International uses in its programs to teach young rebel soldiers about emotional healing. He had started inviting rebels to a local church where he was preaching on Sundays. Some of them were coming to hear him speak and there heard about the love of Jesus.

"They are listening to me, Mum, because I was once a rebel like them before I escaped. If I were not taken when I was young, they would not listen to me now. But I need more Bibles. If I had more Bibles, I could study with more of the rebels, and they might come to know Jesus."

I was just as overwhelmed with awe as I was terrified for this dear one. Sponsoring his care and education from the beginning of our program, I had grown to know and love him deeply. To see him now . . . taking the new life he had been given and bringing it to the violent rebel fighters who had abducted and brainwashed him—it was almost too much to comprehend.

In just a few days, Bibles were purchased to send back with Bahati, along with a cell phone he could use if he found himself in danger. We then, of course, had a long talk about safety.

"Bahati, you know you may be in danger, right? You know the government has begun fighting the rebels there and there may be more fighting soon?" I said. I had cried myself to sleep for three nights wrestling with the very real possibility that I may not see him again.

Looking at me with intensity and purity of heart, he said, "I know, Mum. But this is why Jesus saved me. He saved me in the bush to teach others about Him. To bring them healing from their trauma and help them learn to forgive. This is what I want to do with my life."

He was a man now. He was and is able to make his own decisions. I wondered, *How can I argue with such a surrendered heart? And would I even want to? I wanted to be Bahati when I grew up. There was no denying it.*

This rescued child soldier's life has been transformed. He has become a young man, a leader, and an influencer. He is taking the healing and redemption he has experienced and spreading it to the very rebel group he was once a part of. Distributing it like cups of water to dry bones. Pain becoming purpose. Darkness becoming light.

All of this happened just weeks before this book was first released. I came back to America with a full heart and a restless spirit. I text messaged Bahati regularly to make sure he was safe, and I placed him in God's hands each night before bed. I was back in America preparing for a book tour, speaking engagements, and a floodgate of events. At many of those events, I had the opportunity to sit across the table from leaders and influencers and answer this question over and over: "You mean this is still happening? It is happening now?"

"Yes," I'd reply. "It is happening as we sit here and drink our coffee. It is happening now."

It was about two years before this book was released that a dear friend, Brooke Rosolino, connected me with Matthew Williams—my now husband! Brooke knew that Matthew's personal mission and my own overlapped. He had come to Nashville to visit a friend, and I had just fifteen minutes to chat with him before heading to an Exile team retreat. Fifteen minutes turned into an hour as we talked about what Exile was doing, who we served, and his dreams to provide trauma care to child survivors of war and abuse.

Fifteen minutes turned into an hour as we talked about what Exile was doing, who we served, and his dreams to provide trauma care to child survivors of war and abuse.

At the time I met Matthew, I was planning to head back to Uganda and DR Congo in seven weeks. This particular trip had been postponed multiple times because of the escalating conflict in DRC, but I decided that even if no one went with me, I would move forward with the trip. Exile had been praying for a male trauma counselor and we certainly could use the help on this team, so I asked Matthew if he'd like to join us (myself and a young woman from our operations team). Two days later, he said yes and we began prepping for the trip.

Just before we left, the other young woman had to cancel her trip, and our American team was, unexpectedly, cut down to two. Even though we were with EI's African teammates throughout each activity, we had the evenings to ourselves—debriefing from the day and talking about life.

There was so much about him I did not know, but one thing I did: he radiated *positivity*. He was intentional about remembering the names of practically every person he met and he spoke as if the gospel was fresh to him. He also spoke about love in a way I had never heard before.

"What does your tattoo mean?" I asked.

"*Ahava*. It is 'the will to love.' It is the love that Jesus speaks of as He shares the greatest commandments in Matthew 22, verses 37–40: 'Love the Lord your God with all your heart, all your soul, and all your mind,' and 'Love your neighbor as yourself.' This particular word for love, *ahava*, is not a feeling but a cognitive choice to love God unconditionally and to love your neighbor—no matter what one's emotions may want to choose," he responded.

He was intelligent and soulful. Both of which I respected.

He went on to explain, "When your wife is throwing knives at you and you are hiding behind the sofa for safety, but you're still saying, 'There is nowhere else I would rather be than right here with you right now.' That is *ahava*," he said with a twinkle in his eye.

This was the first glimpse I'd had into Matthew's heart of hearts. There would be many more memorable firsts to come.

The first "test" question I asked Matthew before we started dating was "How patient are you?" I knew it would take time for my heart to open up, and it would also require patience to tolerate my forgetful, unstructured, and uninhibited personality. It would also take a strong man to call me out when needed and wrestle with me through the stubborn pushback.

The first lesson he taught me was about joy. He taught me to see the light in days that seem dreary and to love in the literal way Jesus did—fully, intentionally, and without condition. Seeing the light in everything and loving well was a way of life for him. It was something he saw as his job and his daily ambition.

Another memorable first was the first time I thought Matthew might be someone I could marry. On our first trip together, we were driving in the dark from the mountains of Congo, and it was well past the appropriate (safe) time to be out and about. Our feet were thickly covered with volcanic dirt and our bodies sore from the constant bouncing as we traversed pathways few would actually call roads—often feeling like a shiny ball in a pinball machine. We were weary from a long day of leading Exile International's art therapy and trauma care workshop for recently rescued child soldiers. We'd worked in ninety-degree heat, but we were also emotionally overflowing from washing 120 war-scarred feet and from witnessing young survivors of war pray blessings over one another. A beautiful but exhausting day.

After several flat tires and a stop for our friends to buy chickens and carrots on the side of the road, we would be at least two hours late for dinner. The nuns and priests at the Catholic Guesthouse like to run a tight ship. Dinner is from 6:30 to 7:30. The food is put on the tables precisely on time, and guests are expected to be there. It was 7:30 and we were still an hour away. Stomach growling from not eating all day, I leaned over to ask Matthew, "What do you think we'll have for dinner?"

Both knowing it would be something along the line of cold sardines and eggplant, he didn't miss a beat, "I'm thinking we shall have a Caesar salad, thick-cut pork chops, fresh green beans, and, perhaps, mashed potatoes with gravy. What would you like for dessert?"

He smiled and awaited my response. His charm and kind heart were as indisputable as his good looks, and I thought, *I've never met anyone quite like this man before.*

The idea of "finding someone" had been off my radar for quite some time. Still, what I did know about Matthew was notable. He had graduated with his master's degree in counseling from Dallas Theological Seminary with an emphasis in trauma. He had taken a semester off from graduate school to live in and serve a children's home in Bali. He had worked with survivors of the tsunami in Indonesia and had volunteered in Cambodia and Nepal—serving young survivors of sex

> *The idea of "finding someone" had been off my radar for quite some time.*

trafficking. He had also volunteered with an organization in northern Uganda where he had seen the effects of the LRA. It was there he felt compelled to dedicate his life to serving child survivors of war and slavery by using his gifts as a counselor.

I think back to when I said "yes" to writing this book and how I had *no idea* what I was getting myself into. I had no idea that saying yes to writing down my story, Exile's story, and the story of these brave children was also saying yes to more than a year of reliving trauma, renewed nightmares, sleepless nights, tears, and diving headfirst into vulnerability. When you write a book about your life, your ministry, and the children you love, you really have to open up your heart. In this book-writing process, I literally poured out my soul. I pulled back the curtains and revealed my jagged scars, and I had no idea how the book would be received . . . especially when the only people who read it prior to revealing it to the world are your editor, your parents, and your soon-to-be husband. My parents have always been my greatest cheerleaders, and Matthew makes me feel like my feeblest attempts in the kitchen produce award-winning recipes. But still, I had no idea what to expect from others.

What happened after the book release was beyond anything I could have imagined. More important than the kind reviews were the numerous emails and letters from people wanting to get involved and help these children, and messages from others with their own stories of shame and brokenness who were learning to accept grace and God's love for the first time in their life.

The response was beautiful, but it was also difficult. I am so thankful that I had and still have my teammate, my kindred, my now husband and partner in adventure beside me. Matthew was and is there through it all. Leading Exile International together, we are constantly at the feet of Jesus asking how we can love and live better. Matthew has been my greatest and most unexpected surprise in life.

Matthew certainly is unique and loves the Lord; but, like so many of us, he also had his share of brokenness. His parents had a tumultuous relationship and divorced when he was four years old. His time was split bouncing between homes every other day—each offering their own unique set of difficulties. His visitation arrangements were so unusual that they would have made coping challenging for any child. Still, you won't often hear Matthew speak negatively of his difficulties. One of Matthew's many endearing qualities is his ability to learn from the good, the bad, and everything in between. From his mother, Carla, he learned what it meant to love unconditionally and to forgive freely. His mother also empowered him to believe that he could do or be anything he set his mind to. From his father, he learned to stand up for what's right, pursue justice (even when it's difficult), show respect, have integrity, and refuse to let words hurt you.

Sadly, I never had the privilege of meeting his father. Scott was diagnosed with and lost a battle to cancer in 2008. Matthew was just twenty-four years old. Just a few years later came the deaths of two of his dear friends. One to AIDS. One to suicide.

Unlike me, a preacher's kid, church was not a big part of his younger life. For Matthew, it was a life-threatening four-wheeler wreck at seventeen years old that radically shifted his life. After a week in intensive care to help him recover from eight fractures of the hip and back, he was moved to a hospital bed in his grandparents' living room. Limited to bed rest and unable to walk for more than six months, he would need constant care. It was there, with less of the distractions common to teenagers, that he began seeking out what it meant to follow Christ. His grandfather began discipling him, and Matthew became devoted to serving his Lord and Savior.

The most interesting part about Matthew regarding his wreck and the many surgeries that followed is that he says he wouldn't change any of it—even the pain—if he could. He wouldn't trade any of that pain for something easier. Why? Because he truly believes those experiences were necessary for him to be the man he is today.

The more I heard about the imperfections of his life and how he willfully learned from them—almost using them as stepping stones toward being a better lover of God and others—the more I saw Jesus in him.

We returned from our first trip to Africa together, knowing there was an undeniable spark, and a kindred connection, between us.

Soon after our return, we had an important conversation about three things: First, Exile's mission came first. We were both equally determined that no potential relationship would get in the way of God's plan for the children. If that started to happen, we committed to ending any so-called spark. Second, with the guidance of close friends and mentors, we chose not to date for six months, so we could first build a friendship together. We didn't know what would happen after that, but we were praying for God's guidance. Finally, our relationship would remain pure. We were both committed to upholding sexual boundaries and honoring God through our relationship. This was *not* easy, but we loved Jesus above each other, and that is what kept us grounded.

> *We returned from our first trip to Africa together, knowing there was an undeniable spark, and a kindred connection, between us.*

For the next six months, Matthew worked remotely from Dallas and traveled for Exile International. We talked often by phone, saw each other periodically, and we prayed—a lot. We dreamed together about how we could expand this mission to restore more rescued child soldiers, former sex slaves, and children orphaned by war. We brainstormed on how to ignite people in the West to respond to the cry of child slaves across the world. We traveled to Washington, DC, to meet with national leaders to share stories of LRA child survivors in Uganda.

A few months later, we were back in Africa. We flew to Rwanda and hoped to head to the border to DRC the next day. We were talking about the next steps of our relationship when he slowly leaned over to me.

"Are you ready to try this? Me and you?" he asked with his kind southern charm.

Heart beating. Mind racing.

"Yes," I whispered.

He leaned in slowly and kissed me.

"Are you afraid?" he quietly asked.

"No," I said. "I am terrified."

But I wasn't foreign to facing fears, and he'd told me that this one was worth facing head on.

It's funny. I had given up on love. I believed that marriage was a bonus to life and not a necessity for happiness. God was my soul mate, and although finding a teammate to adventure through life with would be wonderful, I had begun to find contentment without that. I had, as best I knew how, exchanged my will for God's and had thrown my heart into a calling that often consumed me. But it was in that calling that I met someone running the same race—with a tenacious passion to serve God and these children.

I truly believe that when living for something bigger than ourselves becomes our focus, we become less consumed with what we don't have and more fulfilled in living life's adventure. Then, when we look to the right or left and see someone running beside us, we might just have found a partner for life. And, if not, we can say we've lived one rich life.

Eight months into dating and trying to navigate life, I was getting anxious. Matthew knew my story. Every single detail—more than I had shared with people in my closest circle. He had known since that first trip to Congo as I spilled everything into the air one night following a long day of work in the field. But he had not mentioned it again. He had not asked for more details—not once, and he did not seem concerned about my past. But I had reached a point of needing to know how he felt about it.

"You know my past: the unfaithfulness, the brokenness. It doesn't bother you? You don't see me any differently?" I asked.

He smirked slowly. This smirk he has . . . it's a combination of confidence and the ability to see, seemingly, through to my soul.

"May I tell you a story I once heard?" he asked.

I nodded.

"There was once a woman who claimed she was regularly visited by Christ. Many within her church thought she was schizophrenic. One day a priest went to visit her, hoping he could help or just talk some sense into her. The woman remained steadfast, convinced she was truly being visited by the Christ. Unable to sway her, the priest had a bright idea. 'If this really is Jesus coming to you, ask Him what I said in my last confession.' The next week the priest again visited the woman. He asked her, 'Well, what did He tell you I said in my last confession?'

"'He said to tell you He doesn't remember.' The priest was clearly dissatisfied with the response, so she explained further, 'He said to tell you that He doesn't even remember. He told me that because of His death and resurrection, He remembers our sins no more and that you, of all people, should know that,' she finished.

"So, I don't remember," Matthew said, looking gently into my eyes. "I don't see or think about you as your past. I only see Christ's righteousness in you and His love radiating from you. That's all I see."

Tears flowed. Heart swelled. A deep healing comes when we are fully known and still fully loved. When our ugliness is exposed and we are loved in spite of it, we are free to feel accepted—scars and all. I had already felt and accepted God's love and forgiveness, but I had concluded it might be difficult to find that kind of love from a man—especially a man willing to love me for life.

The next year was hard and wonderful and terrifying—full of adventure and lots of laughing. Getting married again was one of

> *"I don't see or think about you as your past. I only see Christ's righteousness in you and His love radiating from you. That's all I see."*

my worst fears, but the process to get there involved some much-needed refinement. It was during this hard and wonderful and terrifying year that I was writing this book.

You might think that being engaged and in love would get in the way of the book writing. And it was certainly difficult to plan a wedding, lead Exile's programming, and finish final book edits all at the same time. But Matthew helped to make it all work. He was my partner, best reader, and encourager. He invested hours reading through the book chapter by chapter; he edited, made suggestions, and listened to me read out loud—over and over. During most of the book-writing process, I was fighting the pain of four herniated disks. I am now quite skilled at strapping an ice pack to my neck while typing into the wee hours of the morning. I'm not sure how I would have finished the book without him. He knew just when to push me a little further and when to insist that I rest. I sure do love that man!

Matthew was not one to shy away from calling me out when I needed it (which is exactly what I needed—whether it was about the writing process and my many deadlines or something else in our lives). I also knew how to call him out. That being said, that year was a season of God's refinement in each of us as individuals and in us as a couple. Throughout that refinement we grew to love each other even more and, equally, the many children God had placed in our lives.

I remember going to lunch with a friend who wanted to know "every detail of our relationship." Matthew and I had a lot going for us and a lot going against us. Writing a book and running an organization together during the dating stage of a relationship was hard enough. We didn't know if our relationship would even work out, but we did know things could become messy if it didn't. It was a heavy load to carry.

My friend finally looked at me, smiled, and said, "This is going to end up as one of two things: a huge train wreck or one of the greatest love stories ever."

I laughed, but she wasn't so far from the truth. There was no doubt God's fingerprints were on this relationship—and it was wonderful! It was also difficult—as most great relationships are.

But in the challenging times, I found myself wanting to retreat. Clouds of anxiety and fear followed me everywhere. Memories of my past marriage came flooding back. My weaknesses triggered his past wounds, and his weaknesses triggered mine. But, through the trials, we grew closer to God and to each other. Jesus uses those of us with skin on to be His hands and feet—and sometimes His chisel. Sometimes He uses our relationships (friendships and kindred spirits) to refine us into the best He has for us. The best we can be. It's not easy, but it's worth it. There was little doubt that God had crossed our paths and that He had placed potential in our united spirits to make an impact on this world. Plus, we had loads of fun around each other and the lens we saw life through was quite similar.

After dating for two years, on a long layover back from a program visit, Matthew proposed in Belgium. He had carried the ring with him for more than six weeks in Africa, waiting for the right time— the day after I turned in the manuscript for *The Color of Grace*.

As was our life, our relationship, and our journeys, my wedding ring was equally unconventional. I was still wearing my "God ring" on my left finger. It was made up of two rings, actually. One thin silver band linked inside of another. They symbolized me and my Beloved. I had seen the Lord as my soul mate for years. I still do.

For my wedding ring, I wanted to add a third thin silver band to my ring—adding Matthew to the duo. One band symbolizing me. One band symbolizing God. One band symbolizing Matthew. We would certainly make a great team!

It was a hot Tennessee outdoor wedding in August 2014. Rain clouds teased all day. They were sure to open up and drench us all by the time Matthew and I would be saying our vows at the stone steps of Percy Warner Park, where we had chosen to be married. A last-minute call was made to move the ceremony to the 1800s farmhouse, where the reception was being held. Friends and family poured in, children blew bubbles, and countless hugs were shared. God even showed up with His umbrella, as He seemingly protected this tiny wedding spot from rain. It was the *only* dry space in Nashville on that evening as torrential downpours covered the area. Guests heard loud clapping thunder as we lit three unity candles: committing our lives to do justice, love kindness, and walk humbly with our God. But my heart was hurting because some of our dearest friends could not be there . . . the children from Africa. The reception hall was full of photos of their faces, but lacked their tender prayers and their sweet singing. And their small hands were not there to hold mine on that special day.

It was nearly time for our vows, and I had held a secret until that moment. A secret only four people knew. I had emailed David in DRC a few weeks prior, asking him if the children would be willing to write a short letter for us to read at the wedding. And, oh, did they come through! I wanted to surprise Matthew with this most special gift of all. Murphy, Matthew's best man, approached the microphone and began to read the letters.

Congratulations, Dear Parents!

On behalf of all the children of the Peace Lives Center in Congo under your care. We, the older Young Peacemakers, wrote this letter after hearing this great news of your wedding. We are very sorry that our poor English will not express very well what is happening in our hearts, but we ask the Holy Spirit to help you know what we are feeling.

Bethany and Matthew,

You are very special, and what you teach us is immeasurable in different ways. Even though we are not yet working in a business, we know it is not easy to spend much time together without having conflict. You have proven that you are led by the Holy Spirit and that you are a strong couple by leading your children in unity. From the beginning we saw many people coming with Bethany to Congo, but they went away and we did not see them again. But Matthew was exceptional. This means God brought him to Exile International to build God's ministry with Mama Bethany through this forever family.

To Matthew,

The Bible says God knew us before we were created. He has a good plan for you. It is the plan to meet the children of Congo, to help villages destroyed by the war, to build a new nation in DRC, and to transform the world. You cannot do this by yourself, that is why, in order to accomplish His mission through you, God said: "Matthew will not be able to do this alone, I will give him someone who looks like him who has the same heart of serving like him so that our nation of Congo may not perish but be transformed, and I will give them both strong hearts in order to build my nation."

To Bethany-Our Mama,

We miss the words to tell you what is in our hearts. You have been a mama before being married. Born from you, we are proud to have a wonderful mama who gives us today a father. We can't wait to see you with our father as one body. You are a team forever. We wish you millions of children.

All the children here wish you a happy wedding, and we pray that you would endure the hard things you will face during your marriage together. We wish you unity and understanding in your home. Let nothing separate you from God's love.

We have but one question: When you arrive here in Congo, can you have a ceremony with us to celebrate this wonderful union for the glory of our Lord?

In Jesus' name,
The Young Peacemakers and Orphaned Hope
Children of Peace Lives Center in Congo

And six months later, we did just that. Thinking this would be a small celebration, we could not anticipate the full-on surprise of a Congolese wedding. In short, it involved a wedding dress surprise, a tiara, a small church constructed from wooden planks, banana leaves adorning the doorway to welcome us, and decorations handcrafted out of paper from the youngest children at the center. Walking in to see four hundred Congolese faces staring back at us, Matthew and I quickly realized this was not going to be a small celebration.

The day involved a lot of traditional dancing and wedding songs performed by children from PLC—all dressed in new clothes. Of course, each song was perfectly choreographed to traditional dance moves. Our groomsmen were recent graduates of the Peace Lives Center, and the bridesmaids were several of the older girls still in the program. This wedding experience and its beautiful details is deserving of its own book! There's just too much to share here.

And as we were leaving the reception at the PLC, I turned around to see Bahati holding the train of my dress so it wouldn't get dirty from Goma's black volcanic dirt. He walked with me to the car and gave me a huge hug. He would return to his village the next day with Bibles in tow for the rebels. We looked at each other and the tears came. There was no stopping them.

"Pray for me, Mum. Pray for my safety. Before, when I was in the bush, I thought I would be nothing. I thought I would die. But Exile has given me education, and you have helped me to heal. I miss the words to thank you."

I miss the words, too. I miss the words to describe this life I have been given. This adventure we are on. But I will say this, God has taught me more about this life than I have room to write, and I have found the greatest treasures through surrender. It is in surrendering to living out the gospel in whatever way we can and learning to see life through spiritual eyes that the romance of life can be found. I totally believe that the Lord waited until Matthew and I had found our complete selves in Him—being willing to be single to serve Him completely, if necessary—before He crossed our paths. God certainly does redeem broken stories and create lifelong adventures. We are living proof.

Bethany Haley Williams, August 2015

A Brief History of the Wars

W hile the issues and contributing factors are too numerous to explore, this brief overview is intended to provide some context for the causes of both previous violence in Uganda by Joseph Kony and the Lord's Resistance Army and the current war in the Democratic Republic of the Congo (DRC).

Throughout decades of war, violence, and oppression in Uganda and the DRC, millions of men, women, and children have lost their lives, and millions more have been maimed, traumatized, or otherwise violently oppressed. Although there are no exact figures, across these two countries, armed forces and rebels have abducted more than one hundred thousand children. As young as age seven, children are kidnapped and forced to join rebel armies. Many are psychologically tortured and brainwashed. Many are forced to commit atrocities against their own families and communities. Young girls are abducted and abused, becoming victims of rape and gender-based violence.

The internationally agreed-upon definition for a child soldier is any person below eighteen years of age who is or who has been recruited or forced by a state armed force or a non-state armed group in any capacity, including but not limited to boys and girls used as fighters, cooks, porters, messengers, spies, or for sexual purposes. It does not only refer to a child who is taking or has taken a direct part in hostilities.[1]

Some of the key factors contributing to years of instability in the DRC are:

- problems left by nearly a century of colonial rule;

- armed conflicts and war with neighboring countries and dictatorships;

- conflict regarding minerals; corruption; and the destabilizing influence of approximately thirty rebel groups.

The Effects of the War

The war has been brutal, and few Congolese are left without its scars. Rape and gender-based violence are rampant and used as weapons of war. Children are orphaned, abducted, and killed. Approximately one in three combatants in the DRC is a child.[2]

Today more than twenty thousand UN peacekeepers reside in

the DRC—representing the largest UN peacekeeping mission in the world.[3] Even so, fighting, coup attempts, and violent clashes continue to displace and harm thousands. Conflicts in 2012–13 led to the displacement of approximately one million people in the eastern Congo.[4]

History

In the 1870s the king of the Belgians, Leopold II, began colonizing the Congo region. Millions are believed to have been killed during his rule of the territory.[5]

The country's first five years of independence (gained in 1960) were hindered by several internal coups. It is believed that these coups were influenced and supported by several outside governments. By 1965, Colonel Joseph-Desiré Mobutu had seized power. Mobutu renamed the country Zaire and changed his own name to Mobutu Sese Seko Kuku Ngbendu wa Za Banga, which translates to "the all-powerful warrior who, because of his endurance and inflexible will to win, goes from conquest to conquest, leaving fire in his wake."[6] His new name fittingly describes the manner in which he accumulated power and wealth for thirty-two years.

The year 1996 marked the beginning of the First Congo War. Supported by a coalition of the Ugandan and Rwandan armies, the anti-Mobutu rebel group the Alliance for Democratic Liberation (AFDL) invaded Zaire. Within a year, Mobutu fled the country, the AFDL leader, Laurent Kabila, was installed as president, and the country was renamed the Democratic Republic of the Congo. Soon after these events, the United Nations pointed to grave human rights violations and genocidal actions committed against refugees in the eastern Congo between 1996 and 1998.[7]

Some refer to the period from 1996 to 2003 as Africa's World War. Successive conflicts have plagued the DRC, and more than five million people have died while nine countries and numerous rebel armies warred on Congolese soil. Tribal disputes and fighting over territories, minerals, and other interests are just a few of the factors.[8]

Joseph Kony and the Lord's Resistance Army in Uganda

In the late 1980s, Joseph Kony took leadership of an opposition force in northern Uganda. Subsequently, he renamed this group the Lord's Resistance Army (LRA), and the brutality of their campaigns increased. As Kony began losing regional support and the ability to maintain his army, he began abducting children and committing brutal acts of violence and oppression against the people of northern Uganda.[9]

Between 1986 and 2006, conflict between the government of Uganda and the Lord's Resistance Army displaced more than two million people.[10] Starting in 1996, the government required the people of northern Uganda to leave their homes and relocate to displaced persons camps (these displacement camps are referred to several times in this book). Sadly, these camps are stricken with high mortality rates, poor health care, and malnutrition.

Kony and the LRA are believed responsible for the deaths of more than one hundred thousand people and the abduction of sixty thousand to one hundred thousand children.[11] Common brutal practices have included forcing children to machete their own parents or siblings to death and raping and abducting young girls—often forcibly giving girls as sex slaves to LRA officers.[12]

In 2005, the International Criminal Court issued warrants for the arrest of five LRA commanders. The warrants stated:

> *[That] the LRA is an armed group that has established a pattern of brutalization of civilians by acts including murder, abduction, sexual enslavement, mutilation, as well as mass burnings of houses and looting of camp settlements; that abducted civilians, including children, are said to have been forcibly recruited as fighters, porters, and sex slaves and to take part in attacks against the Ugandan army (UPDF) and civilian communities.[13]*

From 2006 to 2008, the government of Uganda and the LRA participated in peace talks. After two years of negotiations, a peace agreement was ready; but Joseph Kony failed to sign, and new attacks were launched in countries neighboring northern Uganda.[14]

Today the LRA continues to operate in the Democratic Republic of the Congo, South Sudan, and the Central African Republic. Operating as dispersed groups of fighters throughout the dense terrain of this region, the LRA's attacks and abductions continue. While the size of their force has diminished greatly, they have displaced more than 160,000 people in three countries since 2008 and continue to attack villages and abduct men, women, and children.[15]

Programs and Partners of Exile International

Programs of Exile International

- **Excel Program/Child Sponsorships:** Exile International facilitates child sponsorship programs in the Democratic Republic of the Congo and Uganda that give each child the tools he or she needs to develop and thrive, including food, health care, education, psychosocial support, peace building/leadership development, and spiritual care. These children are empowered to heal and develop into young peacemakers and leaders in their communities. Graduates often continue to study in universities.

- **Extend Program:** Through this program, Exile International partners with other organizations to train leaders who work with vulnerable children and with children in armed conflict. Through Extend, we offer these leaders and organizations training in art therapy, trauma care, and psychosocial support.

- **Hope Counseling Center (HCC) (DRC):** An Exile International partner in Goma, the HCC provides counseling and psychosocial rehabilitation to war-affected children, young girls who have been victims of sexual violence, and women who have survived rape and trauma. Their team of skilled Congolese counselors has been trained in Exile International's care modules and the Empower Trauma Rehabilitation Program, which is a highly acclaimed, evidence-based model for treatment of post-traumatic stress disorder. Exile International and the HCC frequently partner for the rehabilitation and psychosocial support of war-affected children.

- **HOPE Initiative:** Healing and Ongoing Peace through Expression: Exile International fosters healthy, empowered youth through holistic programs that include physical, emotional, and spiritual care, as well as education and leadership development. To restore and empower children to become leaders for peace, Exile International has developed and trains all caregivers in the HOPE

Initiative. The program is composed of an integrated, three-part model: (1) trauma healing, forgiveness, and emotional resilience; (2) peace-building and conflict resolution skills; and (3) leadership development.

- **Peace Clubs:** Care groups serving war-affected children utilizing the Exile International's HOPE Initiative to provide art therapy, rehabilitative care, peace-building, and leadership development—restoring children of war to become leaders for peace. Why call them "Peace Clubs"? Former abductees and former child soldiers are often stigmatized within their communities. Thus the groups adopted this name and seek to re-identify the participants, further empowering them to become leaders for peace in their own communities.

- **The Peace Lives Center (DRC):** An Exile International Care Center in Goma providing physical, emotional, and spiritual care, alongside education and leadership development, to former child soldiers and children orphaned by war. The Peace Lives Center empowers child survivors to become leaders for peace. Graduates of the Peace Lives Center have gone on to become university students, teachers, carpenters, administrative professionals, church leaders, and community leaders. All graduates have continued to volunteer and serve their communities, further fostering healing and promoting peace in a conflict-ridden region of the DRC.

- **The Poza Project:** A venture utilizing the artwork of seven LRA child survivors, Jeremy Cowart's creative collaboration, and the filmed stories of LRA abductees, this project will be used as a means for brave children to share their stories of survival and to amplify the voices of the children of northern Uganda. The Poza Project is a collaborative effort of Exile International, Children of Peace Uganda, Jeremy Cowart, and Composite Films.

- **Young Peacemaker Program (DRC):** This program provides long-term, comprehensive care and leadership development through the Peace Lives Center. Each youth participant (all are former child soldiers and/or children orphaned by war) are identified as and empowered to become young peacemakers in their communities. Throughout the program, these youths benefit from the HOPE Initiative curriculum and programs, receive an education, participate in community service, are involved in a local church, and frequently serve neighboring villages and towns through outreach programs called Village Peace Clubs. During Village Peace Club meetings, young peacemakers use music, drama, and other presentations to share the hopeful message of Christ and to promote sustainable peace-building and conflict resolution within their communities.

Partners and Friends of Exile International

- **Children of Peace Uganda:** A partner organization dedicated to the well-being and empowerment of former child soldiers, children born in captivity, and children orphaned by the two decades of armed conflict in northern Uganda. Children of Peace Uganda offers a variety of mechanisms to support the holistic care and development of youth. Exile International and Children of Peace Uganda partner to provide Peace Clubs (psychosocial support and empowerment groups for LRA-affected youth), child sponsorships, and other peace-building activity programs in northern Uganda.

- **HEAL Africa (DRC):** Through support of a full-service training hospital in Goma, Congo, and its community-based initiatives in public health, community development, and conflict resolution, HEAL Africa works with individuals and communities to restore health, build hope, and help create a better future for all people of the DRC. HEAL Africa partners with the Peace Lives Center, providing needed medical care to the children there.

- **International Criminal Court:** Headquartered in The Hague, Netherlands, the ICC is a permanent, international tribunal established to help end impunity for the perpetrators of the most serious crimes of concern to the international community (including genocide, crimes against humanity, war crimes, and crimes of aggression).

The ICC complements existing national judicial systems and exercises its jurisdiction when national courts are unwilling or unable to investigate or prosecute such crimes. In conjunction with the ICC trial of Thomas Lubanga in 2009, who was charged with conscripting, enlisting, and using child soldiers, Bethany Haley Williams participated in the ICC symposium Understanding Child Soldiers and the Need for Education.

- **Invisible Children (IC):** Invisible Children uses film, creativity, and social action to seek an end to the use of child soldiers in Joseph Kony's rebel war and to restore the LRA-affected communities. Invisible Children creates documentaries, tours them around the world, and lobbies US leaders to make ending the LRA a priority. The organization works with regional partners to build and expand systems that warn remote communities of LRA attacks and encourage members of the LRA to peacefully surrender. IC also invests in rehabilitation, education, and economic recovery programs in the region. Exile International is proud to have partnered with Invisible Children to support and advance international efforts to end LRA atrocities.

- **The Resolve–LRA Crisis Initiative:** This partner organization has worked to end violent atrocities perpetrated by the Lord's Resistance Army and to support the sustainable recovery of communities affected by LRA abuses.

Headquartered in Washington, DC, Resolve undertakes front-line research and reporting focused on identifying policy solutions to the LRA crisis, lobbies influential decision makers in both the United States and international institutions, and designs advocacy campaigns for solutions that save lives and advance the cause of peace. Exile International is honored to partner with Resolve in advocacy initiatives supporting and advancing international efforts to end LRA atrocities and support sustainable recovery.

- **UN-MONUSCO:** A UN peacekeeping force in the Democratic Republic of the Congo that was established by the UN Security Council to monitor the peace process of the Second Congo War. MONUSCO, consisting of 25,698 personnel (including 21,189 UN troops, military personnel, and police), is the largest UN peacekeeping mission in the world. The peacekeeping mission continues with authorization to use all necessary means to carry out its mandate, relating, among other things, to the protection of civilians, humanitarian personnel, and human rights defenders under imminent threat of physical violence and to support the government of the DRC in its stabilization and peace consolidation efforts. Exile International has provided trauma care trainings to the staff at MONUSCO in Goma and continues to work together closely with MONUSCO in efforts to promote successful rehabilitation and reintegration for children in armed conflict.

- **Village of Hope (VOH) (Uganda):** A partner organization that has built villages (communities) of hope for orphans and widows, where children can live with their siblings in safety. VOH provides them with the basics of life: food, shelter, safety, education, skill training, love, and hope. Exile International provides caregiver training, curricula, and consultation to Village of Hope staff and counselors. Exile International teammates work directly with VOH children and teens through a variety of trauma care workshops each year.

Notes

Chapter One: As Sick as Our Secrets

1 C. S. Lewis, *Mere Christianity* (San Francisco: Harper, 2009), http://www.amazon.com/Mere-Christianity-C-S-Lewis/dp/0060652926.

2 Shane Claiborne, *The Irresistible Revolution: Living as an Ordinary Radical* (Grand Rapids, MI: Zondervan, 2006), http://www.amazon.com/The-Irresistible-Revolution-Ordinary-Radical/dp/0310266300.

Chapter Two: I Choose to Live

1 Carl Jung Depth Psychology, May 14, 2013, http://carljung depthpsychology.blogspot.com/2013/05/shame-is-soul-eating -emotion-cg-jung.html.

Chapter Four: Looking Darkness in the Eye

1 http://www.oxfam.org/en/emergencies/congo/in-depth.

2 *The Independent*, May 12, 2011.

3 Evelyn Bromet et al., "Cross-National Epidemiology of *DSM-IV* Major Depressive Episode," *BMC Medicine* 9, no. 90 (2011), http://www.biomedcentral.com/1741-7015/9/90/abstract.

4 Holy Bible, New Living Translation (NLT).

Chapter Five: They Belong to All of Us

1 Kirsten Johnson et al., "Association of Sexual Violence and Human Rights Violations with Physical and Mental Health in Territories of the Eastern Democratic Republic of the Congo," *JAMA* 304, no. 5 (2010), 553–62, http://jama.jamanetwork.com/ article.aspx?articleid=186342.

Chapter Six: "It Is Bigger Than We Are"
1 NLT.

Chapter Seven: A Little Pencil

1 http://www.beliefnet.com/Quotes/Inspiration/M/Mother-Teresa /I-Am-A-Little-Pencil-In-The-Hand-Of-A-Writing-God.aspx.

2 "Factsheet: Child Soldiers," UNICEF, http://www.unicef.org/emerg/files/childsoldiers.pdf.

3 "Children in War," UNICEF, http://www.unicef.org/sowc96/1cinwar.htm.

4 "Genocide in Darfur," United Human Rights Council, http://www.unitedhumanrights.org/genocide/genocide-in-sudan.htm.

Chapter Eight: To Chase Away the Fear

1 HR 2478 (US 111th Cong.): Lord's Resistance Army Disarmament and Northern Uganda Recovery Act of 2009, https://www.govtrack.us/congress/bills/111/hr2478/text.

2 Jihun Sohn, "UNICEF Executive Director, Ann M. Veneman, Highlights the Plight of Children Caught in Uganda's Conflict," July 25, 2005, http://origin-www.unicef.org/infobycountry/uganda_27744.html.

3 "Speaking of Psychology: Molecules and Morals: Learning the Link," transcript, American Psychological Association, http://www.apa.org/research/action/speaking-of-psychology/molecules-morals.aspx.

Chapter Nine: I Am Changed

1 The Justice Conference, Philadelphia, 2013.

2 "Preventing Genocide: A Conversation with Ambassador Susan Rice," United States Holocaust Memorial Museum, December 10, 2009, http://www.ushmm.org/confront-genocide/speakers

-and-events/all-speakers-and-events/preventing-genocide-a
-conversation-with-ambassador-susan-rice.

3 "Cooperative Observations at Nyiragongo Volcano in D.R. of Congo," Earthquake Research Institute, University of Tokyo. Retrieved September 3, 2007.

Chapter Ten: Grace Comes Full Circle

1 http://www.gurteen.com/gurteen/gurteen.nsf/id/X00059ABE/.

Chapter Eleven: With Story Comes Song

1 Siddharth Chatterjee, "For Child Soldiers, Every Day Is a Living Nightmare," *Forbes*, December 9, 2012, http://www.forbes.com/sites/realspin/2012/12/09/for-child-soldiers-every-day-is-a-living-nightmare/.

Chapter Twelve: To Come Back to Life

1 http://monusco.unmissions.org.
2 "Second Congo War," Wikipedia, http://en.wikipedia.org/wiki/Second_Congo_War.
3 http://www.goodreads.com/quotes/3899-out-of-suffering-have-emerged-the-strongest-souls-the-most.

Chapter Thirteen: The Mercy Fast

1 Sunlight Foundation, "Only Four Percent of Bills Become Law," *Huffington Post*, August 25, 2009, http://www.huffingtonpost

.com/wires/2009/08/25/the-vast-majority-of-bill_ws_268630.
html.

2 "LRA Abduction Patterns: Shifting Away from Building Fighting Capacity with Child Soldiers?," ReliefWeb, August 24, 2012, http://reliefweb.int/report/uganda/lra-abduction-patterns-shifting-away -building-fighting-capacity-child-soldiers.

Chapter Fifteen: Peace Lives

1 Gerald G. May, *The Dark Night of the Soul* (San Francisco: Harper, 2005), http://www.amazon.com/The-Dark-Night-Soul -Psychiatrist/dp/0060750553.

Chapter Seventeen: The Voices of Survival

1 Mother Teresa, *Words to Love By* (Leicester, UK: Ulverscroft, 1986,) p. 25, http://www.amazon.com/Words-Love-Linford -Inspirational-Library/dp/0708962548.

2 http://www.goodreads.com/quotes/36738-it-s-the-children-the -world-almost-breaks-who-grow-up.

Final Thoughts: Blood on My Hands

1 Donald Miller, *A Million Miles in a Thousand Years* (Edinburgh, UK: Thomas Nelson, 2009), http://www.amazon.com/Million -Miles-Thousand-Years-Learned/dp/1400202981#.

A BRIEF HISTORY OF THE WARS

1 Paris Principles and Guidelines on Children Associated with Armed Forces or Armed Groups, 2007.

2 J. Gettleman, "Africa's Forever Wars," *New York Times,* April 2010.

3 United Nations Organization Stabilization Mission in the Democratic Republic of the Congo.

4 "DR Congo: Letter to President Joseph Kabila on Prosecuting M23 Leaders and Others for Serious Abuses," Human Rights Watch, January 29, 2014, http://www.hrw.org/news/2014/01 /29/dr-congo-letter-president-joseph-kabila-prosecuting-m23 -leaders-and-others-serious-a.

5 A. Hochschild, *King Leopold's Ghost: A Story of Greed, Terror, and Heroism in Colonial Africa* (Boston: Houghton Mifflin, 2009).

6 "DR Congo: Chronology," Human Rights Watch, August 21, 2009, http://www.hrw.org/news/2009/08/20/dr-congo-chronology -key-events.

7 Ibid.

8 "Congo Crisis Glance," International Rescue Committee, April 2007, http://www.rescue.org/congo-crisis-glance.

9 US State Department, "Fact Sheet: The Lord's Resistance Army," May 23, 2012, http://www.state.gov/r/pa/prs/ps/2012/03 /186734.htm.

10 US 111th Cong., Lord's Resistance Army Disarmament and Northern Uganda Recovery Act of 2009: HR 2478, 2009.

11 United Nations Security Council, *Report of the Secretary-General on the Activities of the United Nations Regional Office for Central Africa and on the Lord's Resistance Army–Affected Areas,* 2013.

12 US 111th Cong., Lord's Resistance Army Disarmament and Northern Uganda Recovery Act of 2009.

13 "Warrant of Arrest Unsealed Against Five LRA Commanders," International Criminal Court, October 2005.

14 US State Department, "Fact Sheet: The Lord's Resistance Army."

15 US 111th Cong., Lord's Resistance Army Disarmament and Northern Uganda Recovery Act of 2009.

Bibliography

Bromet, Evelyn, et al. "Cross-National Epidemiology of *DSM-IV* Major Depressive Episode." *BMC Medicine* 9, no. 90 (2011).

Chatterjee, Siddharth. "For Child Soldiers, Every Day Is a Living Nightmare." *Forbes*, December 9, 2012.

Claiborne, Shane. *The Irresistible Revolution: Living as an Ordinary Radical*. Grand Rapids, MI: Zondervan, 2006.

Congo Crisis Glance. International Rescue Committee, April 2007, http://www.rescue.org/congo-crisis-glance.

"Cooperative Observations at Nyiragongo Volcano in D.R. of Congo." Earthquake Research Institute, University of Tokyo.

"DR Congo: Chronology," Human Rights Watch, August 21, 2009, http://www.hrw.org/news/2009/08/20/dr-congo-chronology-key -events.

"DR Congo: Letter to President Joseph Kabila on Prosecuting M23 Leaders and Others for Serious Abuses," Human Rights Watch, January 29, 2014, http://www.hrw.org/news/2014/01/29/dr-congo -letter-president-joseph-kabila-prosecuting-m23-leaders-and -others-serious-a.

Gettleman, J. "Africa's Forever Wars." *New York Times,* April 2010.

Hochschild, A. *King Leopold's Ghost: A Story of Greed, Terror, and Heroism in Colonial Africa.* Boston: Houghton Mifflin, 2009.

Jihun Sohn. "UNICEF Executive Director, Ann M. Veneman, Highlights the Plight of Children Caught in Uganda's Conflict," UNICEF, July 25, 2005, http://origin-www.unicef.org/infobycountry/uganda_27744 .html.

Johnson, Kirsten, et al. "Association of Sexual Violence and Human Rights Violations with Physical and Mental Health in Territories of the Eastern Democratic Republic of the Congo." *JAMA* 304, no. 5 (2010).

"LRA Abduction Patterns: Shifting Away from Building Fighting Capacity with Child Soldiers?" ReliefWeb, August 24, 2012.

May, Gerald G. *The Dark Night of the Soul.* San Francisco: Harper, 2005.

Mother Teresa. *Words to Love By.* Leicester, UK: Ulverscroft, 1986.

Sunlight Foundation. "Only Four Percent of Bills Become Law." *Huffington Post,* August 25, 2009.

"United Nations Organization Stabilization Mission in the Democratic Republic of the Congo." *MONUSCO Background,* United Nations Peacekeeping, n.d., https://www.un.org/en/peacekeeping/missions/monusco/background.shtml.

UN Security Council. *Report of the Secretary-General on the Activities of the United Nations Regional Office for Central Africa and on the Lord's Resistance Army–Affected Areas,* 2013.

US 111th Cong. Lord's Resistance Army Disarmament and Northern Uganda Recovery Act of 2009. HR 2478, 2009.

US State Department. *Fact Sheet: Democratic Republic of the Congo,* November 8, 2013, http://www.state.gov/r/pa/ei/bgn/2823.htm.

US State Department, *Fact Sheet: The Lord's Resistance Army,* May 23, 2012, http://www.state.gov/r/pa/prs/ps/2012/03/186734.htm.

"Warrant of Arrest Unsealed Against Five LRA Commanders." International Criminal Court, October 2005.

The power of forgiveness is one of the greatest healers and a pathway to freedom. What or whom do you need to forgive in your life today? For what in your past do you need to accept grace and forgiveness? Write a letter to that person or yourself.

Compose your own Creed (pages 44-47) for your life.

Reflect on this quote as Bethany does on page 133, "If we could truly grasp how deeply we are loved by God, we would never feel lonely again." What sort of feelings does this create in you?

Everyone has personal scars of the heart from suffering. Reflect on some of your scars and how they can be transformed into strength (pp. 190–91).

Surrendering is a large theme in <u>The Color of</u> <u>Grace</u>. When was a time you have surrendered to something? What was the outcome? Is there something you need to surrender to God today?

We may each find greater purpose of fulfillment in life when living for something outside of ourselves. To what transcendent purpose might God be calling you—be that a small act or something greater?